WINDS OF CHANGE

WINDS OF CHANGE

The End of Empire in Africa

TREVOR ROYLE

JOHN MURRAY
Albemarle Street, London

First published in 1996
by John Murray (Publishers) Ltd,
50 Albemarle Street, London W1X 4BD

A catalogue record for this book is available from the British Library

ISBN 0–7195–5352 0

Typeset in Bembo by Servis Filmsetting Ltd

Printed and bound in Great Britain by The University Press, Cambridge

Contents

Illustrations

The author and publishers wish to thank the following for permission to reproduce illustrations: Africapix, 18; Associated Press, 17; Camera Press, 7, 9, 16; Central Press, 5, 12, 13; Hulton Deutsch, 14; Imperial War Museum, 1, 2, 3; Kenya Tourist Board, 4; Sport and General, 11; Topham Picture Library, 15; and Topix, 10.

Acknowledgements

First and foremost I should like to thank the many people who shared with me their memories of Africa and who were then prepared to grant me permission to reproduce them in this book. Many extended that kindness to commenting on the text and making helpful suggestions for improvement (although I alone am responsible for any remaining errors). In this respect I owe particular debts of gratitude to W.C. Benson, Trevor Clark and John Trestrail for their helpful comments.

In some instances those interviewed preferred to remain anonymous and I have honoured that condition.

For their professional help and guidance I wish to thank the staff of the Imperial War Museum, the National Library of Scotland, the Public Record Office, Kew, and Scotsman Publications library.

Extracts from interviews from the Scottish Decolonization Project are reproduced by permission of the Librarian of the National Library of Scotland. Extracts from interviews from the Imperial War Museum's Sound Records are reproduced by permission of the Director.

Crown copyright material in the Public Record Office is reproduced by permission of the Controller of Her Majesty's Stationery Office.

I am grateful to the following copyright holders for permission

Acknowledgements

to reprint extracts: Edward Arnold for *A Right Honourable Gentleman: Abubakar from the Black Rock* by Trevor Clark; Harper Collins for *African Laughter* by Doris Lessing and *Titans and Others* by Malcolm MacDonald; the Centre for Middle Eastern and Islamic Studies, University of Durham, for *The Condominium Remembered* by Deborah Lavin (ed.); Mambo Press for *Rhodesia Front War* by Henrik Ellert; Peter Owen Ltd for *Stepping Stones* by Sylvia Leith-Ross; C. Hurst for *Nigerian Kaleidoscope* by Sir Rex Niven; and The Grange Press for *Kenya Walkabout* by Molly Ryan.

Every attempt has been made to contact copyright holders and I apologize for any accidental omissions. Due acknowledgement will be made in later editions if the information is forthcoming.

For help in arranging meetings, providing hospitality and offering advice and assistance I should like to thank Gert J. Grobler, South African High Commission, London; Trevor Grundy, Harare; Sophie Masite, Soweto; Sally Motlana, Soweto; Andrew Brian Mutandwa, Zimbabwe High Commission, London; Ian Smith, Harare; Father Tom Stanton and the Community of the Resurrection, St Peter's Priory, Southdale; and Susan Steedman, the originator of the Scottish Decolonization Project.

Finally I would like to thank one of my oldest friends for his help and hospitality during my visits to Africa. Unfortunately the present political climate in the country of his adoption prevents me from acknowledging in print his many kindnesses but he and his wife know the extent of my debt to them. This book is dedicated to him for old time's sake: *Là a' bhlàir's math na càirdean.*

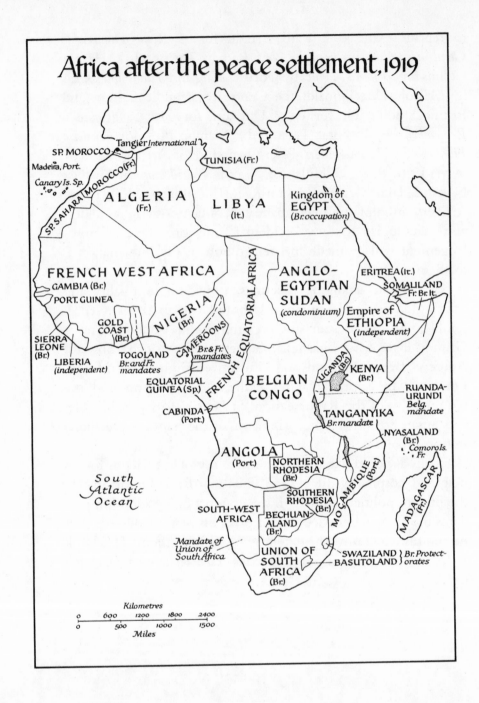

Africa after the peace settlement, 1919

SP. MOROCCO
Tangier *International*
Madeira, Port.
Canary Is. Sp.
SP. SAHARA MOROCCO (Fr.)
TUNISIA (Fr.)

ALGERIA (Fr.)
LIBYA (It.)
Kingdom of EGYPT (Br. occupation)

FRENCH WEST AFRICA
GAMBIA (Br.)
PORT. GUINEA

ANGLO-EGYPTIAN SUDAN (condominium)
ERITREA (It.)
SOMALILAND Fr. Br. It.
Empire of ETHIOPIA (independent)

SIERRA LEONE (Br.)
LIBERIA (independent)
GOLD COAST (Br.)
TOGOLAND Br. and Fr. mandates
NIGERIA (Br.)
CAMEROONS
Br. & Fr. mandates
FRENCH EQUATORIAL AFRICA
EQUATORIAL GUINEA (Sp.)
CABINDA (Port.)

BELGIAN CONGO
UGANDA (Br.)
KENYA (Br.)
RUANDA-URUNDI Belg. mandate
TANGANYIKA Br. mandate
NYASALAND (Br.)
Comoro Is. Fr.

ANGOLA (Port.)
NORTHERN RHODESIA (Br.)
SOUTHERN RHODESIA (Br.)
MOÇAMBIQUE (Port.)
MADAGASCAR (Fr.)

South Atlantic Ocean

SOUTH-WEST AFRICA
Mandate of Union of South Africa
BECHUANA-LAND (Br.)
UNION OF SOUTH AFRICA (Br.)
SWAZILAND
BASUTOLAND
Br. Protect-orates

Kilometres
0   600   1200   1800   2400
0   500   1000   1500
Miles

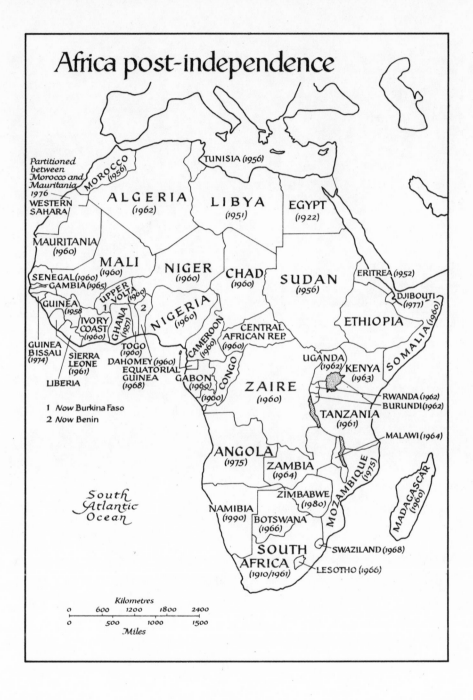

Africa post-independence

Partitioned between Morocco and Mauritania 1976

MOROCCO (1956)

TUNISIA (1956)

WESTERN SAHARA

ALGERIA (1962)

LIBYA (1951)

EGYPT (1922)

MAURITANIA (1960)

MALI (1960)

NIGER (1960)

CHAD (1960)

SUDAN (1956)

ERITREA (1952)

DJIBOUTI (1977)

SENEGAL (1960)

GAMBIA (1965)

GUINEA (1958)

UPPER VOLTA (1960) 1

GHANA (1957)

2

NIGERIA (1960)

ETHIOPIA

SOMALIA (1960)

IVORY COAST (1960)

CAMEROON (1960)

CENTRAL AFRICAN REP. (1960)

GUINEA BISSAU (1974)

SIERRA LEONE (1961)

TOGO (1960)

DAHOMEY (1960)

EQUATORIAL GUINEA (1968)

GABON (1960)

CONGO (1960)

UGANDA (1962)

KENYA (1963)

LIBERIA

ZAIRE (1960)

RWANDA (1962)

BURUNDI (1962)

TANZANIA (1961)

MALAWI (1964)

1 *Now Burkina Faso*
2 *Now Benin*

ANGOLA (1975)

ZAMBIA (1964)

ZIMBABWE (1980)

MOZAMBIQUE (1975)

MADAGASCAR (1960)

South Atlantic Ocean

NAMIBIA (1990)

BOTSWANA (1966)

SWAZILAND (1968)

SOUTH AFRICA (1910/1961)

LESOTHO (1966)

Kilometres

0   600   1200   1800   2400

0   500   1000   1500

Miles

Prologue

Heart of Darkness

AS THE TWENTIETH century rolled towards the end of its final decade, the images from the heart of Africa were stark and deeply depressing. It was not so much the slaughter of half a million Tutsi by their Hutu tribal rivals in Rwanda in the summer of 1994, and the subsequent plight of thousands of Tutsi and Hutu refugees forced to flee into neighbouring Zaire and Tanzania – in a century in which genocide and mass murder have been commonplace, these were relatively modest figures – as the knowledge that during the three decades since decolonization began, things seemed to be falling apart across the African continent. True, the same year, 1994, also saw South Africa finally emerge from the long night of apartheid to hold its first democratic multiracial elections, and countries such as the Ivory Coast, Kenya and Zimbabwe remained relatively stable, but elsewhere the picture spoke of a terrible unpredictability.

Angola, Chad, Ethiopia, Liberia, Mozambique, Nigeria, Somalia and Sudan have all been overwhelmed by catastrophic civil wars, most of which have not been entirely resolved. Even in countries where warfare was not always endemic, the governance has been so brutal that thousands of political opponents – real or imagined – have been slaughtered by leaders who have been little more than self-appointed dictators with age-old scores to settle. Equatorial Guinea, Gabon, Guinea, Mali, Malawi, Sierra Leone, Uganda and Zaire have all indulged in ethnic or communal violence and seem eternally poised on the edge of further bloodshed, with the result that Africa has fallen far, far behind the rest of the world. Add the ravages of famine, AIDS, economic decline and corruption, and the roll-call of disaster is more or less complete.

It was Rwanda and its neighbour Burundi, though, which brought the African nightmare into focus and which forced many Europeans to conclude that Africa was a hopeless case. For a start, it was not just civil war but genocide of a kind which appeared to be peculiar to that particular region. What happened in July 1994 was not the culmination of the fighting between the resident Hutu and Tutsi tribes, but just another stage in a struggle for political domination which had begun in 1962 when the two countries gained their independence from Belgium. Within ten years the rival tribes were at each other's throats. In 1972 the Hutu rose against the ruling Tutsis and killed 10,000 of their number. By way of revenge, the Tutsi Union of National Progress party ordered the massacre of up to 200,000 opponents, including all those who had received an education. There were similar outrages in 1988 and even before the evidence of the mass murders of 1994, rivers flowing into neighbouring Tanzania were often thick with dead bodies, Tutsi and Hutu. Then, in 1993, there was an equally serious bout of tribal bloodletting when hundreds of Hutus were massacred by Tutsi extremists in the capital, Bujumbura.

Although the earlier massacres had rarely warranted more than a brief paragraph in the digest columns of the world's major newspapers, the Rwandan tragedy was too public to be ignored when fighting broke out in April 1994. Not only was it conducted under the glare of television cameras, the new conscience of the age, but it required the standard western response. The paratroops were sent in to evacuate what remained of the white population, in this case mainly Belgian, and the relief agencies did what they could to control the disaster. Charitable relief organizations like the Red Cross, Médecins sans Frontières, Oxfam and Care made fresh appeals for finance, while their workers in the field did their best to save lives and bind up wounds, and then the United Nations invited its membership to contribute towards a new peacekeeping force.

Even so, despite the publicity and the eloquent requests, it was a tardy response. Only six African countries answered the call made by the UN Secretary-General Boutros Boutros-Ghali; and while France sent in a token force for a brief period, the rest of the world shrugged its shoulders and looked away. It was all too intractable, too far away and too dreadful. Even the all-powerful United States made it clear that it would not become embroiled in the problem when the UN Security Council started discussing a possible strategy at the end of June. Stung by the failure of a 1992 initiative to bring stability to a Somalia similarly torn apart by warring factions, the Clinton administration decided against further entanglement in Africa. In *The Times* in London, the political columnist Matthew Parris seemed to speak for many when he washed his hands of the whole continent: 'There is no hope for Africa, no hope at all. And in the end we are going to airlift out our own people, mostly white people, and leave the Africans to their fate. Why don't we just cut out the crap, and say so now?'

If this were a policy of despair, it was one which had been long fermenting. From famine in Ethiopia to civil war in Somalia, the west was becoming immune to the outbreaks of natural and man-made disasters which seemed to be endemic in most parts of Africa. Whereas similar problems in other parts of the world were generally finite and open to solution, the cycle of emergency seemed to be continuous in Africa. Wars rarely ended in peace treaties, famines were never replaced by plenty, the difference between political crisis and anarchy had become blurred, and international aid had taken the place of creating workable

3

internal economies. Africa had become a ramshackle edifice which could be neither propped up for ever nor replaced in the short term with a more reliable substitute.

It was all a far cry from the heady optimism of the late 1950s when the promise of decolonization suggested that Africa was on the verge of renewal, that all would be for the best in the best of all possible worlds. Then, independence seemed to be a universal panacea: democracy and western institutions were regarded as the means of creating a decent and workable system of government. Now, a weary resignation has set in, a belief that hope has been extinguished in large tracts of Africa and that the process of decolonization has been a dreadful failure.

Allied to this sense of abdication is a lingering belief that colonization itself is the root cause of much of Africa's current unhappiness. The drawing of artificial boundaries is frequently mooted as one reason for the anarchy: lines drawn on maps in distant European capitals throughout the nineteenth century did not always correspond to tribal, sociological or linguistic divisions, and the new nation-states were often synthetic creations. Orderly as the new maps might have appeared as boundary lines passed indifferently along rivers or through valleys and over mountain ridges, the people these borders enclosed did not always feel any loyalty to the newly-created state. Worse, the tribes were often age-old enemies.

Nigeria is frequently cited as the poorest example of the imposition of a colonial solution whereby national boundaries were drawn up by white administrators to create a spurious nation-state. A united Nigeria came into being at Britain's behest in 1914, yet fifty-three years later it had been torn apart by a bitter civil war when the Igbo people of the eastern states decided to abandon the federation. At the time of the fighting, the boundary-drawing seemed to provide a plausible enough explanation for the ferocity of the internecine warfare in Nigeria. After all, the country's creator, George Taubman Goldie, founder of the Royal Niger Company, admitted that in

the uncharted regions beyond the Niger coast he found a con-
venient blank which could be coloured red.

The process of bringing Nigeria within the British sphere of
influence involved the proper demarcation of its 350,000 square
miles and the division of tribes, clans and families, not all of
whom were prepared to live in harmony. A system of indirect
rule or dual control allowed the Nigerian chiefs to continue
ruling under British tutelage, but the ethnic tensions remained
and there is little doubt that the creation of artificial boundaries
exacerbated existing antipathies. That being said, it is difficult to
see how those borders could have been drawn rationally. Even
today, the country is home to over three hundred ethnic groups,
many of which are nomadic or minuscule, and the government
has embarked on a process of Balkanization which has divided
the country into nineteen regions with a new federal capital at
Abuja in the interior.

Besides, those who complain about the imposition of borders
during the nineteenth century tend to forget that some of the
worst fighting in Africa has taken place in countries such as
Somalia, which retained some sense of its own separate existence
and is not an artificial creation in the sense that Nigeria is. All
over Africa, the process of colonization was a matter of imposing order on a perceived chaos: trade routes had to be defended,
missionaries required protection and spheres of influence had to
be safeguarded. Much of it was in any case impermanent, for the
British Empire in Africa was itself a mixture of systems where
nothing was uniform. Natal and Cape Colony were self-
governing colonies, white states which were independent in all
but name; Nigeria and Southern Rhodesia were governed by
independent Charter Companies until, respectively, 1900 and
1923; Tanganyika and Nyasaland were protectorates; Sudan was
a condominium ruled jointly by Britain and Egypt. All were
regarded as part of the British Empire and all have survived,
some with different names, as independent African countries.

Come independence, too, those nation-states adopted the

models of government bequeathed by the former colonial power, often with disastrous results. More than all the exercises in cartographical colonialism, this is the baleful legacy of empire. Because colonial rule was usually vested in the hands of a small and élite governing class, incoming governments demanded the same privileges but often without the responsibility. As a result, large bureaucracies were created without the means of sustaining them; money raised from taxation and corruption was siphoned into private hands and participation in the state itself became necessary as a means of personal advancement. The conditions were ripe for the creation of self-perpetuating oligarchies because as long as personal advancement is dependent on the continuation of political power, no parties or individuals will ever agree to give up that authority without a struggle. And those who control the state also control the purse-strings, with the result that the means of making money is usually controlled on tribal or ethnic lines.

All this would have been anathema to the small group of imperial servants who oversaw the British holdings in Africa during the relatively short period of imperial rule. They went there as soldiers, administrators or commercial agents, to make a living or to further their careers, but all were driven by other considerations such as adventure, family tradition and above all by a sense of service. Like their counterparts in India who joined the Indian Civil Service or the Indian Army or who worked in jute or tea, service in Africa was both a duty and a calling. Few could foresee a time when it would all come to an end and even when the writing was on the wall after the end of the Second World War, the servants of empire were often the last to recognize it.

Just as the African terrain and climate swallows up any sign of cultivation which is left untended, so too was British colonial rule a temporary expediency, one whose benefits were quickly forgotten, disregarded or changed beyond recognition. For all that the new nation-states received democratic constitutions and followed the traditions of Westminster and the Inns of Court, the old colonial harmonies frequently evaporated after independence. In some countries, they were replaced by a reliance on the one-party state, itself a symptom of the Cold War years in eastern Europe; in others, they gave way to an oppression and denial of rights worse than anything imagined by even the most fervent anti-imperialist; many put their trust in Soviet aid and bought the arms with which to repress opposition. Small wonder that amidst the mayhem in disaster-areas such as Rwanda, still small voices could be heard claiming that empire was better than independence, an orderly imported administration preferable to local chaos.

'If the peacemaking agencies of the civilized world – and that includes the United States – wish to make their sense of outrage at disorder in the old empires effective, they must overcome their distaste for imperial forms and set about recreating equivalent services.' So wrote the historian John Keegan in the *Daily Telegraph* during the summer of 1994, as the rest of the world was trying to make sense of the bloodshed and carnage in Rwanda and Burundi. Acknowledging that attempts to alleviate the problem through airlifts provided only a sticking-plaster solution, he gave voice to a thought which was prevalent not just in Britain but in many other parts of the developed world: that there was, perhaps, a case to be made for the reversal of decolonization, that the values of the old imperial system could be revived to restore order in the midst of the prevailing chaos.

Of course, the call was hardly new. In the immediate aftermath of the decolonization of Africa, old imperial servants had written outraged or despairing letters to the British press bemoaning the latest disaster to befall countries they had known and loved. Natural though their anguish was, it was also a reaction to the prevailing ethos. Throughout the 1960s and into the 1970s, younger intellectuals would hoot with derision at the notion that the empire had once been considered the strongest and most virtuous institution on earth. The slave trade, economic exploitation of the underdeveloped countries, the wars against unequal native opposition, the reluctance to hand over power, all seemed to be unworthy components of the colonial legacy and any attempt to offer exegesis was fiercely resisted. Imperialists became the butt of satirists' and liberal political commentators' jokes and the blimpish colonel or retired district officer was turned into a stock caricature. It was not surprising that these maligned colonial servants wanted their side of the story to be told.

In time, much of that guilt began to disappear and a calmer view was taken of the process of colonization. Instead of being blindly condemned, the benefits of empire – the sound administration, the law and order, the relative prosperity, the virtual absence of venality – were examined again with interest, and, let it be said, not a little pride. The new mood was as much a reflection of the neo-Victorian revolution in values which swept through Britain during the 1980s when Margaret Thatcher was the Conservative prime minister as it was of a need to understand why the concept of an all-virtuous empire had been so absolute.

The process of revisionism was also helped by problems created by the continuing need to supply aid and assistance to the west's former colonial holdings. In the mid-1980s, Ethiopia was ravaged by famine and civil war and the images of despair from the country encouraged people to give huge amounts of money to charities and aid agencies. Amongst the most popular appeals was the 'Band Aid' movement started by the Irish pop singer Bob Geldof. Although he had little difficulty in raising sufficient funds and even less in finding the food and medical supplies, what failed him was the administration at the end of the line. It was easy enough to prick the world's conscience but it turned out to be exceptionally difficult to ensure that the supplies got through to the people who needed it – the starving people of Ethiopia. As John Griffiths, a former official of the Indian Civil Service, claimed at the time, the emergency called for men of the calibre of the district officers who brought a stable administration and a just rule to large parts of India and Africa. Throughout the British empire, his job had been to collect taxes, settle disputes, attend to public works and to enforce law and order, all of which were essential parts of the *pax Britannica*. Many old empire hands argued that this type of person was needed more than ever if the problems of the old colonies were ever to be solved satisfactorily.

Although good work was being done by the agencies in the field and although large sums of money were being made available both by the public and by a variety of governments, there did seem to be a lack of engagement with the underlying problems of the countries receiving aid. This in turn bred a dependency culture in which the recipients of aid found it preferable to live off donated food instead of attempting to create the means of production. All too often it was forgotten that beyond famine-fighting lay the challenge of building an orderly administration and it seemed to many people that if the civilized world wanted to express its sense of indignation at the disorder in Africa then it must overcome its distrust and dislike of any form of government which smacked of imperialism.

This does not mean reimposing the empire on the former colonies. For much of the time, and in most places where settler influence was strong, the system was paternalistic and blighted by a grudging unwillingness to include Africans in the process of administration and government. Certainly, many former members of the Colonial Administrative Service believe that this denial hindered the development of the African nation-states after they became independent: instead of treating their African colleagues as second-class, they should have trained and promoted them according to the same ideals of service as they themselves had followed. It is also true to say that race relations were rarely perfect and that while most imperial servants liked and admired many Africans with whom they came into contact, there was widespread distrust of African politicians and

9

intellectuals, the very people who would be entrusted with the stewardship of the new countries.

What is required, perhaps, is a realization that the rule of empire in Africa was not all bad; that government, trade and commerce were helped immeasurably by the participation of the white man and that in many African countries he still has a role to play. Only when that happens can the process of decolonization be put into a proper perspective. In 1919, when the League of Nations was founded, there were only two African representatives – Liberia and South Africa. When the United Nations came into being in 1945 they were joined by Egypt and Ethiopia, but by 1960 the number had swollen to twenty-six African members and today there are fifty-one, nearly one-third of the total membership. It is a measure of the success of the empire that most of the countries achieved independence from Britain without much rancour – only in Kenya and Rhodesia were armed struggles a prelude to the process – and that all have accepted the boundaries which were imposed on them during the nineteenth century. In many places, too, the new regimes encouraged white men to stay on because, at its best, British colonial Africa was a true partnership whose ethos is not a dim echo but a reminder that Africa is not yet a lost cause.

1

Scrambling for Africa

FROM THE World's View in the silent Matopos Hills in south-western Zimbabwe, the whole of Africa stretches out to the far horizons. All around, as far as the eye can see, lie miles and miles of rocky, rolling hills, punctuated in the rainy season at least by patches of lush vegetation. In the mid-morning heat, the only sounds are the twitter and rustle of countless insects and the mewing of circling kites; the only people are inquisitive tourists drawn to the site to wonder at the spectacular views and to ponder the two slabs of brass in the red rocks which mark the last resting places of Cecil John Rhodes and his uneasy friend and protégé, Leander Starr Jameson. Standing guard nearby on a rocky bluff is the incongruous stone cenotaph to Allan Wilson and the thirty-four troopers of the Shangani Patrol who died in 1893, wiped out by the avenging Ndebele tribesmen they had been sent to subjugate on Rhodes's behalf.

It is a fitting place for a man who in his day was known as the 'Colossus'. Everything Rhodes achieved was done on a grand scale, whether it was the accumulation of millions of pounds through his dealings in diamonds as head of De Beers, or millions of miles through his grabbing of untamed land as prime minister of Cape Province. His admirers hailed him as the prophet of the New Imperialism; his detractors claimed he was

11

little more than a crook, hell-bent on lining his own pockets. With Rhodes, there could be no middle way.

Even his choice of burial site reflects a sense of grandeur. The barren summit is topped by an uneven crown of massive boulders and Rhodes's grave is marked by a plain brass plate with the simple words: 'Here lie the remains of Cecil John Rhodes.' All around there are other similar whale-backed hills and granite-hard crenellated outcrops; it should be indistinguishable from others in this fantastic moonscape, but Rhodes had a particular reason for selecting his own lair. As you gaze over the savannah to the distant blue hills, there is a cleft in the far horizon where the land stretches north: through this gap Rhodes hoped to see British influence run all the way to Cairo.

By rights and intention, World's View is a place of pilgrimage to the man who gave his name to Rhodesia and who dreamed of creating a new British colony between central Africa and the Transvaal as a prelude to uniting the whole of southern Africa under the British flag. Of course, there were people living in the territory – in Matabeleland the warlike Ndebele, cousins of the Zulu, and the Shona people of Mashonaland – but Rhodes was not a man to be halted by considerations of that kind. The Ndebele King Lobengula was duped by Rhodes's agent Charles Rudd into agreeing a dubious concession for the mining rights in Mashonaland – even though he did not control the territory – in return for a company pension. This prerogative allowed Rhodes to create a Chartered Company, the British South Africa Company, to complete the exploitation of the area.

Just over a hundred years ago, in July 1890, a ragtag column of two hundred pioneers and five hundred military men set out from Motloutsi in Bechuanaland to occupy neighbouring Mashonaland, ostensibly to discover the hidden stocks of gold rumoured to be waiting in the country's virgin reefs, but in reality to expand British imperial interests between the Limpopo and the Zambesi.

12

They were a mixed bunch of adventurers, freebooters, swashbucklers and remittance men. Some were experienced farmers or miners; others lawyers or doctors, but all had been drawn to the column to exploit the wealth of Mashonaland and, just as important, to keep equally acquisitive foreigners, such as the neighbouring burghers of Transvaal, out of the new country. Led by professional soldiers, the column was well equipped and disciplined, and participants like Hugh Marshall Hole regarded it as a piece of empire-building as much as a military operation.

Hitherto they had most been working in offices in Kimberley or Cape Town, or in the De Beers compound. Now their chance had come and almost all of them were destined to make their mark in the years to come. One of them – Pat Campbell – the youthful husband of a lady then making her début on the English stage – was to fall in action ten years later in the Boer War; another was Bob Coryndon, who lived to be the Governor of Kenya and other African colonies.

Within three months of their departure they had raised the Union Flag at Mount Hampden, close to what was to become Salisbury, and had set about colonizing the land. Houses were built, roads cut, a railway constructed and the first mealie fields staked out. Although Lobengula had attempted to rescind the Rudd Concession by appealing directly to Queen Victoria, he also knew that his warriors' *assegais* (short spears) and obsolete Martini-Henrys were no match for modern weapons. At first, the pioneers' occupation of Mashonaland was peaceful enough, but the long-term gamble was soon faltering. The expected gold reefs failed to materialize and Rhodes's company was soon running up debts. When Rhodes eventually visited Salisbury, he found a rough frontier town, not unlike an outpost in the American west. Its inhabitants were equally hardbitten and unimpressed by Rhodes's promises of future wealth. 'I would hae ye know, Mr Rhodes, I didna come here for posterity,' a

13

Scots trader told him when he extemporized on the shining new city that would be built in the future.

The frontier mentality extended to relations with the local black people and confrontation with the Ndebele and Shona was perhaps inevitable if the white presence north of the Limpopo were ever to be cemented. The moment came in 1893 when a Ndebele raiding-party attacked Fort Victoria, thereby providing the company's administrator, Dr Jameson, with a pretext to hit back at Lobengula. In two bloody actions, the proud, though pitifully equipped, native *impi* (army) was cut to ribbons by the Maxim gun, and Lobengula's Matabeleland and his capital Bulawayo were added to the Company's possessions.

As a result of the defeat, Lobengula committed suicide and was buried at an unknown spot in the Matopos Hills. A worse fate befell his subjects. Matabeleland was staked out for white farms and his proud *indunas* (chiefs) found themselves treated with contempt by men who claimed to be their new masters. Rhodes might have argued that he had created a country in which there would be 'equal rights for every civilized man', but there were no doubts in white minds at least about what constituted a 'civilized man'. Few pioneers regarded the blacks as their equals and, as happened so often during the process of colonization in Africa, they concluded that the Ndebele and Shona people were little better than savages or slaves.

In 1896, following a bizarre and illegal attempt by Dr Jameson to annex Transvaal for Britain – the so-called Jameson Raid – the Ndebele started a rebellion but, although the Shona also joined in, it was badly co-ordinated and the forces of the British South Africa Company had little difficulty in restoring order. Once again, the Colossus rose to the occasion, travelling alone and unarmed into the Matopos Hills to speak to the Ndebele chiefs at an *indaba* (meeting) which brought the fighting to an end. The agreement was largely worthless – ownership of the land remained with the white pioneers – but, to placate the settlers, Rhodes gave them seats on the new legislative council for the territory. Rhodesia, as it was named, was set on the road towards settler self-government and to a short history which would make it the last and least welcome legacy of the British Empire in Africa.

Rhodes died in 1902 and within eighty years of his death the country had reverted to its old Shona name of Zimbabwe. By then, too, history had mocked the extent of his imperialist ambitions. His Cape to Cairo railway was fated never to leave the drawing-board, his dreams for a South Africa united under British rule never came to fruition and his inspired vision of the British Empire as an agency for universal good – 'so great a power as to hereafter render wars impossible and promote the best interests of humanity' – had long since disappeared into time's wastepaper basket.

The same is true of Britain's other colonial holdings in Africa. Few lasted more than fifty years and most were grabbed within the last quarter of the nineteenth century, the period which came to be known as the 'Scramble for Africa'. True, Britain had enjoyed trading links with the coastal areas since the seventeenth century; and hardy missionaries, many of them Scots, had ventured into the interior to bring Christianity to people long accustomed to the depredations of the slave trade. There had also been the lure of exploration and British adventurers had made it their business to solve the mystery of the source of the White Nile. James Bruce had identified the beginning of the Blue Nile in 1770 but the headwaters of the larger river provided a puzzle which a whole generation of Victorian adventurers was determined to crack.

Their attempts fuelled as much controversy as they excited public interest. Two explorers, J.H. Speke and Richard Burton, never spoke to each other again over the former's claims that Lake Victoria Nyanza was the true source. The famous Scottish medical missionary David Livingstone, one of the best-known and best-loved men of his day, lost his life in the attempt in 1873.

15

He believed that the fountainhead might be a river further south, known to the Africans as Lualaba. In fact he was wrong – it was the Congo and flowed westwards – but the story of his search and the momentous meeting with Henry Stanley provided the Victorians with one of the great vignettes of empire. It also gave substance to Speke's lyrical description of his own moment of discovery.

> The view was one which, even in a well-known and explored country, would have arrested the traveller by its peaceful beauty. The islands, each swelling in gentle slope to a rounded summit, clothed with wood between the rugged, angular, closely-cropping rocks of granite, seemed mirrored in the calm surface of the lake; on which I here and there detected a small black speck, the tiny canoe of some Muanza fisherman. On the gently shelving plain below me, blue smoke curled above the trees, which here and there partially concealed villages and hamlets, their brown, thatched roofs contrasting with the emerald green of the beautiful milk-bush, the coral branches of which cluster in such profusion round the cottages, and form alleys and hedgerows about the villages as ornamental as any garden shrub in England. But the pleasure of the mere view vanished in the presence of those more intense and exciting emotions which are called up by the consideration of the commercial and geographical importance of the lake.

As Speke foresaw, trade did follow in the wake of exploration and, with it, missionaries who hoped to redeem the black African from his savage past. This movement, too, was central to the colonization of Africa: not without reason did Livingstone claim that the process should be based on what he called the three 'C's: Commerce, Christianity and Civilization.

To those desiderata could be added Conquest. Whether by war and subsequent treaty or by swashbuckling financial negotiations to coerce native people to surrender their homelands, Britain proved to be an enthusiastic grabber of African land. Certainly, both methods played a part in the 'Scramble for Africa', the undignified and frequently confused rush to carve up the 'Dark Continent' which followed the exploration of the interior and which involved the governments not just of Britain but also of Belgium, Germany, France and Portugal. A small degree of legitimacy was conferred on the process by the West African Conference in Berlin in 1884 which confirmed existing 'spheres of influence' and laid the ground rules to be followed by the European powers when colonizing 'protectorates' in Africa. Up until then, Britain's African holdings had come through diplomacy, as a result of treaties following wars with her European neighbours – Cape Province in 1806, Natal in 1835, the Gold Coast in 1843, Basutoland in 1869 – but in the last years of the century it was to add Ashanti, the Gambia, Kenya, Nigeria, Nyasaland, Rhodesia, Sierra Leone, Somaliland, Uganda and Zanzibar, to make it the largest imperial power in the continent.

That Britain was able to add many of these possessions to her world empire was due almost entirely to the energy and vision – some might also say, avarice – of a handful of merchant-adventurers who created Chartered Companies to combine the economic and political exploitation of the new territories. The seizure of Matabeleland and Mashonaland by Rhodes was only one element of that push to claim around ten million square miles of land, but it was entirely typical of the commercial interests which underpinned much of the empire-building. In addition to Rhodes in southern Africa, there was Goldie's Niger Company busy at work in the Niger Basin in west Africa, or William Mackinnon's Imperial East Africa Company with its twin aims of exploiting the Great Lakes and extirpating slavery, or Frederick Lugard opening up Uganda and later Nigeria; all adding to Britain's imperial holdings in Africa without making a charge on the Treasury's funds.

The men who ran these companies were of the type Rudyard Kipling described as 'doers' and the wonder was that so few of their ilk accomplished so much. Rhodes had planted his territory north of the Limpopo with a few hundred pioneers;

there were never more than five thousand settlers in the whole of West Africa; Kenya's British population was a mere 30,000-strong; and in South Africa, the British settlers only numbered 450,000 in 1900. Even at the height of white rule in Rhodesia in the 1970s, the white presence only amounted to 275,000, around the size of the English south-coast seaside town of Bournemouth.

They were a mixed bunch, too. Next to Rhodes, Frederick John Dealty Lugard was one of the greatest theorists of the imperial condition in Africa. A son of the British Raj in India – he was born in 1858 at Fort George, Madras – he followed his father into the army and fought in a number of colonial wars before taking up employment as a mercenary soldier with the African Lakes Company in 1888. The decision was made for him by an unhappy love affair, but it was his own road to Damascus. Finding further employment in the area, this time with the Imperial British East Africa Company, he set about the creation of Uganda by forging treaties with the local chiefs, ending slavery and creating staging posts. Often this was done with the assistance of the Maxim gun, but Lugard survived accusations of winning the country by massacre to see Uganda become a British protectorate in 1894.

Thereafter, his career took him to join Goldie's Royal Niger Company, to help forestall French ambitions on the upper Niger. Both men were very different in character and personality – Lugard a typical Victorian soldier, high-minded and brave; Goldie, a sybarite and something of an outsider – yet both found common ground in their desire to outwit their French rivals in the region. Their concerns were not groundless: France was making headway in securing the Sahara and the hinterland of west Africa and if it succeeded, Britain would be left with the coastal littoral known as the Oil Rivers Protectorate. Following his usual practice of mixing guile with the threat of force, Lugard marched north and made treaties with the kingdom of Nikki but this merely precipitated a fresh French initiative in the region. The

next three years saw a farcical stand-off between the two countries which only ended in 1898 when Lugard took two thousand
men of the newly raised West African Frontier Force into the
northern interior to claim the territory on Britain's behalf.

Within two years, Nigeria had come under Britain's control.
Goldie's company was abolished, Lagos and the coastal area
became southern Nigeria and new boundaries were demarcated
for the new colony of northern Nigeria, whose first governor
was none other than Lugard. Later still, in 1914, the two
colonies were amalgamated with Lugard again at the helm as
governor-general. Britain's holdings in west Africa were now
more coherent: in addition to the new Crown Colony and
Protectorate of Nigeria, Sierra Leone, the Gambia and the Gold
Coast were also controlled by the Colonial Office. But land-
grabbing was not the only concern of the small and wiry soldier
who seemed to the late Victorians to be the very epitome of
British pluck; Lugard was also a visionary. Throughout his
adventures in Nigeria he had been evolving a new system of
British rule which he called 'dual mandate'.

This was the apotheosis of imperial paternalism, a system
which allowed Africans to maintain their own customs, laws and
culture under the tutelage of avuncular British provincial and
district officials. It was similar to the means used by the British
in India to control the princely states where the British political
officers acted the roles of prefects or housemasters and it was
equally effective in Nigeria. As recalled by Trevor Clark, who
worked as a district officer in Bauchi in the 1950s, it was a
humane and practical system which depended on a mixture of
good sense and 'fair play'.

> Every African authority with any capacity for what Lugard's men
> could respect as 'good government' was to be preserved, to be
> enlisted as an agent of 'civilization', to be instructed, supervised and
> supported. Disciplined skills were needed to achieve such a change
> in rulers' attitudes without loosening their control of their subjects.

Lugard's stated purpose, believed unquestioningly at the time although disdained by scholars in years to come, was to induce Africa rulers to rule well, so that their ambitions should lead not to new conquests, but to the prosperity of the people, the efficiency of their services, and the consequential enlargement to their prestige by that means alone.

Lugard produced the definitive interpretation of the system in 1922 in his book *The Dual Mandate in British Tropical Africa* and it was quickly accepted as a blueprint for colonial rule by a whole generation of British administrators and politicians. Two tenets governed Lugard's thinking: first, that Britain had a responsibility to the colonized people to improve their material and moral position, thereby enabling them to rule themselves at a future date; and second, to develop the colony's economy and natural resources on the world market. Properly managed, he argued, there should be no conflict between the two objectives and in time the Africans would be able to govern themselves without British tutelage.

Like Rhodes, Lugard was an iron dreamer, a man who never wavered in his belief that 'the merchant, the miner and the manufacturer do not enter the tropics on sufferance or employ their technical skill, their energy and their capital as "interlopers" or as "greedy capitalists", but in the fulfilment of the mandate of civilization'. Very different in style and outlook was Hugh Cholmondeley, Lord Delamere, the 'uncrowned king of Kenya' who believed that the British colonies in east and southern Africa should become the preserve of the white settlers – a haughty ruling-class of farmers, many of whom enjoyed aristocratic connections. In fact, if any part of Africa conformed to the Marxist notion that empire was based solely on white exploitation and privilege and black subjugation, it was Kenya, or at least the kind of Kenya which Delamere and his followers wanted to create.

As happened in many other parts of Africa colonized by the

British, Kenya, or British East Africa, was just another area of Crown land ripe for development: when Sir Charles Eliot was despatched to report on the possibilities, he recommended introducing 'order in blank, uninteresting barbarism'. This, too, had been Lugard's view when he had explored the Uganda railway route in 1893 and found a country of rich pastures and cool highlands, not unlike the Sussex Downs. On first inspection, Eliot thought that the area could be exploited by smallholders who would be allowed to purchase no less than 120 but no more than 640 acres of land. Wary of large-scale land settlement and worried about Britain's ability to offer protection, his masters at the Foreign Office tended to agree with that assessment.

It was at this point that Delamere intervened. He had explored the country during the 1890s and an extended visit in 1898 convinced him of its potential. On his advice, Eliot changed his tune to propose that Kenya was ideal for investment by men of substance – Delamere himself invested £80,000 and other speculators included Lord Kitchener, the eminent railway-developer Percy Girouard and Lord Cranworth, who wrote *Kenya Chronicles*, an account of his own time in east Africa which was also an amusing guide for would-be settlers. As it turned out, most of those willing to take a risk in the Crown Colony were wealthy aristocrats or well-connected members of the British upper classes who wanted the good life at little personal cost. 'Why did we first go to East Africa?' asked Cranworth. 'My memory puts the answer in a twofold urge. Love of sport, more especially of big-game shooting, and shortage of cash. The former had been whetted by a trip to India the previous year, and the latter looked like being a permanent fixture.'

Not that it was all play and no work. As Elspeth Huxley's biography of Delamere makes clear, the early settlers were hard men and women who were prepared to live rough until the crops or cattle began to pay dividends. Few of the local African tribes knew anything about agriculture (save the Maasai, who knew everything about rearing cattle) and with supplies and equipment at a premium, there was no little guesswork and crossing of fingers. For a while, Delamere and his young wife lived in a mud hut, haunted by bad harvests and lack of capital, but by dint of hard work and perseverance, his ranch Soysambu became a much admired and much envied model. It was also a symbol of a kind, an example of what a man could do if he was prepared to work the land, tame it and then to protect what he held.

But it was not just a working model which Delamere gave to Kenya, it was also style. Part gentleman's smoking-room, part officers' mess – in a good regiment, of course – and part St James's club, life in Kenya was aristocratic in tone, exclusive and refined in practice. (A visiting British cavalry officer quipped, not without reason, that in regimental terms, Kenya constituted the officers' mess, Rhodesia the sergeants' mess, while South Africa provided the other ranks.) Kenyan society was also leavened by an infusion of public-school high-jinks and Delamere was no slouch when it came to leading the way. While he was evolving his ideas of white superiority and laying plans for the development of further white dominions in East Africa, he could be as high-spirited as any unruly subaltern, smashing up the hotel he owned at Nakuru or shooting out the town's lamplights. As more than one visitor confided, Kenya was a place which had no written rules, but if you had to be told them, you would never fit in. And as Cranworth said of the 'old club' which laid the foundation for the exclusive Muthaiga Club in Nairobi, only those who understood that principle would feel at home in the rowdy atmosphere which was an integral part of life in Kenya. Later, the Muthaiga became a byword for snobbishness and entry was strictly controlled, but in its first existence the 'centre of the club was, as it should be, the Bar'.

Here, as the sun went down, assembled the élite from farm and office, from store and counter. Plates of potato chips and monkey nuts garnished the mahogany, and behind it an autocratic Indian marshalled his troop of smiling natives in their white *kanzas*. Drinks flowed freely and so did the conversation, of which one could take one's choice of almost any brand. Here the high official would be laying down the line of some deep Government policy; next, a party of shooters in from safari would be describing, with ever more lurid details, the charge of some tremendous lion or buffalo. Every minute, fresh arrivals would pour in – golfers, tennis players and cricketers; lastly, perhaps, a party of heated and somewhat noisome polo players. If it was a Saturday there would be late arrivals from the neighbouring farms and the 'shop' would slip to coffee, sisal, sheep and cattle. There was an ever-growing babble and everyone knew everyone else, even if for the moment they had ceased to be on speaking terms. For cheer and good fellowship it seemed to conform not unfavourably with, say, the Carlton Club! During this period of the day there was certainly no cleavage between settler and official; they would be indiscriminately mixed up, exchanging chaff and standing each other drinks. Certainly, as the dinner hour approached the babel became louder and the stories taller and even thicker, but unless it was a big night, perhaps six times a year, it was extremely rare to see anyone the worse. And even on those nights, intoxication was of that jovial variety which inspires an over-whelming urge to throw a billiard ball or other handy missile at a stuffed and staring kongoni head, and the damage was invariably made good. Assuredly I had some good times in the old Club, and never ceased regretting when the process of evolution demanded something grander and more dignified.

Men of that kidney worked hard and played hard and although Kenya never numbered many more than three thou-sand whites in the early years at least, they looked to Delamere for their moral and political leadership. (Not everyone was a scion of the upper classes: there was a sprinkling of Boer voortrekkers from the south, roughnecks from Rhodesia and a sizeable Indian population.) As for the Africans, most whites held to the view expressed to the adventurer Richard Meinertzhagen in 1902 that they were 'the master race and [that] the black man must forever remain cheap labour and slaves'. To

23

accommodate the new settlers, the local people were moved off their tribal lands and were only allowed to stay if they agreed to provide a work-force for the new owners. Amongst those most affected were the Maasai, Nadi and Kipsigi tribes, who were forced to give up lands they had cultivated for generations. Just as bad, they were then forced into the kind of labour previously only undertaken by women or slaves.

Also, as happened in other parts of Africa, they were often badly treated because the settlers had reached the conclusion that the blacks were 'constitutionally lazy, entirely ignorant, inconceivably stupid and completely unambitious', and that they had to be worked hard to purge them of those 'defects'. True, in the early days throughout Africa, many white men had black mistresses, but with the stratification of local society and the arrival of numbers of white women (the two not entirely unconnected), a colour bar came into being and most white settlers never dreamed that the blacks would one day rule Kenya.

The Colonial Office did. Although the British South Africa Company had relinquished responsibility for Southern Rhodesia in 1923, thereby transferring power to the white settlers, this was not to be the route taken in Kenya. Delamere and his supporters wanted similar rights of white land-ownership, and campaigned noisily for them, but the British government responded with a White Paper which pointed to the way ahead. One day, once they had been educated and trained to accept responsibility, Kenya would be returned to the blacks.

Primarily Kenya is an African territory, and His Majesty's Government think it necessary definitely to record their considered opinion that the interests of the African natives must be paramount, and that if and when these interests and the interests of the immigrant races should conflict, the former should prevail. As in the Uganda Protectorate, so in the Kenya Colony, the principle of Trusteeship for the Natives, no less than in the Mandated Territory of Tanganyika, is unassailable.

The haughtier settlers responded by blackballing officials from membership of the Muthaiga Club but they could not disguise the fact that Kenya was ruled by the Colonial Office and that its future would be decided in faraway London. A year later, the British government sent an all-party commission to Kenya under the direction of one of Lugard's disciples, William Ormsby-Gore, and it recommended an expansion in health and welfare training for Africans, aimed at improving their economic skills. By then the influence of the planter and the settler in colonial politics was definitely on the wane.

If dual control was the guiding principle of British colonial rule in east and west Africa, it has to be said that it was a system of benevolent paternalism which only survived because, on the whole, the British servant of empire was 'a dedicated person and his integrity was beyond question'. A.J.V. Arthur was typical of that breed in the period between the two world wars of the twentieth century, but he had the added good fortune to serve in two services which many believe represented the high point of British imperial rule: the Indian Civil Service and the Sudan Political Service. With good reason, both considered themselves to be an élite – not for nothing did the former describe themselves, somewhat self-consciously, as the 'heaven-born' – and its members regarded their service in both countries as part obligation and part duty. Sudan was only about the size of an average Indian province such as the Punjab, but applicants to its Political Service went through the same rigorous selection process as those who aspired to be one of the heaven-born.

There was, though, one important difference. For all that Sudan was undoubtedly a British imperial holding, it was an Egyptian possession and ruled by a condominium arrangement whereby the governor-general was appointed by the Egyptian government on Britain's recommendation. It was not until after the First World War that Britain abandoned the pretence of Egyptian involvement and introduced direct rule along the accepted lines of dual control. Sudan was also different in that it was attached to the British Empire by dint of conquest. During the Battle of Omdurman in September 1898, Kitchener's joint British–Egyptian–Sudanese army killed around 20,000 dervishes – Islamic fundamentalists who followed a religious leader known as the Khalifa, son of the Mahdi who had been responsible for the death in 1885 of the mystic General Gordon in Khartoum. Although the slaying of Gordon was one motive for Kitchener's revenge, there were other and more pragmatic reasons for his campaign.

Just as Lugard had fought to forestall French territorial ambitions in Borgu in northern Nigeria, so too was the British prime minister Lord Salisbury concerned about a French intention to occupy the Upper Nile. Led by a Marine captain called Jean-Baptiste Marchand, a small French expedition had laboured across Africa from Gabon to a primitive fort at Fashoda on the White Nile and claimed the surrounding territory in their country's name. Not only would this have threatened Britain's holdings in Egypt – the French would have controlled the headwaters of the Nile – but it would also have caused problems for the anticipated Cape to Cairo railway. It was therefore imperative that Marchand be stopped without risking war between Britain and France. Employing a mixture of guile and superior force, Kitchener convinced Marchand that his position was untenable and relayed this information back to London.

Although there were calls for war on both sides of the English Channel, France backed down in November and Marchand, whom Salisbury described discreetly as 'an explorer in distress', was allowed to retire to Ethiopia. In deference to French pride, Fashoda was renamed Kodok, but this cartographical camouflage could not disguise the fact that Britain had complete control of the Nile from Lake Victoria to the Mediterranean. They also introduced the idea of the condominium, whereby the Egyptian flag flew alongside the Union Flag to signify that the Sudan was ruled jointly by the Khedive of Egypt and the

King of Great Britain. Nothing of the sort, of course: the Egyptian ruler was under Britain's thumb, but the arrangement allowed Britain to control the Sudan and, in due course, to introduce what one district commissioner described as 'peace and security and modest advancement'.

There was one other area of Africa where British control was different from the territories gained during the Scramble: South Africa. The Cape had been known to the Europeans since 1487, when the Portugese mariner Bartholomew Diaz rounded it to open up the main maritime route to the Far East. Throughout the seventeenth century it served as 'refreshment station' for ships bound for the Indies and in 1652 it was established officially by the Dutch East India Company. To begin with, it was meant to be nothing more than a staging post, but the Dutch soon found it necessary to man it with settlers – or 'free burghers', as they were called. Following the wars against revolutionary France at the end of the eighteenth century, Britain assumed control of the colony from Holland in 1815 and continued its development as a staging post on the imperial route to India. However, the annexation also meant that the British had to assume responsibility for the fiercely independent Boer farmers of Dutch, Flemish, German and Huguenot ancestry who regarded the land and its people as their own. For the rest of the century, this collision, cultural and political, was to be a source of constant friction.

One problem was the attitude towards race. When they arrived in the Cape, the Boers had grabbed land in the interior from the local San and Khoi tribes and held it by force of arms. Regarding themselves as God's chosen people, created by divine election, and using the Old Testament as their text, they believed in the absolute right of their actions – black was black and white was white and to compromise was the work of the devil. Invariably, they were convinced that they were superior to the people whose land they had conquered – simple heathen folk beyond redemption – and when the British arrived to rule them, they did not take kindly to their different attitudes to race. (This was a time when evangelism and the anti–slavery movement were particularly strong in Britain.) In 1798, a British traveller, Sir John Barrow, could see at once that the difference in cultures would create problems, when he witnessed a Boer farmer being imprisoned and then flogged by the British authorities for mistreating his Khoi servant.

> For the whole of the first night his lamentations were incessant; with a loud voice he cried '*Myn God! Is dat een maniere om Christian mensch te handlen?*' ('My God, is this the way to treat a Christian man?') His, however, were not the agonies of bodily pain, but the burst of rage and resentment on being put on a level with one of the *Zwarte Natie* [black natives], between whom and themselves the Boers conceive the differences to be fully as great as between themselves and their cattle.

The appearance of Christian missionaries, most notably John Philip of the London Missionary Society, also hastened the tide of reform and the Boers' treatment of their black labourers led to louder calls for British intervention. The arrival of 5,000 British settlers in 1820 provided an additional impetus for change and the administration in the Cape began to introduce internal taxation and to pass laws protecting basic democratic rights. All this was anathema to the Boers, who were further enraged in 1836 when the Colonial Office decided to return a large area of land in the east to the local Bantu people. Although this was a pragmatic solution to the problem of meeting the costs of administering the territory, it was the final straw for those Boers on the frontier who believed that it was every son's right to possess a 6,000-acre farm.

Instead of remaining to fight the changes, the Boers decided to move further away from the meddlesome British with their laws and their newfangled ideas about equality and progress. There followed a mass migration across the colony's eastern frontier, the Orange River, into the new and fertile lands on the other side of the Drakensberg Mountains. Others pushed further north across the High Veld towards the Limpopo. They were all voortrekkers, taking part in the mass migration of peoples which came to be known as the Great Trek and according to Anna Steenkamp, the sister of one of their leaders, they were united in their purpose.

> The shameful and unjust proceedings with reference to the freedom of our slaves: and yet it is not so much their freedom that drove us to such lengths as their being placed on equal footing with Christians, contrary to the laws of God and natural distinction of race and religion, so that it was intolerable for any decent Christian to bow down beneath such a yoke; wherefore we rather withdrew in order thus to preserve our doctrines in purity.

As they moved into the rich grasslands of the coastal plain beyond the Drakensberg, the voortrekkers gave thanks that they were entering a promised land which they believed could be won not by conquest but by bartering with King Dingane, the ruler of the powerful Zulu nation. It was not to be. The voortrekker leader Piet Retief was murdered during talks to find a settlement and his fellow countrymen took revenge, cutting down the Zulu *impis* with modern firepower at a place which came to be known as Blood River. However, even then their troubles were not over. Although the voortrekkers proclaimed the new Boer republic of Natal in 1839, Britain was not prepared to see the creation of an independent regime abutting its holdings in Cape Province. In faraway London the decision was taken to annex Natal, leaving the Boers no other option but to stay put under the detested British rule or to trek on once more.

The need to decide bred within the Boers – or Afrikaners as they also called themselves – an undying hatred of British meddling and duplicity. Those who trekked north founded the independent republics of Transvaal and the Orange Free State and although these were recognized by Britain at the Sand River

Convention of 1852 and the Bloemfontein Convention of 1854, the race-memory of the voortrekking Boers had been permanently soured – even Philip, the missionary, noted that 'the arbitrary government of this colony disgusts them'.

Despite the temporary agreement between Britain and the Boer republics, they were still separated by the great divide of race. By 1872 the liberal Cape Colony boasted internal autonomy with a franchise which gave the vote to men of all races whose income or property value reached a certain standard, whereas in Transvaal only white males had the vote. There was also a difference in economy. Cape Province and Natal were expanding rapidly, first through sheep-farming and then through the discovery of diamonds on the Orange and Vaal rivers, whereas the exchequers of Transvaal and the Orange Free State had been drained by continuous warfare with their African neighbours. The inequality encouraged the British to embark on an expansionist policy: in 1871 Griqualand West was annexed to secure the diamond deposits and Basutoland (Lesotho) was brought under imperial control to preserve the borders with the Orange Free State.

A logical extension of this policy was the creation of a South African federation which would include not only the two British colonies and the two Boer republics but perhaps even the Bantu people. To the British, this seemed a sensible solution and in 1877 the new High Commissioner in Cape Town, Sir Bartle Frere, took over responsibility for the Transvaal. An expansionist by nature, he then moved against the Zulus by reviving a land dispute with King Cetewayo. The resulting war produced the Battle of Isandhlawa in 1879, an inglorious defeat for the British Army, but the Zulus were eventually subjugated by dint of the Maxim gun. All of South Africa could now be brought under the British flag, were it not for the intransigence of the Boers. Under the leadership of Paul Kruger, the Transvaalers rebelled in 1881 and inflicted an embarrassing defeat on a British army at Majuba Hill.

This was the first Boer War and it paved the way for future conflict: when gold was discovered in the Rand in 1886, Transvaal became a wealthy country, the richest in Africa and a prize worth collecting for the British Empire. As we have seen, Rhodes's acquisitiveness, his so-called 'big idea', led Jameson to invade the country on 29 December 1895 with six hundred troopers, to raise a rebellion against the Boers in Johannesburg. The action failed ignominiously, but as the Boer leader Jan Smuts remarked, it was 'the real declaration of war in the Great Anglo–Boer conflict' which followed four years later.

It also marked the beginning of the last phase of the British scramble for Africa. Rhodes was relieved of his post as prime minister of Cape Colony and the direction of Britain's southern African policy passed to the Colonial Office under its secretary of state Joseph Chamberlain and the new High Commissioner in Cape Town, Alfred Milner. The new team came from a very different background from the brash Rhodes – Milner was an intellectual, Chamberlain a political scrapper – but both shared the view that Transvaal should be brought within British imperial control through negotiation or, if that failed, by force.

The outwardly mild-mannered Milner favoured the latter option and he deliberately pushed the Boers into a war over the political rights of the non-Boers, or Uitlanders, in the Transvaal. Protracted negotiations took place, during which neither side showed much adroitness: each new concession was met by further demands until a show-down became inevitable. Ten thousand British troops were despatched to the Cape under the command of General Sir George White and the Boer parliament in Johannesburg made plans for mobilization. After a century of uneasy co-existence and intermittent hostility, Boer and Briton went to war on 12 October 1899, after Boer demands that Britain remove her troops from the frontier had been ignored. 'God hath spoken in His wisdom,' said Kruger, 'I will rejoice.' The sentiment was echoed six thousand miles away by Britain's War Minister, Lord Lansdowne, who scribbled a hasty note to

Chamberlain, 'Accept my felicitations. I don't think Kruger could have played your cards better than he has. My soldiers are in ecstasies . . .'

That first flush of pleasure turned to dismay as the Boer forces swept to a succession of easy victories in the dying months of 1899; the war was destined to last three years and when it ended in 1902 Britain discovered that although it had won the war it had lost the long-term peace. And in so doing, it had set South Africa on the path towards the racial tensions which would disfigure it for almost a century. One of the major concessions of the Peace of Vereeniging which ended the war was the right for the Boers to decide whether or not to extend the franchise to black Africans. Four years later, political power passed back to the Boers, first in Transvaal and then in the Orange Free State, and one of their first acts on becoming self-governing was to exclude non-whites from the vote. As Smuts had foreseen as early as 1892, the question of racial conflict would dominate the future not just of the federal union of South Africa but also of the whole continent.

> The race struggle is destined to assume a magnitude on the African continent such as the world has never seen and the imagination shrinks from contemplating; and in that appalling struggle for existence the unity of the white camp will not be the least necessary condition – we will not say of obtaining victory, but of warding off (or at worst postponing) annihilation.

Smuts's hopes of developing a unified white policy towards the blacks were put to the test when the four south African territories began the process of creating a union to protect the region's economic and strategic interests. The British decision at Vereeniging tacitly ensured that the Colonial Office would not interfere and that the Britons and Boers in the Cape, Natal, Transvaal and the Orange Free State would be free to decide their own future. Negotiations began on 4 November 1908 and on the main sticking-point of the vote a compromise was reached whereby the existing colonial franchise was maintained in each of the four countries. This meant that Africans were excluded in Natal, Transvaal and the Orange Free State, whereas qualified Africans would retain the vote in the Cape. Even so, no African would be allowed to stand as a parliamentary candidate and the African franchise could be overturned by a two-thirds majority of both houses of the Union parliament sitting together. Protection of a kind was offered to Africans in the tribal lands of Basutoland, Bechuanaland and Swaziland, which became protectorates outside the union, but the creation of South Africa was a massive sell-out for non-European inhabitants of the new country.

Aided in part by a Liberal government in London, which had opposed the war and which hoped that appeasement and renewal would create unity, the Boers set about imposing their standards on the new country. Whereas politicians such as Campbell-Bannerman and Churchill put their trust in the healing powers of a 'spirit of charity' and Milner hoped to anglicize the former Afrikaner republics, the Boer leaders dug in. Eight years after Vereeniging, the Union of South Africa came into being, with Botha as prime minister and Smuts his deputy. What they had failed to achieve by military means they had won through the predominantly white ballot box – English speakers also voted for the Afrikaner-led National Party – and their country became a dominion within the British Empire. Tragically for the coloured majority, the British had failed to understand the commitment of Afrikaner nationalism and the flimsy condition of the Cape's liberal traditions. As Milner admitted later, he had underrated the strength of Boer-inspired white intransigence and he went to his death in 1924 regretting that he had been party to the decision to bar non-Europeans from the franchise: 'If I had known as well as I now know the extravagance of the prejudice on the part of almost all Europeans, and not the Boers alone, I should never have agreed to so absolute an exclusion.'

★

The 'Scramble for Africa' was now over and although Britain had relinquished control of the new Union, she and France still had sufficient possessions to make them the most influential colonial powers in the continent. (Britain was responsible for the Gambia, Sierra Leone, Gold Coast, Nigeria, Bechuanaland, Basutoland, Swaziland, Southern Rhodesia, Northern Rhodesia, Uganda, British East Africa, British Somaliland, the Anglo-Egyptian Sudan and Egypt; while France held Algeria, Tunisia, Morocco, Mauritania, Senegal, French Guinea, Ivory Coast, Upper Senegal and Niger, Upper Volta, Chad, Togoland and Dahomey and French Equatorial Africa.) Italy, Portugal, Spain, Germany and Belgium held the rest and by the time of the First World War only two African countries were independent – Ethiopia and Liberia.

And then, following the Treaty of Versailles in 1919, the German colonies were divided amongst the victors under the mandate of the newly-formed League of Nations: Britain gained German East Africa (Tanganyika); South Africa assumed control of South West Africa; Togo and Cameroon were divided up between Britain and France; and Belgium received the tiny central African colonies of Rwanda and Burundi. Britain now had the security she desired for the route to India and the Far East, for although Egypt had been returned to a nominally independent monarchy in 1922, British influence was all-pervasive and a British military garrison guarded the Suez Canal. Although the Cape to Cairo railway was never built, Britain was the supreme power on Africa's eastern flank from the Mediterranean to the Indian Ocean.

However, the hoped-for bonuses of the 'Scramble for Africa' – the investment and economic growth, the settlement and the trade – failed to materialize. During the 1930s only 60,000 Europeans settled in the lands between the Limpopo and the Sahara, and the main European investment of £1.2 million during the same period was centred almost exclusively on mining and farming interests in South Africa and Southern

Rhodesia. Elsewhere, colonies were encouraged to be self-sufficient and little money was made available to them. This was partly due to the prevailing political ethos: governments interfered less in the maintenance of social functions than they do today. Partly, too, it was felt that the colonies should raise their own funds for the preservation of law and order and that education and economic development should be the responsibility, respectively, of the Christian missions and the commercial companies. It was only when colonies such as the Gold Coast and Nigeria began to show a profit over their expenses in the years after the First World War that Britain began to take her colonial responsibilities in Africa more seriously.

In 1925 the Colonial Office began the process of improving medical and agricultural standards in an attempt to make the Africans more self-sufficient. In 1929 Britain took the decision to invest more heavily in the empire, either by loans or by grant-aid, and by 1938 the Colonial Development Fund had spent £4 million on the African colonies. Educational standards were also regularized, inspectors were appointed to improve standards and mission schools were subsidized. Although this did not mean that every African received a primary education, it ensured that children were able to stay at school longer. Standards were also improved and by 1939 Nigeria was able to boast that it had a dozen secondary schools turning out two hundred pupils a year. By modern standards it might seem a drop in the ocean, but the opening up of education in the 1920s and 1930s laid the foundation for a new professional class of Africans and it opened the eyes of future nationalist leaders such as Hastings Banda, Jomo Kenyatta and Abubakar Tafawa Balewa. As the latter's biographer, Trevor Clark, makes clear, the grant of a decent education proved to be a transforming moment in the nascent politician's life: 'He returned to the country town to teach, convinced that the well of fresh knowledge would never run dry, and that an understanding of mankind's bonds, one individual's with another's, was the key to a just civilization under God's will.

Promotion brought him closer to the sources of some of the injustices which he thought to be amendable.'

Yet in spite of the improvements and the attempts at orderliness, Britain had little clear idea about what it wanted from its African colonies. Pragmatists talked about allowing the people to develop along their own lines until some unspecified future date when they could look after themselves. White supremacists hoped that the settlers would take charge of development and assume responsibility for the colonies, while liberals put their trust in the creation of an all-embracing Commonwealth of Nations. Meanwhile, scores of young men and women looked to Africa for a career, not just as a means of making money but also of living a life of public service amidst adventurous surroundings. And in that brief heyday of empire in Africa, as happened to Martin Lindsay, they could go out to a colony under British rule and live to see it become independent after the winds of change had swept through Africa.

> When I left Ibadan in 1929 the white community was tiny. Apart from our twenty-five officers and about the same number of white sergeants and warrant officers, the only white community consisted of three or four traders in Ibadan in charge of different stores and the bank manager and his cashier and the policeman, the district officer who lived not too far away and that was really about the lot. They were talking about building a fine new hospital which they subsequently built and also the University of Nigeria which they built in Ibadan but they were only at the planning stage then.
>
> And then I went out there thirty-five years later [in 1964, after Nigeria's independence]. The difference was astonishing. There was an enormous white business community, I think there were something like two hundred members of a large local club they'd built on what had previously been our polo ground, and white wives – everybody seemed to have a wife – and they all had two or three white children. The difference was really absolutely astonishing.

It was a far cry from the early pioneering days, when eighteen months was the accepted length of service for British officers in the Nigeria Regiment; but by then the connection with Africa was less about service and adventure and more about commercial partnership. Lindsay was the son of an Indian Army officer who had been commissioned in the Royal Scots Fusiliers. In 1927 he transferred to the 4th Nigeria Regiment and, after serving with them for less than two years, he embarked on an expedition across Africa from the Belgian Congo to Uganda, an adventure he described as 'one of the most enjoyable periods I've ever had in my life'. Although his experiences were hardly run-of-the-mill, the same sentiments have also been expressed by hundreds of others who lived through the last days of the British Empire in Africa.

2

The Lives They Always Led

WHEN IT COMES to remembering the days of imperial splendour, Africa occupies a curious place in British affections. It does not have the sepia-tinted sentimentality of the Raj, with its strong sense of imperial guardianship; nor does it pull at the heart-strings as does the long love-affair with the haughty Bedouin of the desert wastes of Arabia. The relationship even lacks the raffish charm of the Levant or the Orient, where merchant adventurers plied their trade as equals with their partners in Beirut or Singapore. Africa was simply too huge and too kaleid-oscopic to create a single bucolic memory; the big skies over the red earth of Kenya being as different as the lush, steaming jungles of southern Nigeria or the sear winds which blow over the dust of the Horn of Africa into Sudan and Ethiopia.

Perhaps because it was so short-lived – except in Egypt and South Africa – the British empire in Africa seems like a vanished world, a place where the voices of the inhabitants are only dimly heard. The accents were different, too. The homely tones of the Edinburgh-educated Scots missionary in Nigeria, the Welsh lilt of the miner who had exchanged Tredegar for the Witwatersrand, the clipped public-school inflections of the young subaltern in the King's African Rifles or the District Officer in the Sudan: all were representative of the brief British involvement in the African continent. Even the systems of

British colonial administration were variegated, the complexion of Crown Colony, mandate, protectorate or condominium changing from one territory to the next. In fact, order and coherence would have been the last things needed by the British Empire in Africa, for it was never intended to be anything other than a temporary arrangement, the countries held in trust until they had been prepared for self-government or, as the League of Nations enshrined the policy, until they were able 'to stand on their own feet in the arduous conditions of the modern world'.

Yet, despite the absence of unity and the apparent lack of method, there was a swashbuckling magnificence to the British colonial connection in Africa: all those millions of miles of scrub, desert, jungle or pastureland neatly divided and controlled by a tiny handful of British administrators, soldiers, engineers, missionaries, businessmen and adventurers. When Britain went to war with Germany in 1939, her African empire consisted of 1.3 million square miles made up of fourteen different territories, yet the Colonial Service in Africa only consisted of several hundred officials. In Nigeria there were only 4,000 European soldiers and policemen in a country of twenty million inhabitants; in the Sudan, throughout the fifty-seven years of the condominium, only 393 officers served in the Sudan Political Service.

Physical constitutions had to be tough, too, for the local conditions were not always conducive to healthy living. The west African colonies were collectively known as the 'White Man's Grave' and there was good reason for the soubriquet. Malaria and yellow fever were endemic, parasitic insects invaded the body, and in the remote country areas there were poisonous snakes, insects and plants which could and did kill unwary human beings. Preventative medicines were either primitive or not readily available and even the monotonous diet conspired to make life more difficult and dangerous. As Martin Lindsay had discovered in 1927, more than any other drawback, the absence of good food was the most debilitating of all the hardships he had to endure in Nigeria.

We were very dependent upon the ships that came to Lagos and they always brought us enormous slabs of ice and also great slabs of beef, because there's practically no food in Nigeria locally grown . . . the only locally grown food was rather scraggy hens and their rather small eggs and yam which was a kind of sweet, second-class sweet, and very unpalatable potato. So food was really pretty poor the whole time and that I think is one of the reasons why towards the end of peoples' eighteen months' tour they got progressively tired, because they'd been so badly fed . . . Food was pretty standard, I mean every single dinner started with a tinned soup, then you had the dish of the day, like, say, chicken, or if you were lucky enough to have beef off the Elder Dempster boats, and then you finished up with either sardines on toast or tinned peaches. Practically never any variety from that.

It was generally accepted that towards the end of one's eighteen months' tour one was getting tired and we used to take artificial stimulants, like somebody had the idea that one should drink claret laced with soda water and that would buck one up. But there's not the slightest doubt of it that eighteen months was plenty in those times. I think not so much from incipient malaria but because the food was so appalling and one had been eating such hopeless food.

Sunstroke, too, was considered a hazard and the whites in Africa went to great pains to shield themselves from the heat of the day. Mostly it was a matter of good sense – rising and working early and sheltering from the midday heat – but there were obsessions about wearing heavy sun-helmets and uncomfortable spine-pads which often exacerbated the problem. So enervating was the climate that exposure to it had to be rationed. Just as Lindsay had found in Nigeria, the period of tours of duty had to be restricted in other harsh environments such as the Sudan, where government officers were not allowed to spend more than nine months of any one year in the country and had to retire at the age of fifty. As Rosemary Kenrick, wife of a British political officer, discovered, service in the Sudan demanded a particular type of hardiness and self-sufficiency from the handful of British colonial servants.

Duty and uncomplaining endurance remained tenets of their faith. Admittedly, out in the wild, be it desert, scrub or swamp, there existed few distractions. In some cases, ambition fuelled ceaseless work, but in general the only reward lay in personal satisfaction. Most members of the Political Service came to have a genuine interest in, and affection for, whatever tribe they happened to have been asked to administer, championing it and vindicating it in any dispute.

Nigeria and the Sudan were extreme cases, or at least countries which contained excesses of terrain or climate. In the highlands of eastern and southern Africa, life for the European could be both temperate and spectacular, provoking heroic literary outpourings in which the adjectives fly like locusts. Anne Louise (Hay) Dundas was not the only wife of a British colonial official to be swept off her feet by Africa's breathtaking natural beauty, in her case in Tanganyika after the First World War.

With the approach of twilight the serrated peaks [of the Usambara highlands] rise higher against the fast purpling sky; one thinks of Valhalla and almost expects to see the Valkyrie hosts float from some dark recess into the flaring afterglow of the sunset, which succeeds the darkening shadows for a brief moment and then quickly fades into night.

There are no half-tones in Africa to bridge her changes, the notes are sharply defined. The hot tropical day follows fast on the sunrise; the evening shadows are hovering about before the sun has fairly set, and the black mantle of night is quickly silvered with countless stars, not arriving singly as in European countries, but appearing suddenly, as if a curtain had hastily been drawn from the face of the heavens, revealing the stage set for the night.

Anyone who has lived in Africa knows how awesome are her hours of darkness; a stillness of death pervades the sleeping world of humans, yet one is ever aware of the wildlife which silently creeps from cover with the approach of night, and imagination peoples the thick bush with crouching lions and velvet-footed leopards, and every dancing firefly becomes a glowing eye set in the head of some savage beast.

41

Of course, it was not all poetry. With her newly married husband Kenneth Dundas, Anne Louise Hay was stationed at Chagga, a few degrees south of the Equator where mosquitoes brought malaria and the maintenance of good health was a daily battle. Although the Dundases were only in Tanganyika for two years, Anne was frequently unwell – despite wearing unlovely knee-length mosquito boots, even with her ballgown, she was a prey to malaria – and was forced to spend time in a nearby Roman Catholic mission hospital. None the less, like the increasing numbers of people exposed to Africa in the years following the First World War, she was captivated both by the sheer scale of life there and also by the curiously English suburban atmosphere imported by the European colonial servants and planters. Throughout her diaries, complementing her sense of wonder, there is a feeling of self-satisfaction about the preservation of standards: the creation of golf courses and tennis courts where once had been scrubland, the ritual observation of the sundowner on the verandah and the absolute necessity of changing for dinner. Outside the verandah of the club, in whatever savagery lay beyond, the climate might be demanding and the people primitive, but here in the pool of light, certain standards had to be kept. The Dundases were in Chagga, 250 miles away from the east African coast, but the prevailing ethos could just as easily have been Worthing or Wimbledon.

> One of the saving graces of life in a British station is the unvarying observance of the small conventions which mark the society of civilization. A man may be the only European official, with no neighbour nearer than one hundred miles, but he and his wife (if he has one) will dress as carefully for their lonely dinner as if in the midst of a London season, and the gleaming candles, the flowers and quiet unobtrusive service are considered as essential in Africa as in Mayfair or Upper Fifth Avenue.

And then there was another extreme, the places where white civilization had been imported the better to enjoy Africa: the cool, green highlands of Kenya; Cairo's broad avenues and the solid elegance of Zamalek; the homely suburban spirit of Salisbury with its bracing highveld air; and the smart homesteads and rolling acres of white Cape Province. This was very different from life in the boma up-country where paraffin lamps and tin baths were considered luxuries; but these scenes, too, are part of the panorama of colonial life in Africa.

For example, cosmopolitan Cairo with its variety of cultural styles – Coptic, Greek, Levantine, Jewish and Islamic – possessed enclaves which were unashamedly British. In addition to the island suburb of Zamalek, where the polo-playing acres of the fashionable Sporting Club reflected the British obsession with all things equine, the official British imperial presence was centred within a few square miles. Here on the Nile's east bank was the solid mass of the Kasr-el-Nil barracks, home to the thousand-strong military garrison; here, too, within walking distance, although out-of-bounds to the British other ranks, was Shepheard's Hotel with its famous Long Bar where every secret was a matter of gossip; also within walking distance was the Continental Hotel and the equally exclusive, all-male Turf Club. In the Garden City, the trim lawns of the British Embassy ran down to the banks of the Nile and the Anglican cathedral was a satisfyingly extravagant late-Victorian pile designed by Adrian Gilbert Scott.

Nominally independent since 1936, to all intents and purposes Egypt was run by the British and possessed in its ambassador Sir Miles Lampson a suitably gubernatorial administrator of the old school who believed that King Farouk and the government of Egypt had to be kept firmly in check. No other imperial presence in Africa was so determinedly British in influence and authority: Cairo also had a sizeable and urbane population drawn from all over the Mediterranean, many of whose members were seriously rich or aristocratic, but from the Union Flag flying over the Kasr-el-Nil barracks to the sentries outside the embassy building, British supremacy was paramount.

Running it a close second was Cape Town, with its lush,

white-dominated hinterland of rich pastures and vineyards. It
might have lacked Cairo's pell-mell sophistication and its strong
sense of history – Milner's private secretary described it as a
fourth-rate provincial town peopled by the 'most awful cads' –
but there is a grandeur in its physical setting which even the most
world-weary traveller could hardly ignore. With the dramatic
backdrop of Table Mountain and its horseshoe ridge from
Devil's Peak to Signal Hill, Cape Town itself is surprisingly
compact with a pleasing architectural mix of Dutch domestic
and British imperial. And, like other cities in South Africa, there
were also other divisions and other mixes – the cosmopolitan
cafés and restaurants at Sea Point were light-years removed from
the bleak townships at Khayelitsha or Mitchell's Plain. Here the
schisms were not just between rich and poor but, during the
apartheid years, between white and black. Fired by her child-
hood reading of the novels of Rider Haggard and having won a
Rhodes Travelling Fellowship (the first woman to have done so),
Margery Perham visited South Africa in 1929 to study the
country's 'race problem'. She proved to be a sturdy and independent critic of the racial divisions in the country – strict
segregation was not introduced until 1948 but outside the Cape
the Afrikaners practised *baaskap*, or white domination – but even
so, she found it impossible to ignore Cape Town's natural beauty.

> I found myself every now and then looking up to catch my breath
> in astonishment at the mountain wall rearing up behind the town,
> so high that not even the tallest buildings in the main street could
> shut it from view.
>
> I engaged a room in the part called Seapoint [*sic*] where the open
> sea breaks on the rocks and rows of hotels and pleasant villas cluster
> along this favourable site like shellfish. The Lion Mountain, as
> rounded as Table Mountain is square, lies behind, and its couchant,
> rocky lines against the brilliant South African sky save this suburb
> from looking commonplace. Also, the architecture is good; simple
> houses are washed in pale grey or lemon: they have gardens and per-
> golas brimming over with blossoms, wide, pillared verandahs, and
> often a red-flagged terrace garden climbing up the hill.

44

In later diary-letters home, Perham reveals that her natural inquisitiveness about the lives led by the black people had made her many enemies – 'You wait until you have been ten years in the country before you advance an opinion' was a constant refrain – and her observations on life in South Africa were one of the first attempts by an outsider to understand the country's growing racial tensions. Later, during and after the Second World War, she was to become one of the most trenchant but always constructive critics of the colonial system in Africa.

Geographically and socially, Cairo and Cape Town represented the extremes of British colonial life in Africa. Elsewhere, the contrast with Europe, or indeed with British India, could be startling. Accra, the capital of the Gold Coast, was described by Queen Victoria's granddaughter Princess Marie Louise in 1925 as 'just an ordinary tropical town, with a picturesque native quarter and, in strong contrast, ugly modern buildings and stores with corrugated-iron roofs and some very fine Government offices'. The renowned explorer Rosita Forbes thought that the 'violent contrasts' of Addis Ababa were typical of the Abyssinian people: 'There are a few modern buildings – a hotel, the Bank of Abyssinia, the Legations, and, of course, the palaces of the royal family, but the huts outnumber them, smother them, as a self-sufficient simplicity outweighs the influence both of Africa and Europe.' As Martin Lindsay had discovered when he left Nigeria in 1929, there were fewer than one hundred Europeans in Ibadan and the place itself had a frontier-town atmosphere. Even a relatively well-developed place like Salisbury in Southern Rhodesia had a spirit all of its own, part suburban, part outpost: according to the novelist Doris Lessing, its charm lay in the fact that it was a 'one-horse, one-storey town'.

Other countries, other customs. If society and architecture had failed to create a hegemony over Britain's colonial holdings in Africa, the closest thing to standardization was provided by the men who worked in the Colonial Service. Like their brethren in the Indian Civil Service or the Sudan Political Service, they were an élite group, selected for their academic achievement at school and university and sometimes, too, for their prowess on the sporting field; many regarded their service as being more of a calling than a well-paid job. (In the 1930s a young officer was paid £450 a year and was able to retire on full pension when he reached 55.) True, military men who served in the British South Africa Police or the King's African Rifles could be equally Jesuitical about their calling, but the District Officers of the Colonial Service were in a class of their own when it came to producing uniform standards of professionalism in colonial administration. For one thing, the virtue best remembered by Briton and African alike, they were completely incorruptible.

> In thirty-one years in Nigeria, I was only once offered a bribe. I was sitting in the office in Aba in eastern Nigeria during the war, working overtime in the afternoon and a local lorry-owner came up to try to get a permit for his lorry which he had difficulty in getting. I was then DO, Aba, and he came in to see me and he said, I can't get my permit, can you help me, please. And he produced an envelope and I thought it was just something showing what his lorry's faults were. But when I opened it up, there were two five-pound notes.
>
> I seized the telephone, got on to the local British Commissioner of Police and said, 'Josh, a man has just offered me a bribe.' The police came along, arrested him and next day in court he was sentenced to three months' imprisonment.

One reason for the preservation of the ethos remembered by Johnnie McCall was the selection process. Just as the India Office had created a well-oiled system for assessing candidates for the Indian Civil Service, so too did the Colonial Office take considerable pains to choose the right kind of young man for service in the colonies. Few formal rules existed: considerably more important were the possession of favourable references from school and university, an interest in sport and outdoor activities and a reasonable degree. Otherwise, everything depended on the candidate's ability to 'fit in' and sublimate himself to the service of empire; or as Lugard put it, the best men should be all-rounders who possessed 'an almost passionate conception of fair play, or protection of the weak, and of playing the game'.

What the process meant in practice was the candidate's ability to convince the Colonial Office's Patronage Secretary that he possessed the right qualities to live and work in a small and tightly-knit service, often in harsh or primitive surroundings. For thirty-eight years, from before the First World War until after the end of the Second World War, the Patronage Secretary was Sir Ralph Furse, a conservative imperialist of the old school who was responsible for interviewing thousands of candidates for the service. If they were successful they proceeded to a final, formal interview before a board at Burlington House, but everything depended on making a good impression on the Patronage Secretary. A tall, kindly man with the air of an efficient housemaster, Furse was ideally suited to the task of putting candidates at their ease; in fact, even before the interview had taken place, he had gone to considerable pains to ensure that the young man sitting in his office possessed the qualities he was seeking. As one of them, Kenneth Bradley, remembered in later life, Furse 'looked neither for brilliance – men with firsts went into the ICS anyway – nor for Blues, but he did want people who had learned at school the elements of leadership'.

From a wide network of the great and good in British education – headmasters of the leading public schools and tutors at Oxford, Cambridge, London and the ancient Scottish universities – he had discovered everything there was to know about the most suitable young men, and he claimed in later life that this ability to spot talent saved the Colonial Service no end of trouble. Far better, he reasoned, to know a man's strengths and weaknesses before appointing him than to discover them once he was out in the field.

Taking his text from the seventh book of Judges, in which God instructs Gideon on the selection of the Midianites, Furse insisted that qualities of character, personality and physical bearing were as important as intellectual ability and that these could often only be deduced by the personal contact of a private interview.

A man will not reveal himself till he is at ease and natural. This is one of several reasons against interviews by board alone. Before a board, a man is seldom quite himself: I have often proved this by watching a man before a board whom I had previously seen alone. But the combination of board and personal interview is valuable. It serves as a useful check, and tells you both what a man is really like and how he will behave in public. Normally he comes in all strung up and on the defensive: you must give him time to relax before you can really begin. The more I learnt of the business, the longer my interviews lasted: at first, perhaps quarter of an hour; towards the end of my time, three-quarters, an hour, an hour and a half. Beware of the fellow who says he can judge a man as soon as he comes into the room: he is probably lazy or does not know his job. It *can* be done sometimes, but rarely. Often you must correct your early impressions.

And the system worked. During one interview with a highly recommended candidate who seemed to have all the qualities required by the Colonial Service, Furse's telephone began to ring. The man was obviously startled and upset by the interruption. Later investigation by Furse revealed that the man had been buried by a shell-burst during the First World War and still suffered from anxiety attacks. Such a fellow might crack up in front of the natives and he failed to proceed to interview by the board. Another candidate was almost rejected because he had a 'languid handshake' but redeemed himself by responding well to Furse's firm grip at the conclusion of the interview. In the 1930s at least, it was also considered a solecism to prefer Virginia to Turkish cigarettes and all candidates were expected to answer in the affirmative when asked if they played cricket. By these means, a mixture of common sense and social condescension, Furse was able to fill the Colonial Office's list of vacancies for service overseas with 'good types'. As W. R. Crocker, one of his better-known appointments, reminded him: 'The most dangerous man you can have in the Colonial Service is the clever cad.'

Candidates were free to make known their own preference of posting but this was not necessarily accepted by the interviewing board which met at the Civil Service Commission at Burlington Gardens. Much depended on availability; and the candidate's own temperament and ability had also to be taken into account. For example, a good horseman might be sent to Northern Nigeria where the absence of the tse-tse fly meant that horses could be kept and polo was a popular sport. Although its presence was always denied, there was an unofficial social pecking order which meant that candidates had to be acceptable both to the local British and to the existing native population. Kenya, with Lord Delamere and his set, and Northern Nigeria, with its polo and Muslim Fulani aristocracy, considered themselves to be a cut above the others; claims which were hotly denied by Tanganyika and Nyasaland. Sudan, like India, had its own service and such was the prevalence of good sportsmen amongst its officers that it was known as the service where Blues ruled blacks. Length of tour was also a factor: west Africa was a year to eighteen months on account of its debilitating climate; healthier east Africa two to four years. All these factors played their part, although it was commonly assumed by all candidates that if they did not receive the posting of their choice, selection had been made by way of sticking a pin into the list. In 1935 Kenneth Simmonds was given his preference of Kenya – his adventurous vacation work at sea on whalers and trawlers made a good impression – but even so he found the interview an unsettling experience.

Across a semicircular table sat a row of six or so elderly (to us) gentlemen, the Commissioners. One of them used an ear trumpet and exhorted me to speak up, which I did manfully, whereupon another Commissioner with a very up-to-date electronic hearing gadget said, 'Don't talk so loudly – you'll damage my instrument'; a ploy, which if nothing else, was a test of one's character.

Once selected, the candidates proceeded to the Colonial Service Course which was run jointly by the universities of Oxford and Cambridge and which had been designed to give a broad introduction to the demands of the service. Separate courses were run for those entering the specialist Agricultural, Forestry and Police services. Because most new Assistant District Officers (ADOs) would be required to spend much of their time in solitary stations or on tours of duty in remote areas, they had to be self-sufficient: as a result, one part of the course was strictly practical, with training in basic engineering, hygiene and agricultural techniques. Another important element was a grounding in legal procedures: in his district, the officer had to be both lawmaker and law-enforcer. By way of introduction to the individual colony, there was an elementary language course; although it was commonly agreed that the best training would start when the cadet actually arrived in the colony to take up his post.

Once kitted up with tropical clothes and basic camping equipment, itself an experience, especially before the Second World War when retailers such as Griffiths McAllister and the Army and Navy Stores supplied lists of clothing 'necessities' – everything from Bombay or Wolseley pith helmets to palm beach suits – the fledgeling ADO travelled out to Africa by sea. For those going to west Africa, this meant a voyage by an Elder Dempster mailboat from Liverpool; while the east African service travelled by the British India and Union Castle lines from London. While standards on board were never those of the lordly Peninsular and Oriental which served India, there was a definite pecking order. Government officials, trading managers and missionaries travelled first class, public works officials second and there was even a third class for Africans. The main difference between P&O and Elder Dempster or the lines serving South Africa was one of style. Whereas India-bound travellers were encouraged and indeed instructed by the purser to maintain strict standards of behaviour, Harold Franklin discovered the atmosphere was more relaxed on the *Glengorm Castle*, the ship taking him to join the colonial service in Northern Rhodesia in 1928.

There was the excitement of the Fancy Dress Night, when a husband on honeymoon, dressed as a policeman, accused another young man, robed in the habit of a monk, of lasciviously stroking his wife's legs, temptingly exposed beneath her fringed Robin Hood jerkin. The accusation, scarcely doubted by the rest of the male passengers who had had the legs under admiring but discreet observation, was hotly denied by the accused. Robin Hood burst into tears, which further incensed the husband. In the ensuing fight the monk was much hampered by his long habit and the police-man, appropriately, won. The opponents shook hands and Robin Hood was revived with champagne. All three became the best of friends and the party reached great heights; such heights that the husband suggested a swim before bed. It was, he said, a certain guarantee against hangover.

Once in Africa itself, drinking was more restrained – except for the incurable alcoholics, rarely during the day and moder-ately after sundown – but as many colonial servants found, the two-week voyage was a time out of life with deck-games during the day and dancing and flirtations in the evening. As the pas-sengers realized they were travelling to work in Africa by the only means available and were therefore out of contact with Britain and Africa for a fortnight, the enforced idleness created a strange limbo as they passed between one life and the next.

For those going to central or southern Africa, the landfall was Cape Town, whose spectacular scenery more than compensated for the three weeks at sea which Franklin felt had been 'too long'.

Despite the superb food and drink, the deck-games and the inter-esting amour in which my cabin-mate was engaged, for the last week of the voyage I was bored. There was too much sea in the Atlantic Ocean. I felt it ought to be punctuated with interesting islands, and in any case I was in a hurry to get on with the job of civilizing my noble savages.

For those travelling to west Africa, such as Philip Allison, who joined the Nigerian Forestry Service in 1931, the first port of call was Freetown in Sierra Leone, then Accra, Gold Coast's capital, where the passengers had to be rowed ashore in surf-boats and finally the landlocked lagoon of Lagos which Allison described as

> the worst day of the tour; suddenly stepping off the boat into real life; haggling through the customs (perhaps to be introduced to the husband of your shipboard sweetheart); trans-shipping a pile of crates and tin trunks on to the branch-boat to Port Harcourt or up-country by rail or road; to come to rest at your station where, with luck, you would be welcomed by the familiar grin of your steward, prepared again within his limited capacity to organize your comforts (with the inadequate materials at hand) for the next year or two until, once again, you set out on the long voyage home.

For first-timers, the physical shock of Africa was even greater. To begin with, the oven-hot temperature on land was quite different from the balmy day spent at sea along the coast. The smells were strange, too, and most one-time residents have little difficulty in conjuring up Africa's multitudinous aromas: pungent mangrove woodsmoke; decaying vegetation; the reeking, damp soil after torrential rain; rancid palm oil; or the sweetness of mimosa. And then there were the sounds: the distant drumming from the native quarter; the rustle of hidden animals in the bush; the whine of mosquitoes and the constant chirrup of countless crickets. After the senses had been assaulted by this strange, new world, its different customs had to be learned, too. Before the Second World War it was considered insane to walk in the sun without a hat or a spine-pad – a padded strip of cotton drill to protect the spine from the heat of the sun. Most old hands refused to drink alcohol until after the sun had finally gone down and then usually with quinine to ward off malaria.

There was also a question of protocol, which was still important in the years between the two world wars. On arrival in the capital, the new ADO was supposed to sign the governor's book and if his new station was large enough he was supposed to make his presence known through the system of 'calling' at the various residences. Normally bachelors or unattached married men did not warrant a call but, as every wife found, the social atmosphere in their station seemed to be about fifty years behind the times.

Africa was probably never as rigid as India; nevertheless, the newcomer had to learn the code and abide by it. On arrival, the mysteries of calling were first performed, especially in the smaller stations. You called on your seniors, while your equals and juniors called on you. This involved the whole paraphernalia of hats, gloves and stockings, not to mention visiting-cards. The most senior officials in any town or boma kept a visitors' book on a table at the door which you duly signed; the more lowly had a silver or brass tray for the receipt of cards.

In fact, despite the strict rules surrounding the custom, 'calling' helped to break the ice for a newcomer and usually resulted in invitations to drinks or dinner. Even so, social occasions could be a minefield for the unwary, as many hostesses paid a good deal of attention to precedence, especially as it was laid down by the Colonial Service's Civil List which not only listed a man's seniority, but also his age, qualifications and current salary. Although some people placed an importance on protocol and precedence which might seem ridiculous to modern eyes – hostesses went to great lengths to ensure that the wife of the Forestry Superintendent should not be outranked at table by the younger and prettier wife of a policeman – there was a good reason for the hierarchical nature of British social life in Africa. Because it was usually a small, clannish society and because everyone knew everyone else – and how much they were paid – some sort of formal order had to be introduced, particularly at government receptions or official dinners.

★

Only in the club were the rules sufficiently relaxed to allow people to let down their hair amongst their own kind. On one level it could be a grand, formal place like the English Club in Zanzibar or the Muthaiga in Nairobi which reflected the aristocratic, or at least upper-class, interests of Kenya's white settlers. On another level, the one best remembered by most people, it could be a solidly unpretentious establishment offering good sporting and recreational amenities which were available to most Europeans in the vicinity, the very fact of residence granting eligibility to all but the most antisocial. Such was the club at Chagga. It had its own tennis courts, nine-hole golf course and swimming-pool; there was also a decent dining-room and bar, and for Anne Louise Dundas and her friends, social life revolved round drinks on the verandah after sundown.

> After the games of golf or tennis, small parties gather for the evening drink, which is rated as indispensable to health in the tropics, where the evening air calls forth the lurking germs of fever. 'Small chop' (sandwiches) accompany the sundown medicine of Scotch or rye, and the time from six-thirty to eight o'clock passes in the telling of tales (some 'out of school'), the recounting of varied experiences in other parts of the world, and discussion of the happenings, political or otherwise, 'at home'. A name is casually mentioned by a newcomer: 'Oh yes, he was stationed with me on the Gold Coast', breaks in the 'old timer', and so the circle ever widens, and new links of interest are forged in that human chain of younger sons who have gone forth to represent the empirical Mother.

In the main urban centres, clubs could be stuffier places which denied membership to those in trade or to lowly 'B'-class public works officials but in the out-stations up-country, the social code was not so strictly enforced. Military messes were equally relaxed, if usually somewhat smaller establishments. Again, the rules were unwritten but understood by every officer who was a member, just as they would have been in the regiments of the

British Army. At Ibadan, the 4th Nigeria Regiment's mess was a bungalow with mud walls and a thatched roof, but it was still a place of 'jolly talk and lots of jokes' for the fifteen or twenty British officers who used it.

> The officers' mess was a very jolly place, everybody was full of fun and jokes and thoroughly enjoyable company, and of course we were all in the position of being unmarried officers. There may have been three or four officers who were married, with their wives at home, but it was just a very pleasant bachelor establishment. Except of course the Colonel was treated with great respect.
>
> The mess carried on very informally. Except for the Colonel, nobody was called sir; the young officers didn't call the majors sir. We used to put on a white mess dress with a scarlet cummerbund in the evening and a soft shirt and black tie. We used to have a guest night once a week when the local District Officer, or the local policeman, or perhaps the bank manager, whoever you'd made friends with in the community, would come to dinner and the band used to play. Somebody would perhaps go out and conduct the band afterwards, to which the band paid no attention at all and went on playing as they would have done normally.

For Martin Lindsay and his fellow officers, the day had begun with a morning parade at six o'clock, followed by field work or administration until lunch-time. Afternoon was pre-ordained for rest, followed by a brisk game of polo between four o'clock and six o'clock. Before gathering in the mess for drinks at seven-thirty, most officers used the time to study Hausa, it being a requirement of the regiment that sufficient knowledge of the language be learned within nine months of arrival. (There was an official oral examination which tested officers on their ability to give basic orders and to converse colloquially with local chiefs.) Although there was considerable heavy drinking up-country – at Degema on the Niger delta, Philip Allison was told that the lunchtime gin-drinking sessions took place because 'Christmas lasts from Armistice Day until Easter' – Lindsay and his colleagues were more restrained.

55

The usual thing was to have a pink gin before dinner and then perhaps a whisky and soda at dinner, there was very little serious drinking. Beer of course was drunk on Sunday mornings before lunch and that sort of thing, a good deal of beer was drunk because it was a hot country and iced beer is extremely good in a hot country.

Unfortunately, though, alcoholism took its toll all over Africa. The heavy drinking sessions at Degema were mirrored in other out-of-the-way areas where men lived alone or in tiny communities. Not only was it common for them to become depressed by their surroundings and the absence of company but even the strongest minds could wilt before the very presence of Africa. Some took to drinking heavily to allay the boredom and frustrations of everyday life and had to be repatriated by the Colonial Office or their trading firm for their own good. Others developed eccentricities or went 'native', abandoning the pretence of dressing for dinner and maintaining social standards. Cullen Gouldsbury, a District Officer at Malale in Northern Rhodesia before the First World War, called the mood 'Africitis' and suggested that its onset could be caused by the slightest setback.

If there is anything more solidly depressing than perpetual rain, I should be glad to hear of it. The drizzle of London streets is bad enough; but when the rain is falling steadily over the untidy wilderness of tropical bush, when the wife of one's bosom has retired to the fastness of her bedroom with pronounced 'Africitis' (for which there is no known cure save the healing lapse of time), and the English mail is eighteen hours late – then, indeed, the matter becomes a tragedy meriting the attention of the High Gods.

Fortunately, in the Gouldsburgs' case the affliction was not terminal, Africa's 'marvellous recuperative qualities' allowing them 'to rise at dawn radiant with an energy just as wonderful in its own way as the overnight depression'. Others were not so fortunate. In the worst cases, some committed suicide either in desperation or in shame: one officer in the Nigeria Regiment sent home before the outbreak of war shot himself during the retreat to Dunkirk in 1940. Like Marlow in Joseph Conrad's novel *Heart of Darkness*, they had asked and failed to answer the question: 'What were we who had strayed in here? Could we handle that dumb thing or would it handle us? I felt how big, how confoundedly big was the thing that couldn't talk and perhaps was deaf as well.'

There were, of course, compensations. There was ample sport, from birds to big game. Rough shooting at the end of the day was a pleasant form of relaxation and officers serving with the King's African Rifles in Kenya, Uganda, Tanganyika and Nyasaland considered safaris and the opportunity to shoot elephant or big cats to be the highlight of their posting. Here they were following in the footsteps of such well-known big-game hunters as Chauncey Hugh Stigand, Dennis Lyell and James Brander Dunbar, who were keen hunters and writers on the subject of big game during their service with the King's African Rifles before the First World War. Others revelled in the district's natural life and became experts in the local plant, bird or insect life, frequently contributing the result of their discoveries to learned journals. A few became interested in ethnology or undertook expeditions. Indeed, for army officers, leave could be refused if it resembled a holiday and in the Sudan Defence Force, British Army officers of the calibre of Hugh Boustead and Orde Wingate undertook expeditions, respectively, to climb Mount Everest and to discover the Oasis of Zerzura in the Libyan desert.

A substantial handful found solace in the local women. This tended to happen up-country or in remote outposts where there might only be two or three Europeans living in a twenty-mile radius. In the Nigeria Regiment between the two world wars, it was estimated that about one-third of the officers and two-thirds of the NCOs had slept with native women. Officially, abstinence was the order of the day. Older members of the Colonial Service and the army claimed that the separation of boys from parents and the female sex implicit in a public-school education could be useful preparation for a life of service which could be lonely and chaste for long periods at a time. Others asked their servants to bring back a local woman for the night: this was the advice given to Harry Franklin shortly after he took up his first appointment in Northern Rhodesia.

> I never did have a black girl, at Serenje or anywhere else, partly because I never saw one that seemed sufficiently attractive; partly because I couldn't imagine what I would do with the girl or say to her, outside the bedroom; and partly because I thought it would be letting down the Service. On the last point I was hopelessly wrong. As I was to discover, any bachelor official or grass widower who did not take on a native girl was regarded as queer by the people. He had the *droit de seigneur* of a chief, and there could only be one (unflattering) reason why he did not exercise it.

In addition to loneliness, the absence of white women also encouraged men to take on native mistresses. For all young men in Africa, whether they were in government service or trade, the rules of engagement in the Colonial Service prevented them from getting married until they had reached a position of seniority. In the Sudan Political Service, no officer could get married until he had completed four years of service and no one was permitted to become engaged until he had reached the age of twenty-seven. This was less draconian than it first appears. Apart from the capital, Khartoum, life in the out-stations could be tough, unyielding and, more than anything else, dominated by men. As most were bachelors who regarded duty and uncomplaining endurance as tenets of their faith and who looked for little reward other than personal satisfaction in their service, they were unlikely to welcome a married woman into their monastic society. It was also thought that in some places the climate might be too enervating for women. Asked if he would ever bring his wife out to Africa, a District Officer replied incredulously: 'Why, my wife has such a delicate complexion that she has to wash her face always in distilled water.'

Not that white women were entirely missing from the African scene. Indeed, some of the doughtiest travellers and missionaries were women, and their distaff reminiscences frequently provide more detailed and certainly more personal insights into everyday colonial life. Whereas a man might dwell on his manly exploits as an explorer, soldier, administrator or trader, their wives or independent visitors, like the Australian May Mott-Smith, noticed small domestic details of life – in her case, the problem of finding accommodation for guests in the more remote areas of Africa before the Second World War.

> There are no hotels either for the traveller, the trader or for the government official. No place for anyone except at the homes of friends or at the home of a resident representative of his firm or of his country. Therefore any day a local agent must be prepared to share his bed and board with some visitor. Sometimes it is literally his bed unless the one who must depend upon his hospitality is put up in the dining-room. There are few bungalows with guest-rooms. This is all right if the stranger is of a congenial temperament to his host. It is a lonesome country at best and life for the gregarious person is hard, but one can imagine in such an atmosphere of imposed care and close association how antipathies and prejudices become magnified and how quickly they grow.
>
> The situation is complicated rather than softened by the presence of a wife. In a land where so much of the food supply is dependent on cold-storage stuff from ships, an extra mouth to feed, if one is caught when the larder is bare, becomes an embarrassment. Not that I heard any murmurs or complaints about this problem from those who are there.

A man might have noticed the problems of accommodation – and laughed it off – but it is difficult to imagine him making any reference to the provision of food for the sudden visitor. True, some of the letters and diaries written by the many female missionaries or wives of missionaries tend towards maternalism – the African treated as a holy innocent, part savage, part booby, but wholly lovable – but they did typify a difference of attitude.

59

Mott-Smith, for example, was aware of the sexual tensions between whites and blacks and wrote about it sensitively. In one case, reminiscent of Kipling's short story 'Georgie Porgie', she encountered a British official who had become so attached to his Nigerian mistress that the arrival of his wife brought genuine agony: 'the night before her arrival the negress and the white man spent the hours together in tears.'

However, Mott-Smith was less sensitive about the other side of the relationship, where white women lived with black men. Although she had been assured that no minister in Africa would ever carry out such a marriage, she did know of seven women in Lagos who were married to Africans. 'What their life is can only be conjectured,' she wrote. 'They are pariahs to both races. Usually the woman was some hard-working girl from England who had been won by tales of the riches and princely importance at home of her dusky suitor. Too late she learned the real conditions.' It was not an uncommon experience: stories were legion on the Elder Dempster line of young girls travelling out to west Africa to marry their 'prince', only to find that he was a shop assistant in Freetown or Lagos.

Such behaviour was abhorrent to the white community. Another Australian visitor, Mary Gaunt, travelling in west Africa some fifteen years before Mott-Smith, expressed the distaste in pseudo-Darwinian terms: 'The native who has had contact with the white man is but on the first rung of civilization. Between black and white there is that unbridgeable gulf fixed, and no man may cross it.' Some women did, though, and found themselves ostracized by the white community. As Gaunt also noted: 'tall, stalwart, handsome as is many a negro, no white woman may take a black man for her husband and be respected by her own people.' Racism was one reason for the obloquy, the clash of cultures another – many of the girls found themselves living in simple mud huts with a polygamous husband – and sexual anxiety yet another, but throughout the period of colonialism in Africa, a double standard prevailed. A white man might take a black mistress – at least before the Second World War – but woe betide the British girl who married into African society. Occasionally the local authorities would intervene by helping with repatriation; but as J.E. Hodge, an officer in the Nigerian police, discovered, it had to be done sensitively to avoid hurting the Africans' feelings.

> Well, they didn't like to make a fuss, the Africans would feel they were being insulted because they hadn't been able to treat her properly. I mean, a girl who had never lived in this country had not the least idea of African food that she had to eat or provide from the market. And no idea of the language; quite often she'd be abused or other people like me just laughing with her – and she'd think laughing at her. And there were definitely cases where husbands had beaten their wives good and proper and did so regularly. Or when she got out here she'd find that he'd already got a wife according to native law and custom and that she wasn't strictly married.

The shortness of the time spent in service in Africa also gave a different edge to life in the colonies. Apart from the settlers and planters in Kenya or Rhodesia who regarded Africa as their home (while retaining strong sentimental links with Britain), most British colonial servants were birds of passage, many of whom might flit from one colony to another during the course of their career. To aspire to the dizzy heights of a governor, the district officer had perforce to aim for the secretariat in a colonial capital and that could entail changes of colony. Alan Burns, for example, served in the Leeward Island and the Bahamas as well as in Nigeria and the Gold Coast. For those with ambitions it could be a congenial move, particularly as amenities began to improve, but others, drawn by the attractions of working alone in an area where their authority would be absolute, preferred the life of the District Officer. Not that aspiring for the stars was an easy lot. Africa was divided into three classes of governorship, the first being Nigeria, Kenya, the Gold Coast and Tanganyika; the second, Sierra Leone, Uganda and Northern Rhodesia; the third, Nyasaland, the Gambia, British Somaliland and Zanzibar.

One consequence was that great store was placed on the level of appointment – the Colonial Office kept a constantly changing list of suitable candidates for gubernatorial appointments – and on the level of public reward in the New Year's Honours List; a knighthood being the preferred prize.

Another consequence was that there was a distinct gulf between the DOs in the country areas and the secretariat officials in the capital. The first might possess a strong, even tribal loyalty to the people in his district and see the local problems through their eyes, whereas the administrator might think he had a clearer and more objective idea of their actual needs. While Burns was serving in Nigeria, he noticed a tendency for secretariat officers to write sarcastic or critical comments in the margins of reports, knowing that they would be seen by the District Officers who had filed them. When he became Governor of the Gold Coast in 1941, he laid down guidelines to put a stop to the practice.

> The secretariat officer, who has seen previous correspondence and precedents, often knows much more than another officer regarding a subject under discussion, but this is a reason for being helpful and no excuse for impatience or discourtesy. But the secretariat officer, knowledgeable as he may be in the matter of rules and precedents, sometimes has little knowledge of problems which rise in 'the bush', and little sympathy for the officer who has to deal with them; and it is this lack of sympathy which provokes the not-infrequent anti-secretariat complex which one finds in stations away from headquarters.

Tribal loyalties were equally pronounced in the armies which served in the British colonies in Africa. Just as the regiments of the British Army place a strong emphasis on the concept of 'family', so too did British officers and NCOs serving with colonial forces create strong bonds of friendship and trust with the men they commanded. In the West African Frontier Force, an officer serving with a Hausa regiment, for example, would regard his men as being superior to an Ashanti unit and the same was true vice versa. The force enlisted men from all of Britain's west African colonies and incorporated such doughty formations as the Royal African Colonial Corps (1816), the Sierra Leone Frontier Police (1829) and the Hausa Constabulary, or 'Glover's Horse' (1865). It came into being in 1897 and by 1901 it consisted of the Northern Nigeria Regiment, the Southern Nigeria Regiment, the Gold Coast Regiment, the Sierra Leone Battalion, the Lagos Battalion and the Gambia Company. By then, the King's African Rifles had also emerged through the amalgamation of the Central Africa Regiment, the Uganda Rifles, the East Africa Rifles and the levies in British Somaliland, including the Camel Corps.

The Sudan Defence Force also enrolled men from such a multiplicity of tribes – Sudanese Muslims, Baqqara Arabs, Somalian negroes – that it was not uncommon for British officers to be fiercely loyal to the men in their Idara (company). 'They were delightful people,' wrote Orde Wingate of the men under his command at Kassala in 1929, 'and I should have been perfectly happy to concern myself with their affairs indefinitely.' Indeed, according to Hugh Boustead, the close relationship with the men was one of the main attractions of secondment to the SDF.

> The family atmosphere of the company, the manliness and intense fun of the Sudanese soldiers and the complete reliance on his officers produced a feeling of affection between the British company commander and his men which formed one of the main charms of African service with an irregular corps.

For that reason, the SDF took considerable care over the selection of officers. All candidates had to have completed at least five years' service with a British regiment and during the 1920s and 1930s selection depended almost entirely on the old boy network.

Nearly always the officer serving in the SDF knew of someone (usually in his British regiment) who he thought would get on well with SDF life, and if his friend would like to apply for secondment he would recommend him. It was not easy to get selected if you did not know somebody serving, or someone who had just finished serving with the SDF.

Although to modern ears the 'need to fit in' smacks of a closed shop or private club, it was an important qualification. With a roster of only 4,500 men, the SDF was a compact organization and its small band of officers had to work harmoniously in remote areas, usually without the amenities of modern life. In Darfur Province alone, there were only twenty-three British civilian and military personnel to govern and control an area of 192,000 square miles, four times the size of Britain, with a population of 1,005,000. All officers were expected to ride and to play bridge, both necessary requirements in postings where entertainment had to be home-made. Three months' leave was granted each year and this had to be spent outside the country, preferably in Britain or at least in Europe, a wise precaution given Sudan's enervating climate. In addition, each new officer had to learn, and be examined in, enough rudimentary Arabic to understand his men. Above all, they had to be single. Unless the newcomer was prepared to accommodate himself to these local conditions, life for his colleagues would have been intolerable.

Despite the physical discomforts and the monastic life, it is not difficult to understand why British officers enjoyed serving in the more remote parts of the empire in the years before the Second World War. Far away from the rigid discipline and protocol which surrounded regimental life in the garrisons at home or the cantonments in India, they could develop their own ideas and interests and were able to exercise authority well beyond their age and experience. A young subaltern could find himself in charge of around 200 men in an isolated area where conditions might be crude or dangerous. If communications were primitive or the chain of command flexible – as was the case in the majority of places – he was supposed to show initiative, and survival was frequently a matter of forgetting the rules and acting according to local conditions. In short, it was what the more adventurous officer called 'real soldiering'. Africa offered all this in abundance. In the vastness of Sudan, a young subaltern with the local rank of *bimbashi* had to combine the attributes of a military commander and a colonial administrator.

> He had to be a man of spirit, initiative, reliability and resourceful-ness: above all, he had to be an energetic type with a good sense of humour, for he was on his own now, with no CO, no other company commander, adjutant or quartermaster with whom to discuss his problems or to guide him.

But as Colonel J. H. R. Orlebar, the SDF's historian, also makes clear, soldiering in the Sudan, as in other parts of Africa, had its compensations. Each Idara was supposed to carry out a number of treks or patrols to show the flag in remote areas of the country and because much of it had not been explored or the maps were rudimentary, these expeditions took on the aspect of an adventure. Setting off in the cool morning – in the cold season, temperatures could fall to as low as two degrees Fahrenheit – the men would swing into the march, lu-luing their rhythmic tribal songs. Ahead lay a long slow trek in the ever-growing heat, broken at midday, until the shade of the evening brought a welcome rest for the night. A *zeriba*, a tem-porary fortification cut from thick thorn bushes and sage brushes, would be constructed for the Idara's protection, a camp-fire would be lit and dinner prepared as darkness fell. The night would be alive with a mixture of sounds: the soft padding of the camels as they walked into the lines, the steady thumping to restore the circulation after the day's march and, later still, the chatter of the men laughing and joking around the camp-fires. Beyond the *zeriba*, the immensity of the hills or plain stretched in darkness and a silence so intense that it was impossible not to hear the slightest sound. And overhead the sky was speckled with the sharp brightness of African stars.

If the scene is touched by romance, then on one level it was a fabulous existence: men on secondment to the colonial forces in Africa felt that they had tasted the salt of life and that its savour would never leave them.

Many of the traders in the colonies also shared those bucolic memories of life in the bush, on trek, or up-country, particularly in the early days when they had to be part explorer, part soldier and part colonial administrator. In the nineteenth century, the 'coasters' who traded in west Africa had to be both hardy and assertive, such was the harsh nature of the local environment and the cut-throat competition. In the creeks of the Niger delta – known collectively as the Oil Rivers – the trade in palm oil was lucrative for the traders, but it also extracted a heavy price. A popular saying had it that every bar of soap made from the oil contained a drop of English blood: conditions on land were considered so bad that the traders lived in the reconstructed hulks of superannuated ships where it was supposed to be healthier than living ashore. Described as huge Noah's Arks, the vessels were elaborately designed or even fortified, and in the estuaries of the Niger delta, at Calabar, Bonny and Nun, many remained serviceable until the Second World War.

During the nineteenth century, traders in the interior of Africa had to be jacks-of-all-trades. In Sierra Leone the major trading routes were not securely guarded, ambushes were common and one eminent trader, John Whitford, recommended that newcomers from Britain should possess 'sound constitutions combined with a knowledge of Manchester, Sheffield and Birmingham goods, also able to handle a rifle, cook food, do anything rough and enjoy doing so, as well as eating heartily'. In west Africa, it was a hard life, the dangers no different from those shared by the other inhabitants, but if a man was prepared to work hard and look after his own and his company's interests, he could be well rewarded. One of Whitford's Scottish colleagues explained that 'in this region every man does what

is right in his own eyes, and obeying no law but his own pleasure, is accountable to no one – so long as he makes the factory
pay'.

To survive and survive profitably, the trader had to learn how
to barter, bargaining the exchange of Manchester cotton or
Sheffield cutlery for elephant tusks or palm oil, or ensuring that
most of the cash paid out for goods was returned with the sale
of his own products. Many took on local chiefs as trading partners but the relentless free-trading conditions created an intense
rivalry which often led to violence. In 1875 the traveller and
writer Mary Kingsley came across a trader in Nigeria who
defended his trading station with a Gatling gun and it was not
uncommon for traders to barter guns and alcohol for oil and
ivory. And, as we have seen, the companies run by men like
Rhodes and Goldie also made war on tribal opposition, seizing
land for the British crown in the name of trade.

By the beginning of the twentieth century, the fighting was
restricted to commercial wars and among the first casualties were
the palm-oil rivals in Nigeria, including Goldie's Niger
Company, which were bought up and consolidated by Lord
Leverhulme as the United Africa Company. The economic
recession of the 1930s also encouraged young men to a commercial career in Africa, where pay was higher and expenses
lower and many a clerk or cadet, as they were known, followed
much the same path taken as the fledgeling ADO. However,
although conditions of service had improved with the introduction of better salaries and pensions, their social position in the
colony faded – perhaps one reason why the 'old coasters'
deplored the arrival of white women. With the increasing social
stratification of colonial life in Africa, men in commerce or trade
occupied a lower position in local society than the colonial
administrators and army officers and in some centres they were
often prevented from joining the local club until they had
reached a reasonable seniority. In Kenya and Tanganyika, to be
in trade was to be in a position similar to the jute-wallahs in

Bengal who were usually looked down upon by the 'heavenly ones' of the Indian Civil Service.

For all that the white colonies in Africa tended to create their own local snobberies, often reflecting those found in any middle-class suburb in Britain, there was one redeeming factor which touched everyone: a common love of Africa and the lives they led in the colonies. A man might suffer temporarily from Africitis, his wife might complain of MMBA – miles and miles of bloody Africa – but were it not for the weirdly fascinating natural beauty of the place and the friendliness of most of the people, few colonial servants, of whatever social hue, could fail to admit to a lasting love for whatever corner they served. You can take the man out of Africa but, as Mary Gaunt and others discovered, you cannot take Africa out of the man.

> Africa holds. The man who has once known Africa longs for her. In the sordid city streets he remembers the might and loneliness of the forests, by the rippling brook he remembers the wide rivers rushing tumultuously to the sea, in the night when the rain is splashing drearily he remembers the gorgeous tropical nights, the sky of velvet far away, the stars like points of gold, the warm moonlight that with its deeper shadows made a fairer world. Even the languor and heat he longs for, the white foam of the surf or the yellow sand of the beaches, the thick jungle growth densely matted, rankly luxuriant, pulsating with the irrepressible life of the Tropics. All other places are tame.

3

The Beginning of the End

WAR, THE GREAT source of social and industrial change, was also responsible for many of the moves which led to the demise of the British Empire. In fact, even before the Second World War broke out, it was clear that India, the 'Jewel in the Crown', was on the road towards independence. The Government of India Act of 1935 had loosened British power by granting the franchise to thirty million Indians and by giving virtual autonomy to the provincial governments, whose ministers were mainly Indian. The pattern of recruitment to the Indian Civil Service also altered: between 1931 and 1935, only ninety-one British officers were appointed, as opposed to 130 Indians. This was largely due to a policy of gradual Indianization of the service, but the shortfall of British appointments was also caused by a realization amongst younger officers that they might not see out their service in India. John Christie, who had joined the ICS in 1928, likened the wartime atmosphere in the hot-weather station of Simla to 'the gaiety of the Duchess of Richmond's ball before Waterloo'.

Seen from the vantage point of today, the Government of India Act seems only to have provided a puny set of reforms, offering only safeguards, reservations and a division of responsibility, but at the time it was considered to be a major experiment in the division of power within Britain's major imperial holding. At the subsequent elections, the Congress Party dominated the polls in the provinces – they were the main focus for nationalist aspirations – but recklessly refused to form coalitions or alliances with the rival Muslim League, thereby paving the way for the future creation of the Muslim state of Pakistan. The declaration of war against Germany on 3 September 1939 brought the constitutional experiment to an end, but, in truth, by then Britain was growing tired of the imperial connection with India. 'For those of us who were serving in India during the last five years of British rule, the experience was not unlike that of runners in the last stages of a long-distance race,' remembered Christie. 'The earlier stages may have been exhilarating, but the last lap, which will end with triumph or disappointment, inevitably has its grim moments.'

Besides, before the winning-post could be reached, a war had to be won and, as Britain had shown before in her history, everything had to be bent to that goal. In a world-wide conflict, Britain was fighting for her life and could not afford to have a large portion of her empire suborned by seditious behaviour. This was especially true after Japan entered the war in 1941, when it seemed to some Indian leaders that the very presence of the British in their country was attracting the attention of a vicious enemy. Britain's initial setbacks against the Japanese in South-east Asia also helped to undermine her position not just with the Indian people but also amongst nationalist opinion in Africa. Hong Kong fell on Christmas Day 1941; Singapore followed two months later, on 15 February 1942; and in Burma the Japanese armies had swept forward on a tide of conquest from Rangoon to the Assam border, which threatened Britain's last imperial holding in Asia.

The Viceroy of India, Lord Linlithgow, had already declared war on India's behalf in 1939, without consulting the Indian leadership, a move which caused a great deal of offence to Congress. None the less, unlike the Irish republicans in 1916 who held to the Fenian axiom that 'England's difficulty was

Ireland's opportunity', in the first stages of the war Congress leaders did not attempt to use Britain's problems to destabilize India. Although Gandhi and his followers continued to push for independence, there was no trouble until the 'Quit India' campaign of August 1942 which led to widespread rioting and subsequent repression. Altogether, 763 Indians lost their lives in 601 violent incidents in which firepower had to be used to restore order; at the same time, sixty-three policemen were killed. In other actions, 208 police stations were destroyed and there were 664 bomb explosions. The estimated financial loss to the Government of India was over £1 million.

Although these figures suggest not all-out rebellion but a thinly spread revolt which was halted before it became too serious, the Quit India campaign did give a taste of things to come. While the politicians talked, the police and military authorities would face the consequences of riot and civil unrest until such time as they reached agreement on the handover of power. For the time being, India had been secured, but only by force, and it had become obvious that once the war was over, the process of dismantling the raj would begin in earnest. And once that happened, the writing would really be on the wall. As Lord Curzon, a former Indian Viceroy, had foreseen in 1901, the loss of India would herald the end of the British empire: 'As long as we rule India, we are the greatest power in the world. If we lose it, we shall drop straight away to a third-rate power . . . your ports and your coaling stations, your fortresses and your dock-yards, your Crown colonies and protectorates will go too.'

So it came to pass: within a dozen years of the end of British rule in India in 1947, the first African colony had become inde-pendent, yet on the outbreak of war all of Africa had been under European rule of one kind or another and thoughts of immedi-ate independence were but a distant dream. As had happened in India, attempts had been made to introduce the Africanization of the administration of government – Africans were admitted to the Colonial Service and there was a handful of African ministers in the legislative councils or assemblies which advised colonial governors – but it was a slow and parsimonious process. According to W. R. Crocker in his study *On Governing Colonies*, the watchword was: independence, soon, yes; but no, not yet.

> British policy starts from the point that the African is the end himself. There is no *arrière-pensée* about it. Whatever its shortcomings may be in conscious theorizing, it does seek to achieve for him the maximum welfare possible now and to give him self-government as soon as he can exercise it. We may be muddled but we see ourselves as Trustees who are to hand over their trust at the earliest practicable moment.

Crocker had been a district officer in Nigeria and Sierra Leone and wrote his book while serving as a lieutenant-colonel in the army during the war. Although he did not foresee independence being granted in the short term, and even then only as a dominion within the framework of a commonwealth, he insisted that the interests of the Africans had to be paramount and that Britain's long-term aim was to hand over power to them.

> The British colonies contrast sharply with both the French and the Belgian, for our aim and also our practice is to eliminate ourselves. We shall not disappear tomorrow, nor the day after tomorrow, but the governor of each British colony is in fact presiding over the liquidation of that colony – as a colony. It is to become a self-governing dominion.

For the time being, though, any political movement towards dominion status had to be put on hold for the duration of the war. It was also imperative to harness the support of the commonwealth, especially the white dominions whose manpower and industrial base would be needed to wage the global conflict. Although Australia, Canada and New Zealand had no difficulty in aligning themselves with Britain, there was greater resistance in South Africa where the ruling National Party favoured a policy of neutrality. Opening the debate in the House of Assembly in Cape Town, the prime minister, J. B. Hertzog, told fellow members that there was no proof that Hitler sought 'world domination' and that they had 'no right' to 'plunge' the country into war. Many of his countrymen agreed with him – thousands of ultra-right-wing members of the Ossewa Brandwag were active Nazis – but following a split in the government, Hertzog was forced to resign. Smuts's South Africa Party took office and declared war on Germany on 5 September.

His country's help was badly needed and South African forces saw action in the campaigns in Ethiopia, north Africa, the Middle East and Italy. The African colonies proved to be equally enthusiastic allies and provided some 375,000 soldiers either through conscription or voluntary enlistment: amongst them, Nyasaland contributed 20,000 men to the armed forces, Kenya 67,000, Nigeria and the west African colonies recruited 150,000 men as soldiers and war-workers, and regiments such as the King's African Rifles, the Rhodesian African Rifles and the Royal West African Frontier Force gained distinguished war records. Over 90,000 soldiers from east and west Africa saw service in Burma, many of them Nigerians who fought behind enemy lines with Major-General Orde Wingate's élite Chindit forces. Others, often led by white South Rhodesian and Kenyan officers, took part in the campaigns to oust Italian forces from Ethiopia and Somaliland and in the war against General Rommel's Afrika Korps in the western desert of North Africa. (But none saw service in Britain. In January 1942 the Foreign Office indicated that 'the recruitment to the United Kingdom of coloured British subjects, whose remaining in the United Kingdom after the war might create a social problem', was not considered desirable.)

The war also came to the African continent. British Somaliland fell to the Italians in August 1940 and Egypt, with the strategically important Suez Canal, was threatened first by the Italians and then by the Germans. The war in the western desert of Libya and Cyrenaica provided the British imperial forces with their first victories over the Germans but it was not the only cockpit of the fight against the axis powers. In the Sudan the immediate threat came from the Italian forces over the border in Ethiopia, where Eritrea was an Italian colony and Abyssinia Italian by conquest, but in the early stages of the 'phoney war' in Europe, a period which lasted from September 1939 until May 1940, there was considerable doubt as to whether Sudan would be dragged into a war with Italy and what would happen if it were. Partly, this was due to the international situation: although Britain had declared war on Germany, there had been no subsequent declaration against Hitler's principal ally, Italy. Partly, too, it was due to the fact that Italy was considered to be a rival colonial power which posed a worrying threat: in Abyssinia and Eritrea there were 300,000 Italian and native troops and Mussolini had boasted that his African empire would one day stretch from Libya to Somaliland and would include both Egypt and the Sudan.

Opposing him in the Sudan and British Somaliland, there were only 10,000 men of three resident British infantry battalions, three companies of the Somaliland Camel Corps and the regular troops of the resident British-led Sudan Defence Force, which had been raised as a home defence force in 1925. Of course, there was the 63,000-strong British garrison to the north in the Suez Canal Zone but it was earmarked for the defence of Egypt and the Canal as well as the general defence of the Middle East. In the Sudan the first line of defence was the lightly equipped, though mobile, SDF. From 1935 onwards, a rapid process of reorganization and rearmament had strengthened it but, as the force's historian Colonel J.H.R. Orlebar admitted, it was a case of creating a 'highly mobile David to meet and attack from every conceivable direction the ponderous Italian Goliath'. To do this, the force received armoured cars and new weapons including the Boyes anti-tank rifle, Bren light machine-guns and two-inch mortars. Equally importantly, Sudanese officer cadets were granted governor-general's commissions. This process was also used to commission a handful of African officers in Nigeria, the Gold Coast and Sierra Leone.

At the outbreak of hostilities, the younger political officers were released for service in the SDF and many saw action with Wingate's Gideon Force, which returned the Emperor Haile Selassie to the throne of Ethiopia. Amongst these were such well-known men as Hugh Boustead, a noted mountaineer who had served with the South African Brigade and the Gordon Highlanders in the First World War before joining the Sudan Political Service, and his colleague, the noted explorer and big-game hunter Wilfred Thesiger. Under the command of General Sir William Platt, Sudanese forces distinguished themselves in action at the Battle of Keren in 1941, when the back of the Italian occupation was finally broken. However, in the early days of the war, there was no sign of any impending confrontation – at Gallabat, on the border with Eritrea, Colonel P.G.L. Cousens found that his relationship with the Italian garrison at Metemma was most cordial. The officer commanding the Italian troops, Maggiore Garoldi, was particularly sympathetic and the two men frequently dined together. Indeed, when Cousens was stricken with malaria in early November 1939, the Italians came to his aid.

> Our *tamargi* had nothing but liquid quinine to offer, the most nauseous fluid I have ever tasted. The Italians were better equipped but nothing did any good and I was glad to get out of Gallabat in early November. Garoldi had invited me to spend the New Year up in Asmara with the idea that altitude might help clear the malaria, and shortly after Christmas, he collected me in Kassala. Johnny Gifford also came up on his own. We were thus able to have a good look at Keren though we were both of us elsewhere when the battle came to be fought almost a year later. We were very well entertained and enjoyed everything which Asmara had to offer, which was a lot, even if I myself, still plagued as I was by a misleadingly

named 'benign tertiary', was hardly in a position to do full justice to certain aspects of what was on offer.

It was all too good to last. On 10 June 1940, heartened by German successes against the allies in France and hoping to gain a seat at the victory table, Mussolini declared war on Britain and France. (Even Hitler was not taken in: 'First they were too cowardly to take part. Now they are in a hurry so that they can share in the spoils.') The forces in the Sudan responded immediately to the challenge – on the same day as the declaration, Wing-Commander McDonald, RAF, signalled British defiance by flying a Vickers Wellesley bomber to attack the Italian garrison at Asmara. Suddenly war had come to Africa.

In the opening stages Italy seemed to hold all the aces. To the west in Cyrenaica superior Italian forces under Marshal Graziani were massed on the frontier with Libya, while in Italian East Africa equally strong forces under the command of the Duke of Aosta posed the threat of a massive two-pronged attack on the Suez Canal. When the Italians captured the Sudanese frontier towns of Gallabat and Kassala on 4 July and completed the conquest of British Somaliland on 17 August, it became difficult to see how Britain could hold on to Sudan unless it was substantially reinforced. And if the Sudan fell, not only would Egypt's southern border be at risk but the way would be open for the Italians to invade the British colonies of Uganda and Kenya.

There the threat was taken seriously and reservists enlisted for service in the King's African Rifles or the Kenya Regiment. For many of the white settlers this meant leaving their farms in the care of their wives and foremen: Tony Ryan had arrived in Kenya during the 1930s, but as his wife Molly remembered, the call to protect Kenya's frontiers meant that farming had to take second place. Having received his call-up papers – including the injunction to 'please bring with you revolvers, binoculars, gumboots and any money required' – he called his farmworkers together and told them that as war was coming he was leaving his farm and family in their care. As he raised his arm in salute, they responded in kind.

> With sudden and precise movement, each man must have bent over and lifted from the long grass at his feet his gleaming spear and his heavy leather shield. The clash of steel against steel, of steel against the deep thud of the rawhide shields – the noise and the din of their ringing battle-cry had all the elements of true drama, and was almost as terrifying as the complete hushed silence that followed it. Tony and I turned back to face them squarely, completely mystified and our hearts beating madly. There before us stood our stern-faced rigid army, 200 strong, their spears razor-sharp, polished like burnished steel, and their heavy battle-shields held firmly in position! In their own amazing fashion they had known long before we had ourselves of the certainty of war, and we were quick to note the incredible thoroughness that had gone into their preparations.
>
> Once more, Tony raised his arm in silent and appreciative salute, which raised the tremendous cry '*Tutajuenda nawe, Bwana, tutasi-mama kando yako*' ('We will go with you, Bwana, we will stand beside you'). Our hearts leapt into our throats!

But it was against Egypt that the Italians chose to attack first and by September they had taken possession of Tobruk and Sidi Barrani. To combat the threat to Egypt, General Archibald Wavell, the newly appointed commander of Britain's forces in the Middle East, ordered a swift counter-attack and by the beginning of February 1941 Cyrenaica had been cleared by Lieutenant-General Richard O'Connor's XIII Corps. The respite allowed Wavell to redeploy his forces to meet the southern threat and as early as December 1940 he had felt confident enough to transfer the 4th Indian Division to the Sudan. At the same time, another Indian division, the 5th, also arrived in the country, while in Kenya a large African army, consisting of the 1st South African Division and the 10th and 11th African Divisions was formed under the command of General Sir Alan Cunningham.

Wavell's plans were simple but effective: 'to maintain pressure from as many directions as possible, thus forcing the Italians to use up their resources.' To do this, a northern force commanded by Platt and consisting of the two Indian divisions and the SDF would launch an assault on Eritrea from Kassala while Cunningham's southern force would tackle Abyssinia and Italian Somaliland from Kenya. In addition, a British force from Aden would attack and recapture British Somaliland. At the same time, a 'Patriot Force' commanded by Wingate and directed by Dan Sandford, for many years British consul in Addis Ababa, would foment a rebellion in the western province of Gojjam with the intention of restoring the Emperor Haile Selassie to the throne he had lost in 1936.

After an initial setback – the attack on Gallabat by the 10th Indian Brigade faltered under heavy Italian aerial bombardment – the Italian East African campaign proved to be a brilliant success. By the beginning of May 1941, Haile Selassie had been returned to Addis Ababa and although Italian resistance continued in the remote Gondar province until November, the reconquest of Ethiopia and Somaliland provided the British with a convincing victory. Some of the fighting had been hard and arduous, particularly at Keren in Eritrea, where it had taken place in the high mountain passes, but it ended Mussolini's dreams of creating a cohesive empire in Africa. It was also a war of extremes in which modern aircraft and armoured cars were used with the same effectiveness as camels and cavalry. And contrary to the wartime myth that Italian soldiers lacked courage or fortitude, SDF officers like Bobby Popham (later Brigadier R.H.S. Popham) learned to respect their opponents both for the courage and the sense of élan they demonstrated after being pursued on to an open plain near Keren.

We ran into trouble on the outskirts of Keren – an open plain and big mountains on both sides. We stopped there temporarily because a new plan had to be made . . . when from the left came out of the

78

hills a great cloud of dust. Now this was something extraordinary. There we were, fighting a modern war with aeroplanes, tanks, modern artillery, armoured cars, and out of this cloud of dust came two squadrons of Italian cavalry, *ventre-à-terre*, completely flat out, led by two Italian officers on white horses, throwing their little hand-bombs and firing their carbines from the saddle. Now they were straight at the gun-lines and we then discovered later on that their orders were to disrupt and get into the gun-lines and cause havoc, and they very nearly did.

Fortunately, the British and Sudanese gunners were able to turn their artillery pieces to fire point-blank into the cavalry, but even this display of superior force did not deter the Italians. A second attack was made and the ensuing battle lasted two-and-a-half hours. Afterwards, Popham called it one of the most gallant actions he had ever seen, fit to stand alongside the Charge of the Light Brigade, which also attacked a superior force of Russian guns during the Crimean War. And, like all SDF officers, he also recalled with gratitude the courage and forebearance of his own Sudanese men who fought at Keren.

I always remember one Sudanese soldier coming out of the armoured car helped by a comrade. He hobbled up and I noticed he'd got no foot. And he said, 'I've come to say I must go; I've got no foot and I had to come and say I must leave.' Now that, I thought, was marvellous. It showed that stoic endurance of the Sudanese soldier and it was a thing we found the whole way through [the campaign].

The Sudanese men of the SDF belonged to what the British had learned to characterize as a 'martial race', from whose membership could be drawn regular or irregular native forces for frontline combat duties. In the Indian Army the belief in the superiority of martial races had been adopted almost as a creed, with preference being given to Punjabi Muslims, Sikhs, Gurkhas, Rajputs and Pathans; in Transjordan, the British-led Arab Legion consisted of Bedouin Arabs; in Iraq, the Iraq Levies were recruited mainly from Assyrian Christians; and in Aden, a similar force was based on the warlike Awlaqi and Awdhali tribes. This concentration was accompanied by a belief that races which had been subjected to modern industrial life were second-rate; an Indian Army instruction-book in the 1930s warned that even those Muslims who 'live in cities, owing to a life of ease and to inbreeding are an effete race'. For that reason, too, Bengali Hindus and Madrassis were considered suspect in India and, similarly, in the Middle East it was generally thought that town-based Arabs and Jews would never make decent soldiers.

By way of thanks for its wartime service, the SDF was rewarded in the immediate post-war years by the creation of a scheme which allowed selected officers to attend specialist training course in Britain. This was partly an investment in the future – by the early 1950s, Sudan was moving towards independence – and partly an acknowledgement that the Sudanese made good soldiers. (This had already been recognized in the 1890s, during Kitchener's reconquest of the Sudan, when a large part of his army consisted of Sudanese infantry battalions commanded by British officers.)

During the campaign to oust the Italians from Abyssinia, the native troops of the SDF continued – and enhanced – that tradition by fighting alongside the men of the British and Indian armies. So too did the *askaris* of the East African forces who had served in Cunningham's southern army. Together, they had given notice that African infantrymen were the equal of whites but, even so, their feats were not given much prominence by the War Office in London. A post-war report on the military abilities of the men in Britain's African colonies concluded that they took longer to train and were temperamentally or educationally unsuited to serve in the army's technical corps or the Royal Air Force. As such, they were regarded as bad value for money and would never be able to replace the British Indian Army whose disappearance in 1947 would leave an uncomfortable gap in Britain's strategic options in the Middle and Far East. Only by leavening the forces with a substantial cadre of British officers and non-commissioned officers could an African army be operationally effective, but this was considered to be too expensive an option and the idea of raising a pan-African force to replace the Indian Army was quietly dropped in 1949.

Lack of funds was one reason for the decision not to proceed with large-scale African colonial forces – post-war retrenchment and the possibility of financial bankruptcy had led to massive cuts in Britain's defence budget; the RAF Estimates alone shrank from £255.5 million to £173 million between 1946 and 1948 – but bigotry, too, played a part. On one level this was simple racism: although the African colonies provided impressive numbers of men to support the war effort, all too often they had been used as labourers or in support services to enable white men to be released for combat duties. On another, there was the not ungroundless fear that properly trained and armed Africans might one day use their military expertise to rise against white rule in armed insurrection. Following Japanese naval operations off Madagascar in 1942, Smuts declared that in the event of a Japanese invasion he would arm and train black soldiers. Afrikaner nationalists were horrified and there was no more talk of African military prowess. Indeed, after the victory in Abyssinia, Douglas Dodds-Parker, an SDF staff officer, had been shocked by the racist attitudes prevalent amongst South African officers in Kenya and on his return to London he was advised not to discuss the campaign in detail: 'Later I found that South African pressure had been brought to play down the victory of mainly non-white troops over a largely white army.'

It was not an idle fear. The easy Japanese victories over British, Australian and British-led Indian forces in South-east Asia and Burma had severely dented the myth of white superiority, thereby enabling the Japanese propaganda machine to reinforce the idea that they were liberating the oppressed peoples of Asia from white rule. This represented an enormous loss of prestige to the European colonial powers and Africans sent to Burma were presented with direct evidence of Britain's inability to defeat the Japanese invaders. Other experiences were equally unsettling: 'for the first time in their lives these Africans had met a number of Europeans less educated than themselves'. Sylvia Leith-Ross had known Nigeria since 1907 and despite her husband's death three years later she had spent the better part of her life in the country. Between 1941 and 1943 she was working with the Political and Economic Research Organization in Lagos and was well placed to notice the Nigerians' sense of bewilderment at the eclipse of the white man's 'power and wealth and knowledge and their air of authority'.

> They had always taken it for granted all Europeans were educated men. Had we not prated of our universal compulsory education system, our magnificent schools and colleges? Yet here were grown men whose English was more limited, less grammatical, worse pronounced than their own, men who never seemed to read anything except a newspaper and who were more ignorant of history or geography than themselves. In their conversations with me, the speakers took pains to be tactful. They spoke tentatively so as not to hurt my feelings: 'We thought all Englishmen were educated . . . ?' They were careful to show no disdain, only sheer amazement that they should have been mistaken. You could not help feeling that this discovery was perhaps the final insidious blow which shattered the crumbling edifice of white superiority.

Many of the men to whom Sylvia Leith-Ross refers went on to serve with the 81st and 82nd West African divisions in India and Burma between 1944 and 1945. (The other African division to serve in the same theatre was the 11th East African Division.) Of their number, three battalions – 6th, 7th and 12th Nigeria Regiments – formed the 3rd West African Brigade in Wingate's second Chindit force which was officially entitled the 3rd Indian Division (Special Force). Their presence in Wingate's Chindits was due to the rapid expansion of his long-range penetration forces following the Quadrant Conference in

Quebec in August 1943. Anxious to placate US fears that the British were refusing to prosecute an aggressive campaign against the Japanese in Burma, Churchill supported Wingate's idea to launch a long-range thrust into Japanese-held northern Burma. Following his brilliant advocacy, Wingate's plans were accepted by the allies – the US promised air support – and the Commander-in-Chief India, General Sir Claude Auchinleck, was ordered to find the necessary eight brigades.

It was at this point that the West Africans were proposed. Auchinleck was anxious to maintain the strength of his British and Indian divisions for offensive operations against the Japanese in 1944 and 1945 and he felt that the manpower resources should be found from the two West African divisions which were due to arrive in India between March and May 1944. Although adamant that Wingate's 'proposal is unsound and uneconomical', Auchinleck was forced to compromise, mainly because Churchill fully supported the idea that aggressive operations should be mounted against the Japanese. Initially Wingate was dubious about the quality of the troops – not on racist grounds, but because 'the West Africans, and particularly their officers, have not been tried in battle, and it would be a mistake now to base the whole plan on their being a success in battle'.

Eventually he was persuaded to accept a brigade and as a result five thousand men of three Nigerian battalions saw service in Burma behind enemy lines wearing the special griffin badge of the Chindit forces. That they were able to do so owed everything to the energy of Lieutenant-General Sir George Giffard, who planned the expansion of the West African Frontier Force into two divisions complete with full logistical support. Whitehall planners had misgivings about raising native forces, but manpower shortages and the success of a Nigerian and a Gold Coast brigade in the Ethiopian campaign persuaded them to accept Giffard's proposals in 1943.

None the less, the creation of the west and east African forces did cause problems for the British. The first was the difficulty of

83

providing suitably trained leaders. Before the war, service in the Royal West African Frontier Force or the King's African Rifles was an eagerly contested honour for ambitious British officers and NCOs. The wartime expansion of these forces introduced a different kind of leader – British emergency commissioned officers and conscript NCOs who did not always hold the parade-ground or regimental ethos of the regular officers. This did not mean befriending Africans or supporting the idea of independence, as frequently happened in India during the same period, but many time-honoured shibboleths, such as wearing sunhats and spine-pads, were cheerfully discarded.

Officers were also recruited from the armies of Poland and Southern Rhodesia and, according to Trevor Clark, the former brought with them 'cross-fertilized English grammar-school and Scots high-school ideas of duty with a feudal sense of aristocratic responsible for peasantry', while the latter 'cajoled British townsmen into a readier adjustment to bush life . . . [and] moderated the British parade-ground distinctions between the cadres of the leaders and the led'. Steps were also taken to create African officers by offering suitable candidates a wartime 'governor's commission' similar to the Viceroy's Commissions provided by the Indian Army. Although some Africans were commissioned during the war, the idea was not as successful in the Royal West African Frontier Force or the King's African Rifles. Even as late as 1958 there were only fifty African officers in the whole of the Royal West African Frontier Force.

For most African soldiers, though, the war was not without benefit. The experience of wartime service abroad helped to widen horizons beyond the comfortable world of home where the District Officer, trader or missionary provided the only contact with Europeans. Most of the soldiers left not only their home districts but also their countries for the first time in their lives; they were given training and met soldiers from other allied nations. Even the children at home had been affected by patriotic fervour, but Hitler and Nazism were little more than distant

and unimaginable concepts. In the Gold Coast, the future writer
Cameron Duodu had another reason for remembering the outbreak of hostilities.

> The Second World War and I entered the classroom together, for
> we impressionable little tots were psyched by our teachers into
> believing that the skies would fall if someone called Hitler won the
> war. To prevent that calamity, we were instructed to bring a ciga-
> rette-tinful of palm kernels to school each day. It was never actually
> revealed to us how palm kernels would win the war. But our teach-
> ers so hyped up the competition between those of us in Class One
> and the other classes – and also between the junior and the senior
> school – that many of us were induced to spend part of each
> morning hunting for palm kernels in the bush before going to
> school.

There had been other changes at home. Roads and airstrips had
been constructed and major bases had come into being at
Freetown, Mombasa and Accra; in return, there had been an
unprecedented demand for copper, tin and groundnuts, all of
which provided employment and wealth. Southern Rhodesia
was used as a base for training allied flying crews and in
Kenya Africans were treated to the novel sight of seeing white
prisoners of war – a quarter of a million Italians from Ethiopia
– working in the fields. For Kenneth Simmonds, now based in
the secretariat in Nairobi, these changes could never be undone,
once instituted.

> The war years 1939–45 brought about decisive changes which
> accelerated the whole progress of the African territories towards
> decolonization and independence. Hundreds of thousands of
> Africans, many living in remote tribal areas on a pastoral or
> agricultural subsistence economy level, were recruited into
> Government and military or quasi-military service and as members
> of pioneer corps and worked not only in East Africa but also in the
> north as far as Egypt. In many cases such recruits had never previ-
> ously seen even the relative sophistication of Nairobi, and what they
> saw of life in other lands with its contrast to their own simple way

of life opened their eyes to the possibility of change and independence. The demand for increased production of crops and meat
for the war effort and the need for new and different crops to a
greater or lesser extent affected the agricultural pattern in all save
the most remote and primitive districts. By the time the war was
coming to an end there existed a political ground swell which led
irresistibly to independence.

The Americans, in particular, left an indelible impression with
the prodigality of equipment and luxury items they took to war
with them. Within hours of setting up camp, they had refrigerators and ice-cream machines working, their stores were well
stocked and they had vast reserves of equipment and spare parts
– all in stark contrast to the hard-pressed British.

There were other divisions: not only were the Americans
better-equipped but they operated from a different viewpoint.
Most US servicemen had no time for Britain's imperial trappings
and higher up the command chain their senior officers made it
clear that they were not fighting the war to help Britain hold on
to its colonial holdings in the east and Africa. (The view had
been articulated in an editorial in *Life* magazine in 1942: 'One
thing we are sure we are *not* fighting for is to hold the British
Empire together.') Extreme sceptics such as the acerbic General
Joseph Stilwell even questioned Britain's moral right to run a
world empire and mocked the stiff-upper-lipped supercilious-
ness he never tired of finding in the senior ranks of the British
Army. 'The more I see of Limeys the worse I hate them,' was one
of his more temperate criticisms; his immediate superior commander Admiral Lord Louis Mountbatten was a 'fatuous ass',
Wingate an 'exhibitionist', and British soldiers 'pig-fuckers'.

Imbued with the spirit of 1776, American liberals regarded
the British Empire as a dead letter which was not worth the
bones of one American fighting soldier. They also believed that
the British operated a colour bar – while conveniently forgetting that segregation was a way of life in the southern states of
their own country. The first appearance of black US servicemen

in Britain led to riots in the ports of Liverpool and Cardiff and, throughout the empire, steps were taken by the Colonial Office to ensure that the African troops did not mix with black US servicemen whose superior education and wealth were considered to have an unsettling effect. As evidence, the Colonial Office cited the stationing of 2,000 black US servicemen in Trinidad in 1941, an experience which led to social tensions created by the Americans' greater spending power. Eventually they were withdrawn and replaced by racially more acceptable Puerto Ricans.

Racism was certainly not absent in Britain – C.L.R. James argued in 1939 that even 'the English revolutionary movement is eaten to the marrow with a most dangerous anti-Negro chauvinism' – nor in the British colonies. Gordon Jamieson, an official in the Sudan Customs Service, took a Sudanese colleague into the Grand Hotel in Khartoum 'and the whole conversation just stopped and they looked at this black and this white man eating together. Very strange, very strange to look back on.' At the time there was a gradual process of 'Sudanization' within the service and the sight of two colleagues of different-coloured skin eating together should not have caused surprise, but all over Africa old ideas of racial superiority died hard. While the Sudanese officials were slowly being admitted into white-only clubs, Jamieson and his wife noticed that during the final of a tennis competition the whites were seated with the sun behind them while the Sudanese had the sun in their faces.

Behaviour of this kind was not organized racism of the kind that had led to the increased number of segregation laws in South Africa – as early as 1927, the Immorality Act had made sexual intercourse outside marriage between blacks and whites a criminal offence – but it was an expression of an implied superiority. Throughout the Colonial Service in Africa, white officials recognized that they had a duty towards the people they served, and most lived and worked happily enough with their own black officials and the local chiefs or emirs. As A.J.V. Arthur had discovered in the Sudan – and his experience was by no means unusual – there was also a tendency for DOs to prefer the local Africans in their own districts, whose bucolic way of life offered little threat to the *status quo*.

> The District Officer was more successful in rural areas than he was in the towns, and more successful in dealing with unsophisticated peasant farmers whose main concern was to earn their livelihood in peace with their neighbours, than with the urban educated intelligentsia, whose members naturally resented this paternalistic system and were more interested in the political development of their country and the eventual attainment of its independence.

Although the colonial officers were not opposed to the idea of Africanization, most agreed that the process should be gradual not just because it would take time to implement but also because it was frequently opposed by the Africans themselves. Not a few DOs experienced difficulties in having their African colleagues accepted by the local African dignatories, although the degree of acceptance often depended on the country. Africanization was relatively well advanced during the war in the Sudan and Nigeria – where such officials were known in Yoruba as *oinbo dudu*, 'black white man' – but less so in Tanganyika or Kenya.

British reserve or phlegm could also lead Africans to believe that they were being haughty or stand-offish (and that such behaviour implied a racist attitude). One day an official, officer or manager could be cool and officious to the point of rudeness; the next, he could be open and humorous and the model of fair play. As more than one former DO has admitted, the relationship with the Africans was too much that of the prefect with the lower fourth and did not recommend itself to working together for the common good. It was also considered bad form to talk politics. Another Sudanese official, E.W.T. Morris of the Sudan Medical Service, was discouraged from discussing the concept of independence, not because the subject was taboo, but because it was considered unattainable within the foreseeable future.

It was in the middle of the war and we had two of my Sudanese medical officers to dinner, which was becoming more and more common, but certainly not their wives, and it was not considered the done thing to discuss the question of independence with the Sudanese because at that particular stage it looked as though it was going to be a long way off. It was pointless to discuss something that was not going to be implemented in the near future and I remember this chap saying to me, 'Do you really mean to tell me that we are not fit to govern ourselves when we have been instrumental in putting Haile Selassie back on his throne? Do you consider that we are less competent than the Abyssinians?'

'No, certainly not.'

'Well then, why aren't we getting independence?'

'The answer is that it's a pointless discussion because it doesn't rest with me and what I think has no influence whatsoever.'

Aided by a revolt of tribes loyal to the emperor, Sudanese troops under Wingate had been instrumental in restoring Haile Selassie's crown. At the time, the action was considered to be a legitimate act of war, in that he had been deposed from his rightful throne by the Italians, but the significance of the action was not lost on African nationalists. To them, it seemed that after the war there would be a return to the *status quo* and that although Africans might be useful as soldiers, that did not make them ready for independence.

It was that kind of attitude which led the American Walter Lippman to complain that Britain was fighting to defend the 'archaic privilege' of its world empire. Not that US society was any more liberal. Racial inequality was prevalent throughout the country and on the outbreak of war the State Department attempted to restrict black recruitment to 10% due to what the Secretary of State Henry L. Stimson called 'the insoluble problem of the black race in this country'. The US administration also went to great lengths to manage the presence of black servicemen in Britain and to encourage a policy of 'separate but equal'. Even General Dwight D. Eisenhower, no racist himself, reported to Washington in September 1942 his concerns about black US servicemen and white British women.

> To most English people, including the village girls – even those of perfectly fine character – the negro soldier is just another man, rather fascinating because he is unique in their experience, a jolly good fellow and with money to spend. Our own white soldiers, seeing a girl walk down the street with a negro, frequently see themselves as protectors of the weaker sex and believe it necessary to intervene, even to the extent of using force, to let her know what she's doing.

Not all racial fighting was between British whites and US blacks: as Eisenhower predicted, white US servicemen were frequently enraged by the sight of British girls with their black colleagues and friction between GIs was common. Seven GIs were executed by the US forces for rape or murder while stationed in Britain during the war. Several more had death sentences commuted to life imprisonment following an outcry in the British parliament.

Although the Americans' double standards infuriated the British in India and Africa, there was substance to their complaints about the size and influence of the empire. On paper, Britain and her colonial empire combined were larger than the US or the Soviet Union and exuded an aura of power which was beyond question, but the reality was harsher. For all the trappings of empire, the dominions, the colonies and the mandates, it was mainly illusion: even by 1941 Britain had become largely dependent on US funds and supplies. So perhaps Stilwell and his cohorts were right to hold such anglophobic views; perhaps the empire was becoming an anachronistic encumbrance; perhaps it was just a myth and British imperial power was a façade, hiding behind all the blotches of pink on the map of Africa and elsewhere. If so, it was an expensive luxury and despite the continuation of an imperial ideal, the empire itself had become a costly liability. At the war's end, in a remarkable analysis of Britain's overseas financial policy, the distinguished economist Lord Keynes estimated that Britain had to find £725 million a year to meet the military costs of policing the empire and that the figure had been overstretched to the point where 'our external policies are very far from being adjusted to impending realities'.

> The *prima facie* evidence of the global statistics is that unless it is advisable and practicable to bring this expenditure under drastic control at an early date (and perhaps it is not), our ability to pursue an independent financial policy in the early post-war years will be fatally impaired.

Keynes had prepared his paper for the Cabinet during the dying days of the war, having served the government both as special adviser to the Chancellor of the Exchequer and negotiator for US aid. He was well placed to comment on Britain's parlous economic state in the post-war world but his warnings were not widely accepted. Indeed, during the war the government continued its policy of providing development money through the Colonial Development and Welfare Acts, the first of which had been passed in 1929 to supply up to £6.5 million in development finance for selected colonies during the 1930s – Northern Rhodesia, for example, was given £136,000 to develop its mining facilities in the copper belt. Further legislation under the same act in 1940 and 1945 permitted funds to be spent on improving education and the infrastructure so that the colonies could one day become self-sufficient. After years of balancing its books between national expenditure and revenues raised from the production of sisal, Tanganyika was given £90,000 to spend over a five-year period.

With the benefit of hindsight, the cost of waging the Second World War should have spelled the end of Britain's colonial holdings in Africa, but the plans for post-war reconstruction envisaged a rosy future for them. As we shall see in the next chapter, not only would they play a role in contributing to their own and Britain's economic growth but they were still considered to be loyal to the imperial cause. During the war a secret report on Africa prepared by Lord Hailey in 1940 advised that there was no evidence of political discontent and that, apart from parts of the Gold Coast and southern Nigeria, nationalism was in its infancy. In May 1943 the War Cabinet reached a similar conclusion.

> Many parts of the Colonial Empire are still so little removed from their primitive state that it must be a matter of many generations before they are ready for anything like full self-government. There are other parts inhabited by people of two or more different races, and it is impossible to say how long it will take to weld these so-called plural communities into an entity capable of exercising self-government.

And yet, despite the official view that the goal of self-rule would not be attained for many years and that there were still mutual economic and social benefits to be gained from Africa, a tiny number of imperial servants looked into the future and realized that the colonial philosophy was changing subtly and that the new mood was being caught by African intellectuals. Edward Aglen had entered the Sudan Political Service in 1930 yet he believed that although his fellow Sudanese officials 'were very friendly, nevertheless, there was this feeling that there was a wind of change'. This was particularly true of the Atlantic Charter, the declaration signed by the British and the Americans in August 1941, which supported the general principles of national self-determination and prepared the way for the creation of the United Nations.

> I do remember that in 1942 the Governor-General said that we would be leaving in twenty-five years. Why people will not accept the Atlantic Charter I do not know. I think that the greatest influence to change was the Atlantic Charter. I know for a fact that some

of the more educated Sudanese sat up and said, 'Do they really
mean this for freedom? Come on, chaps.'

And from that moment there were winds of change. I've said this
dozens of times. People have forgotten the Atlantic Charter but it
really meant something to the Sudanese.

Sudan was different from the rest of Africa in that it was linked
to Egypt by the condominium arrangement, but that did not
mean that it was tied to Cairo's coat-tails. On the contrary, the
war saw a growing sense of nationalism, inspired not just by the
Atlantic Charter but also by the Graduates Congress which had
come into being in 1938. Created by former students of Gordon
College in Khartoum, mainly from northern Sudan, it became
a focus for nationalist aspirations and received a boost when Sir
Stafford Cripps visited the country in 1942 on his way to India
to discuss the creation of a constituent assembly with the
Congress Party. Although his mission failed, his visit to Sudan
left a lasting impression on Sudanese intellectuals such as
Meccawi Sulaiman Akrat, who had entered the Sudanese
Political Service in 1927.

> The continuous hammering on the radio from America and
> England on the Four Freedoms – how everyone was going to be
> free; Sir Stafford Cripps passing through the Sudan on his way to
> India and being met by journalists and telling them not to worry –
> all this made the Sudanese feel that a change was definitely going
> to take place and that they were going to be independent.

Although many of Akrat's colleagues, British and Sudanese,
feel that eventual independence owed more to the growing
nationalism of the northern intellectuals and to the process of
Africanization, the Atlantic Charter did exert a profound influence on the growth of African nationalism across the continent.
With its sonorous call to the allies to 'respect the right of all
peoples to choose the form of government under which they
will live', it seemed to promise freedom for everyone, Africans
included, once the war was over. Its message was propagated by

radio and newspapers and, encouraged by the allies' wartime propaganda that the war was a struggle for freedom, African nationalists began to dream of throwing off colonial rule. An unknown Nigerian soldier spoke for many in the two West African Divisions in India and Burma when he wrote to the nationalist leader Herbert Macaulay in 1945.

> We all overseas soldiers are coming back home with new ideas. We have been told what we fought for. That is 'freedom'. We want freedom, nothing but freedom.

As yet, voices of that kind were muted and their influence confined to small circles in urban centres, but the war had given them some impetus. As Charles Meek discovered when he was seconded from the Argyll and Sutherland Highlanders to serve in the Colonial Service in Tanganyika, the returning soldiers were also interested in what happened in the wider world. His study group at Shinyanga where he was DO yielded some surprising results.

> My object in running the group really was to make the audience better aware of what the war was all about and why we were engaged in this terrible conflict, but I found that they were much more interested in questions about democracy and even about the party system in the UK and about Russia and large political questions generally than the mere course of the war.

Meek was one of the first of a new generation of officials in the Colonial Service, men who were interested in discovering what the younger, educated Africans thought. He owed his appointment to a chronic shortage of officers during the war – his father had served in Nigeria, where he was a distinguished anthropologist – and in 1941, at the age of twenty-one, he found himself posted to the 'scruffy little port' of Lindi on the Tanganyikan coast. In addition to starting his study group, he also came to know a young student called Julius Nyerere who had been educated at Makerere College in Uganda and at the University of Edinburgh and was rapidly making a name for himself in the ranks of the Tanganyika African Association. The discussion group founded in 1929 was the forerunner of the Tanganyika African National Union (TANU) which emerged in the post-war years as a political party committed to independence.

> I used to go out to Nyerere's big meetings at the old aerodrome and sit on the ground amongst the African crowd and get the feel of things. All being very good-natured, they used to pull my leg in a perfectly friendly fashion and I was very impressed with the party's organization. I was very impressed with Nyerere's delivery and so on.

Equally impressive political changes were beginning to take place elsewhere in wartime Africa. In 1944, the National Council of Nigeria and the Cameroons was launched as a political party, with Herbert Macaulay as president. In the Sudan, left-wing students formed the Sudan Movement of National Liberation which later became the country's Communist Party; and pre-war youth leagues in Nigeria, Sierra Leone and the Gold Coast became more closely associated with nationalist politics. Although wartime emergency measures meant that several of the political groupings were banned or repressed and leaders such as the Sierra Leonean militant E.T.A. Wallace-Johnson were interned, the burgeoning nationalist movement was able to continue in Britain, where a handful of African students were attending university courses. The numbers were pitifully small – Nyasaland, for example, only introduced secondary education in 1940 – but throughout the war London acted as a focus for their political aspirations.

At the centre was the International Africa Service Bureau (IASB) which had been founded by two Caribbean activists, George Padmore and C.L.R. James, to co-ordinate anti-colonial activities through the trade union movement. Amongst its membership, it attracted a number of Africans living in Britain who would later emerge as leading players in the post-war struggle for independence. Jomo Kenyatta had arrived in London as early as 1929 and although the authorities regarded him as being little more than a naïve activist for the rights of the Kikuyu tribe in Kenya, his political skills were sharpened during a visit to Moscow, where he studied at the so-called University of the Toilers of the East. Recruited into the Comintern, the organization of world Communist parties to bring about the world revolution of the proletariat under Leninist principles, he returned to Britain in 1933. For the next twelve years, with Padmore's help, he continued his studies at summer schools and the London School of Economics, wrote a book on Kenyan landownership and indulged his tastes in good clothes and attractive women. During the war, he worked as an agricultural labourer in a Sussex village and married an English girl, Edna. As he said later, he was merely waiting for the moment when actions would speak louder than words.

Another of George Padmore's associates was Kwame Nkrumah, a student from the Gold Coast who arrived in London in May 1945. He, too, had sharpened his political mind, having spent ten difficult years in the United States where he had to work as a labourer to fund his studies at Lincoln University in Pennsylvania. For the next two years, again under Padmore's tutelage, he was to become involved in plans to develop a revolutionary brand of pan-Africanism which would eschew the 'respectable', educated view in favour of the mass politics of the uneducated majority. Also involved in the movement was Hastings Banda, a doctor from Nyasaland who had been educated in the United States and Scotland and whose views had been moderated by exposure to the middle-class life-style led by a doctor in Britain. During the war he had attempted to return to his native country as a medical mission-ary but the nurses at the Church of Scotland's 'Livingstonia' mission had given notice that they were not prepared to work under an African doctor and his war had been spent in towns in the north of England.

All three were present at the Pan-African Congress which met in the town hall of the Manchester suburb of Chorlton-on-Medlock on 15 October 1945. It was only the fifth meeting of the Congress in some twenty years and most of the hundred or so delegates came from the Caribbean or West Africa, but it was a watershed of sorts. Instead of simply petitioning the British government for an improvement in their political rights, the little group around Padmore insisted that the time had come for overt action. Their message was simple: the war was over and in the new world made fit for democracy, the peoples of the African colonies should also be granted the right of freedom and independence even if they had to fight for it. A 'Declaration to the colonial workers, farmers and intellectuals', prepared by Nkrumah, echoed the new militancy which was being ushered in by the Congress.

> All Colonies must be free from foreign imperialist control. The peoples of the Colonies must have the right to elect their own governments, without restrictions from foreign powers. We say to the peoples of the Colonies that they must fight for these ends by all means at their disposal.
>
> The object of imperialist powers is to exploit. By granting the right to govern themselves that object is defeated. Therefore, the struggle for political power by Colonial and subject races is the first step forwards, and the necessary prerequisite to complete social, economic and political emancipations.

It was a heady vision which Nkrumah insisted could become reality if the people used the weapons at their disposal – 'the strike and the boycott' – but as yet it was little more than a political day-dream. The Congress proceedings went largely unreported by the British press and they had no influence on the first British steps to provide new and more democratic constitutions for Nigeria and the Gold Coast which were regarded as the first steps towards training Africans for eventual independence. Although the Colonial Office had been invited to send a delegate, they declined the invitation and the only 'official' representative was a Special Branch officer who prepared a report claiming that the congress was 'of little importance'.

None the less, the wartime experiences of Padmore's group and the rousing speeches for 'positive action' in Chorlton-on-Medlock were to have a lasting effect – Joe Appiah, one of the Gold Coast delegates, later claimed that it 'evoked in [me] all the emotion and sentiments of a Muslim pilgrim to Mecca'. Within the next twenty-four months, Kenyatta and Nkrumah had returned home to Kenya and the Gold Coast respectively, and a disillusioned Banda was to follow them back to his native Nyasaland in 1958. All three were to be branded as extremists by the British and to suffer imprisonment for their political activities, and all three were destined to lead their countries to independence from British colonial rule.

4

Keeping the Flags Flying

NO SOONER HAD the Second World War come to an end – on 8 May in Europe and 15 August in the Pacific – than there seemed to be a case of 'business as usual' at the Colonial Office. Its civil servants continued to maintain a sense of social responsibility towards the colonies and, as far as Africa was concerned, it was considered that another sixty or eighty years would have to pass before independence could be granted to them. This view remained dominant even after the Labour government came to power following their general election landslide in July 1945. By tradition and political ideology, Labour were anti-imperialist and for thinkers such as Hugh Dalton, who had done so much to shape post-war Labour policy, the idea of empire was anathema. If Britain was creating a New Jerusalem with the welfare state, it seemed wrong to keep so many peoples in the colonies in a state of subjugation – for so it seemed to many Labour supporters on the left. Dalton went even further: to him, the African empire was not just a political embarrassment, it was an expensive albatross whose demands could never be met. This remained his belief even as late as 28 February 1950.

I had a horrible vision of pullulating, poverty-stricken, diseased nigger communities, for whom one can do nothing in the short term and who the more one tries to help them, are querulous and

ungrateful . . . of white settlers, reactionary and as troublesome in
their way as the niggers; of ineffective action at a distance, through
telegrams to and from Governors whom one has never seen; of all
the silliness and emotion about the black man who has married the
typist . . .

This was a private diary entry not meant for public consump-
tion, but Dalton's concern did echo fears within the Labour
party that the empire was an anachronistic encumbrance.
(Others were not sure: during the war, Herbert Morrison had
declared that the granting of independence to the colonies
would be 'like giving a child of ten a latch-key, a bank account
and a shotgun'.) To assuage the more tender consciences, the
government insisted that its colonial policies would be strictly
reformist, even though it was still acknowledged that the
changes would not bring self-rule within the foreseeable future.
Instead of 'exploiting' the colonies, though, Britain would invest
in them, using money from the public exchequer, until such
time as they could stand on their own two feet. The Colonial
Secretary George Hall said as much when he reminded his
parliamentary colleagues on 9 July 1946 that Labour was intent
on guiding the people of the colonies to the same brave new
world promised to the British at home.

> To my honourable friends on this side of the Committee, the idea
> of any people dominating or exploiting another is always repug-
> nant. It is not domination that we seek. Nor, on the other hand, is
> it our intention in any way to abandon peoples who have come to
> depend on us for their defence, security, development and welfare.

Hall was succeeded as Colonial Secretary by Arthur Creech
Jones in 1947. A trade unionist who had been National
Secretary of the Transport and General Workers Union between
1919 and 1929, Creech Jones was one of the few Labour ministers who was knowledgeable about the colonies – he was
known as the 'Unofficial Member for the Kikuyu' – and he
brought to the job both enthusiasm and commitment. Earlier,

he had been a leading member of the Fabian Colonial Research Bureau, which had been formed in 1940 to campaign for colonial reform through economic progress, and African nationalists living in London had high hopes that he would introduce measures which would lead to independence for their countries. Here they were to be disappointed: Nkrumah said of him that 'He was an old Fabian. But more gratitude will be shown to the Fabians when they do more, when they put into practice their high-sounding principles.'

Creech Jones's interest in colonialism had been fired by the revelation of atrocities in the Congo in 1905, but his liberal sentiments did not stretch to granting immediate home rule to Britain's African holdings. Like his officials, he held the view that before independence could even be discussed, the first stage was to improve the economic and social welfare of the peoples of the colonies and to eradicate 'their ignorance and poverty, their disease and widespread malnutrition, their primitive cultivation and harsh natural conditions, their hopelessly inadequate revenues'. According to him, this was not paternalism but a measured progress towards democracy and freedom. And this was certainly the view propagated to Trevor Clark and his fellow cadets of the post-war administrative service.

Late in 1946 Arthur Creech Jones succeeded [George] Hall as Secretary of State for the Colonies, very conscious of having referred in a Fabian publication on Labour's colonial policy to the 'slow work of nation-building'. He was widely admired for his sincerity beyond party boundaries, but his civil servants observed that he had not the personality to fight cabinet battles and achieve material change. Not long after his appointment, he told certain administrative cadets in training at Oxford that independence for west Africa was a hundred years off, and shared with them his perception that economic and social development must precede political freedom. His parliamentary under-secretary Rees Williams said the same to the combined Oxford and Cambridge cadet courses when they united for a final academic term in London.

101

The senior civil servants who worked in the Colonial Office in the immediate post-war years also admit that the 'the general assumption' was that 'we had control of the timetable, that history would march according to what we thought, that we had the time and the power and the resources to do all this splendid development'. In private, some might have admitted that the chances of Britain remaining a major power were bleak; but in its 1948 annual report, the public face of the Colonial Office remained optimistic about its future development which would be based on sound economic principles.

> The central purpose of British colonial policy is simple. It is to guide the colonial territories to responsible self-government within the Commonwealth in conditions that ensure to the people concerned both a fair standard of living and freedom from oppression from any quarter.

Under Creech Jones' stewardship, the Colonial Office introduced plans for rapid expansion to meet the new demands. Before the war, it had been staffed by 465 civil servants: by 1950, the number had been increased to 1,289. Recruitment into the administrative service also increased, having slumped before and during the war, when it had been necessary to recruit officers from the armed forces. During the five years of the post-war Labour government, the numbers recruited into the service were: 1,715, 806, 957, 1,341 and 1,510. There was also an expansion of scale. In 1947 the Colonial Office moved from its cramped Downing Street headquarters into new premises at Church House in Great Smith Street. Imposing though the Church of England's brick building was, it was only a temporary measure until a new purpose-built office could be constructed by Westminster Abbey, the site occupied today by the Queen Elizabeth II Conference Centre. Although plans for the building were stillborn – the economic recession in 1949 put paid to its development – the fact that it was envisaged at all underlines the sense of permanence surrounding the Colonial Office. As

Peter Hennessy expresses it in his history of post-war Britain, '[the Colonial Office] in the mid-1940s at least had nothing of the undertaker about it'.

But the expansion was not just about buildings and people. Under the 1945 Colonial Development and Welfare Act, the Colonial Office was given £17.5 million a year 'aimed at maintaining and improving the standards of living of the Colonial peoples'. Three years later, a Colonial Development Working Party reinforced the need to spend substantial amounts of money to aid the development of infrastructures in the African colonies. Unless they were provided with better internal communications, modern agricultural methods, improved health services and education, they would remain 'as they have always been, on the margin of subsistence'. The change of policy was in direct contrast to the pre-war belief that the colonies should pay their way by raising taxes and not be a burden on the British exchequer. It signalled a move towards greater intervention and called for a more structured approach to the economic and political management of the colonies, with the creation of ten-year plans for each of the fourteen territories in Africa. In 1948 the Overseas Development Act laid plans to 'build up good living conditions' and two new bodies came into being – the Colonial Development Corporation and the Overseas Food Corporation (administered by the Ministry of Food).

Although they were hardly the sign of an empire in decline, not all of the new schemes were successful. Under the aegis of the OFC, a scheme was introduced to produce eggs in the Gambia but despite the expenditure of £5 million it failed miserably and not one egg was ever exported. Equally disastrous was the groundnuts scheme in Tanganyika. Constructed at a cost of £36 million, to grow groundnuts for margarine, the plan quickly ran into insuperable difficulties. Despite the best efforts of modern bulldozers and converted Sherman tanks, insufficient ground was cleared and the Tanganyikan countryside was soon littered with rusting debris. As Robert Gordon Scott, an officer

103

in the colonial administrative service, admits, hasty improvisation, lack of preparation and insufficient will all played their part in the disaster.

> They did a brief survey, found places where they thought the soil was good for growing groundnuts which eventually turned out to be patchy. They bulldozed thousands of acres of land. Without any trees or shade it caused not a drop of rain to drop and the whole thing was a disaster, a sort of dust bowl.

When his wife Joan joined him, she quickly noticed that the Africans were completely unimpressed by what had happened. 'They just thought, "the stupid British".'

Farcical though the egg and groundnut schemes were, they represented a very different attitude from the radical changes demanded by the Americans during the war. Far from dissolving the empire, the post-war government was determined to manage it successfully, as if it were a piece of real estate in need of improvement. In return, the African colonies would be a market for British goods and would provide Britain with raw materials. Although only Nigeria and the Gold Coast made profits on the export of cocoa, the idea that the African colonies were a huge, untapped resource reinforced the idea that reformist policies represented a good investment. This was the point of view put forward by President of the Board of Trade Stafford Cripps to the African Governors Conference on 12 November 1947.

> We should increase out of all recognition the tempo of African economic development. We must be prepared to change our outlook and habits of colonial development and force the pace so that within the next two to five years we can get a really marked increase in production in coal, minerals, timber, raw materials of all kinds and foodstuffs and anything else that will save dollars or will sell in a dollar market . . .

Foreign Secretary Ernest Bevin took the concept even further. In October 1948 he wrote to Dalton, claiming that the colonies could not only free Britain from its post-war dependence on the US, but they could also help return the country to its position as a leading world power.

> If only we pushed on and developed Africa, we could have the US dependent on us and eating out of our hand in four or five years. The great mountains of manganese are in Sierra Leone. The US is very barren of essential minerals, and in Africa we have them all.

This part of the policy was largely make-believe. The annual payments deficits remained high, due to the level of investments in development, and the export of cocoa did little to improve dollar profits. It would take time and huge investments for the natural resources of the African colonies to be exploited and Bevin's hopes for a quick return on the investment were never to be realized. Instead, the colonial expenditure represented a huge drain on the national exchequer at a time when Britain could least afford it. According to the Economic Survey for 1949, the previous two years' payments deficits for expenditure on all the colonies had been, respectively, £195 million and £57 million – and this at a time when the government was facing a potentially disastrous inability to meet its dollar loan repayments.

Simple altruism was one reason for the implementation of a policy which the country could ill afford. The annual report for Nigeria in 1947 warned that 'over twenty million people are living on an agricultural subsistence of a very low order, and malnutrition and disease are widespread'. Only by helping the Nigerians in the short term and by organizing them to help themselves in the longer term, could the government's policy be warranted. Not only was it practical but it seemed to be morally justified – an important consideration for a government intent on creating the New Jerusalem.

Political pragmatism also played its part. In the uncertain post-war world, the coming of the Cold War had polarized east–west relations and gradually locked the US and her allies into confrontation with the Soviet Union. Although the Colonial Office noted that Britain was forced to play 'second fiddle' to the US in strategic planning, the threat of communist expansionism, especially in the colonies, could not be ignored by Whitehall. Of particular concern was the birth of trades union movements in Northern Rhodesia, Tanganyika, Kenya, Sierra Leone and Nigeria where it was feared that the development might lead to strikes, unrest and political destabilization. (In 1946, a miners' strike in South Africa was broken by police with considerable brutality.) These fears were fired in 1947 when the Colonial Office reported signs of communist activity in Nigeria; a year later, there was serious rioting in the Gold Coast's capital, Accra, following a boycott of European goods. While there was little evidence to suggest that Moscow was extending its influence into Africa during the 1940s and 1950s, the British government was sufficiently concerned to take steps to counter it. By settling the local economies and creating decent living conditions, it was hoped that the threat would be kept at bay long enough for the African politicians of the future to be trained in democracy.

In this respect, the British Council was also considered to be a force for good. Founded in 1934 to provide a wider knowledge of British culture, it was financed by the government to teach English abroad, to develop the teaching of science and to maintain libraries and information centres. In Africa, not only was it considered a useful means of furthering knowledge about democratic institutions and creating cultural bonds with Britain, but also of countering Communist propaganda. Often its resources were meagre both in terms of staff and equipment, but in many African colonies the most important service was offered by the library. When he arrived in the Gold Coast in 1955 to work for the British Council, A.C. 'Bert' Davies was struck both by the 'inadequacy' of the education system and by the Africans' hunger for knowledge.

My job in Sekondi-Takoradi was to get in touch with schools, to have meetings with the teachers, talking about their problems, suggesting reading for them, going over and giving them little lectures on British writers and trying to encourage them to do plays . . . We had quite a good library and a large number of local people, lawyers, tradesmen, young fellows wanting to improve themselves and so on and every night the place was open to about eight or so. Very often I was there myself, just hanging about, speaking to people, having a look at what they were doing and helping them.

At the end of the war, the majority of schools were primary schools run by Christian missions and it was not until the 1950s that provision was made for a larger number of secondary institutions. Later, university colleges were founded in Ibadan (Nigeria), Achimota (Gold Coast), Khartoum (Sudan) and Makerere (Uganda) and these helped the British Council to expand its activities, even though a commission into African education had warned in 1943 that their creation was 'an inescapable corollary of any policy which aims at the achievement of self-government'. In time, as George Patrick Hall, an educational missionary, found in Nyasaland in the 1950s, the British Council itself became suspect amongst white settlers who thought it was 'left-wing and communist and a harbinger of independence'.

Other steps taken by the Colonial Office included the sale of subsidized radios for the African colonies. Built by Ever Ready and nicknamed 'saucepan specials', they proved to be an immediate success, with one thousand being sold each month in 1951.

That they came into being at all was pure serendipity. During the war, Harry Franklin had been placed in charge of the department of public information in Northern Rhodesia, one of whose functions was the operation of a modest broadcasting service. However the absence of readily available wireless receivers meant that the service could only be heard by the white population. (The cheapest receivers available in the protectorate cost £45, an impossible sum for the average African family income.) Undeterred, Franklin used his leave in 1948 to ask a radio engineer to design a basic receiver which would operate off batteries and be robust enough to withstand the rigours of the African climate. The result was a sturdy prototype made of aluminium alloy which he admitted 'looked like a saucepan without a handle'.

The next stage was to find a manufacturer and Franklin was fortunate enough to convince Magnus Goodfellow, the chairman of the Ever Ready battery company, that the 'saucepan radio' could be an economic proposition 'on the Gillette razor and blade principle: sell the receivers at cost and leave the profit to the resulting expansion of the battery trade'. Backed by the Colonial Office, Franklin made an initial order for 1500 sets which quickly sold for £5 plus twenty-five shillings for the batteries: 'They loved what they called the "*wayleshi*" (wireless). It was wonderful white man's magic, and for once it was for them.' While Northern Rhodesia was the first to benefit, the 'saucepan specials' were sold throughout the colonial empire, bringing not just entertainment but also, as Franklin noted approvingly, enlightenment.

> I learnt that Africans were no longer almost exclusively interested in local and tribal affairs. They wanted to read and hear more about other parts of the territory, other countries in Africa and in Europe. Something new was stirring in their minds and hearts. Their letters sometimes referred to 'living in a new environment', to 'waking up', to 'the modern world'. '*Though some of us are very poor and worthless* [the writer meant without possessions], *but yet we bought our dignity through the wireless sets which the European brought to all Africans.*' In one respect at least that correspondent was equal to the white man (and that was what he wanted); he owned a radio.

In addition to schemes aimed at improving the colonies' economic, educational and social infrastructures, there were moves to give Africans a greater say in the government and administration of their countries. When he came to office, Creech Jones identified three main areas for taking forward Britain's colonial policy in Africa – the Colonial Development and Welfare Acts, the introduction of local government, and constitutional advance. Here he was helped immensely by one of his principal civil servants, Andrew Cohen, the Assistant Under Secretary in charge of the Africa Division, whose knowledge about, and concern for, the continent had earned him the Colonial Office nickname of the 'King of Africa'. Cohen had joined the Colonial Office in 1933 and under Creech Jones he became one of the most influential colonial innovators of his generation. It was his view that Britain had a duty to provide a watertight policy for its colonies which would not only lead them to independence but keep them within the fold of the Commonwealth, the great gathering together of Britain's imperial holdings.

> The change and improvements which are needed cannot be made in a day; they will take years to accomplish in dependent territories which we want to leave as strong as possible when they get their independence, the tasks of economic and social development have a special urgency, because we no longer have indefinite time in front of us. But countries which have achieved their independence also need outside assistance. The social and economic problems which face them are not solved by independence, nor can the grant of independence be delayed until they have been solved.

This was a different kind of language from the delays and hesitations of earlier policy papers. One immediate result was the Local Government Despatch of 25 February 1947, largely Cohen's work, which heralded the end of indirect rule and introduced the devolution of powers to local authorities to take fiscal and financial responsibility for their own areas. Based on the English county council model, this was regarded by Cohen as 'the key to all future developments in our African territories'.

> Local government must at once provide the people with their political education and the channel for the expression of their opinions. An efficient and democratic system of local government is in fact essential to the healthy political development of the African

Territories, it is the foundation on which their political progress must be built.

This was particularly relevant in the west African colonies of Sierra Leone, Nigeria and the Gold Coast which had already made a number of democratic advances with the aim of moving towards dominion status. In all three countries, Africans had been appointed to the executive councils advising their governors during the war and in the Gold Coast the Africanization of the Colonial Service had already begun. The process was simply accelerated in 1946 when Nigeria was given a new constitution which permitted two Nigerians to sit on the legislative council and created regional councils for the Northern, Western and Eastern provinces. It was much criticized by nationalists such as Chief H.O. Davies for failing 'to secure greater participation by the Africans in the management of their own affairs', but it was a step forward. Two years later saw another constitutional change which devolved power to the regions. One of the new members of the northern regional council, Abubakar Tafawa Balewa, warned his fellow Nigerians – and the British officials – that the time had come for Nigeria to be responsible for its own destiny.

> Since the war years, things have been moving at a tremendous speed. We have our own laws and forms of government; we have our own traditions and our much-respected customs. I am quite aware that many of these need reform and that some of them must be abolished altogether if we are really to compete with the rest of the world in the race towards modern progress. We are fortunate in having the British here as our guides and teachers. They are great colonial administrators and they have great experience in developing and administering many tropical dependencies. I want all our British officers to realize that now is the time when we, as their pupils, need all their patience and courage, and the use of their knowledge and experience . . . We have our own leaders whom we have chosen. We must do all we can to help the success of the new constitution by co-operating with the government and by creating among ourselves an atmosphere of mutual understanding and trust.

110

Abubakar's address also gave a veiled warning to the British that the northern Nigerians were not prepared to stand by and allow future political power to fall solely into the hands of the Igbos and Yorubas of the south – a problem of which much more would be heard later.

Although the constitutional experiment failed to please every-body, it was a statement of intent that Britain was prepared to begin the business of decolonization. In London, the process had already been taken several steps forward – albeit only in theory – when Creech Jones asked his officials to 'chart a new approach to Africa'. One of those entrusted with the task was Cohen. The results were startling. Instead of maintaining the idea that inde-pendence was a far-off dream which could only be realized by continuing the dual mandate with the tribal chiefs, Cohen and his colleagues recommended a rapid Africanization of the Colonial Service and the creation of a new partnership with the educated, mainly middle-class, élite. In four distinct phases, the colonies would move towards, first, internal self-government, and then full independence once the African politicians were ready to take over the reins of government.

There would be no attempt to hold on to power and the report recommended that the Colonial Office, particularly the governors, should recognize the inevitability of self-government. Unless this happened, and mindful of what had occurred in India, Britain would find itself increasingly in conflict with the new generation of nationalists and, when it happened, the transfer of power would be marred by violence. Not only was this a radical reappraisal of Britain's policy towards Africa, but it also recommended a new timescale for independence: 'Perhaps within a generation many of the principal territories of the Colonial Empire will have attained or be within sight of the goal of full responsibility for local affairs.'

Not unnaturally perhaps, Cohen's report got a stormy

welcome when it was discussed by the conference of African governors in late 1947. Nigeria's governor Richards called him 'the intellectual dreamer of Whitehall' and in his diary entry for 10 November, Sir Philip Mitchell, the governor of Kenya, gloomily thought that Cohen and Creech Jones had lost touch with reality.

> The CO has got itself into a sort of mystic enchantment and sees visions of grateful independent Utopias beaming at them from all around the world, as if there was – yet – any reason to suppose that [an] African can be cashier of a village council for three weeks without stealing the cash.

Even the formal memoranda about the report were scathing about the proposed policy.

> I should like it to be borne in mind that apart from men who have retired after long service in Colonial Administration, no one in England knows anything at all about native administrations in West Africa, though unfortunately there are some who have no compunction in using Africa for the purpose of exploiting their crackpot views.

The opposition from the governors was little different from the clash of views experienced in their own colonies between the District Commissioners and the officers in the secretariat. Those in the field inevitably believed that they were closer to the Africans' problems than the men in Government House and, after considerable discussion, the report was never adopted, even though its findings were to influence future Colonial Office thinking. Cohen himself continued his career in the service, was knighted and spent some time as governor of Uganda, where he came into an unseemly conflict with the Bagandan king, or Kabaka, Edward Mutesa II.

However, events in west Africa were soon to render the opposition to his recommendations redundant. In the Gold Coast the reform programme was moving steadily forwards but it was not just being driven by the authorities. A younger and more restless generation, many of them ex-servicemen, showed themselves to be anxious for change. Not only did they want independence, but they were also prepared to challenge the authority of the chiefs, Britain's traditional allies in ruling the country. The political focus for their disaffection was the United Gold Coast Convention (UGCC) whose principal spokesman was the veteran lawyer J.B. Danquah. Although he and his colleagues had welcomed the changes in the legislative council which had given Africans a majority, they were sceptical about the pre-eminent role enjoyed by the chiefs and in August 1947 they called for independence in the 'shortest possible time'.

A few months later, in December 1947, Kwame Nkrumah accepted the appointment of UGCC secretary and returned to the Gold Coast. It was the beginning of a time of political instability and although he was not always responsible for the events which followed, Nkrumah quickly found himself at the centre of a younger generation of nationalists who demanded an end to British rule. The starting point was the rioting which took place in Accra in February 1948. Initially little more than a protest about the high price of European goods and low local wages, it turned ugly when a group of urban protesters marched on the governor's residence at Christiansborg Castle. Amidst scenes which were to become drearily familiar as Britain began to withdraw from empire, stones were thrown and the security forces opened fire, killing two demonstrators and wounding several more. In the subsequent rioting, twenty-nine people were killed and hundreds more injured.

The violence shocked the British government. Not only was the Gold Coast considered, wrongly perhaps, to be a model of sobriety and political stability, but it was thought to be the one African colony capable of early self-rule. The response was badly handled. In the immediate aftermath the new governor, Sir Gerald Creasy, blamed the UGCC, especially Nkrumah who was branded a Communist agitator. He, Danquah and four others were arrested. They were quickly released when no evidence of a plot was uncovered but matters in the country would never be the same again. A commission of enquiry headed by Aiken Watson, the Recorder for Bury St Edmunds, confirmed that the riots had not been begun by Communist agitators but it did suggest that they had political undertones, in that the post-war reforms were 'outmoded at birth'. Instead of attempting to halt the pace of progress, Watson's commission recommended that the constitution be amended further to give Africans executive power. The die was now cast: to counter the threat of extremist infiltration, the British would now work with the middle-class intelligentsia to train them to take over the reins of power, sooner rather than later.

Although the Colonial Office argued that the Gold Coast was a special case, in that it had an advanced education system and a stable economy based on cocoa production and was therefore reasonably politically sophisticated, the change of tack did not please everyone. The veteran official Ralph Furse claimed that the new generation of African political leaders were no different from other politicians in that they were pursuing their own agendas and pointed out that 'because African crowds shout slogans at the behest of such leaders it does not follow that they understand what the slogans mean'. Other older officials were equally bemused by the policy adopted for the Gold Coast and were not reassured by claims that the experiment could be controlled if matters got out of hand. (Curiously, some African nationalist leaders also regarded the Gold Coast as a laboratory: Hastings Banda told Nkrumah that it was the ideal place to test British resolve to hold on to the African colonies as it had more mosquitoes than any other territory.)

Once again, the British response to the Gold Coast riots had been guided by fear of Communism – local officials claimed that Nkrumah intended to establish 'a Union of West African Soviet Socialist Republics' – which many believed would enter Africa through the increasingly nationalistic conduit of Egypt. The Americans were particularly concerned lest British intransigence should force Cairo into an alliance with Moscow. It was not an idle fear. Relations with Egypt had not been good since 1942, when the British unilaterally assumed control to preserve their security in the fight against the axis forces in North Africa, and, with the 1936 Anglo-Egyptian treaty due to be revised in 1956, there were still tensions over the British military presence in the Suez Canal Zone and the condominium arrangement with the Sudan. Since 1924 the Egyptians had been prevented from holding any responsibility for the government of the Sudan – which was in the hands of British political officers with increasing Sudanization – and it was British policy to protect the country from 'the political ambitions of Egypt until such time as it might be able to decide its eventual status'.

For the Egyptian nationalists, though, the return of the Sudan and its independence from British control were popular policies, and in 1950 King Farouk abrogated both the 1936 treaty and the condominium agreement when he proclaimed himself King of Egypt and the Sudan. Although the move was welcomed by Sudanese nationalists in the recently formed (1944) Ashiqaa Party, Farouk's proclamation was only a gesture which could never be put into effect. According to Sir Gawain Bell, whose career in the Sudan had begun in 1931 and who was working for the Sudan Agency in Cairo in 1949, Egyptian thinking on the position of the Sudan was guided more by emotion than any pragmatic policy.

> Of all the foreign peoples I have known, none was more paradoxical than the Egyptians at this extraordinary period of their *fin de siècle*. No other people in my experience, then or since, could combine so many qualities and shortcomings in such a perplexing mosaic. Most foreign governments represented in Cairo were quite ignorant of what was happening in the Sudan, but most were prepared to try and learn. Not so the representatives of the United States of America. None was so ignorant, so adversely prejudiced

115

and so obsessed with out-of-date conceptions of colonialism as the Americans. Their prejudices were partly, but not entirely, removed when in 1952 they sensibly posted a representative to Khartoum. The Egyptian government had no excuse for ignorance, for a great many Egyptians lived in the Sudan and constantly came and went. But the Egyptians possessed a remarkable ability to believe passionately whatever they wanted to believe, even if they emphatically knew it to be untrue.

As it turned out, though, Egypt was to influence the course of Sudan's moves towards independence when Farouk was deposed in 1952 and replaced by a military government under General Mohammed Neguib. Half-Sudanese by birth, he promoted a policy which accepted Sudan's right to independence provided British influence were scaled down. As Bell saw it, 'Once the British were out of the way, he was confident he would be able to engineer close constitutional links between Egypt and the Sudan. In order to ensure his objective, he sent to the Sudan a great many representatives who distributed much in the way of material inducements.'

Unfortunately for the British and for many Sudanese, Neguib concentrated his efforts on Northern Sudan, the mainly Islamic area whose people were more advanced, politically and socially, than their Southern neighbours. Historically and geographically, there was little to link the two territories but it was a tenet of British policy in 1946 that they should be brought together in an equal political partnership as the Sudan moved towards self-rule. It was an admirable sentiment but, as Edward Aglen found, it was introduced too late in the day because most Southerners were badly educated and were ill-prepared to fight their own corner.

> We were too optimistic about the length of time we had. The result was that we left the South to tick over. There is no question of that, I think. Our plan, as far as I could make out, was to make the North viable, which we did, and then train people to administer; then, when we had enough money to do more, to train the South.

1. For King and Country.
As happened throughout the empire during the Second World War men of military age were called up for service in their countries' armed forces. Recruiting propaganda stressed the unity of the British Commonwealth of Nations, a point being reinforced to these young men who are about to join the Royal West African Frontier Force

2. Over there. In the latter stages of the war against Japan African troops played a major
role in the Indian and Burmese theatre of operations. West African medical orderlies of
field ambulance wait for their train to take them to an up-country station in India

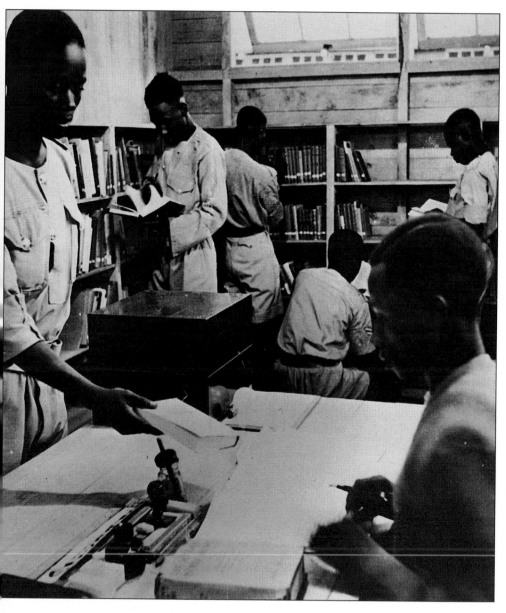

3. War the bringer of change. The experience of wartime service abroad helped to widen horizons beyond the comfortable world of the village. Soldiers borrowing books from a lending library run by the East African Army Education Corps

4. From scenes like these. A farmer in the White Highlands of Kenya contemplates his flock. The post-war cultivation of sheep in the colony was one of the business interests of Molly and Tony Ryan

5. The good shepherd. Throughout Africa the district administrative officer was the most important point of contact with the government. During the 1961 famine in Kenya Masai children in the Kajiado district relied on their District Commissioner Tom Edgar to supply them with vitamin pills and medicine

6. Kwame Nkrumah, the first African to lead his country into independence from British rule. A supporter of the idea of pan-African unity, he visited Britain in 1960 and was welcomed by admiring African students. Six years later he was deposed by the army after declaring Ghana a one-party state

7. Dr Hastings Banda became prime minister of an independent Nyasaland in 1964 and was made president of Malawi two years later. Educated in Scotland and the United States, he enjoyed several close political relationships with Church of Scotland missionaries

8. Alhaji Sir Abubakar Tafawa Balewa, the first prime minister of Nigeria. Considered to be one of Africa's emerging statesmen, he travelled to New York to address the United Nations in October 1960, a week after his country became independent

9. Jomo Kenyatta with his daughter Margaret in 1961 while serving a period of politica internment at Maralal for his alleged connections with the Mau Mau terrorist movemen Two years later he led Kenya to independence and did much to heal the breach betwee the country's white and black populations

10. Ian Smith, the Rhodesian prime minister whose unilateral declaration of independence in 1965 took his country out of the Commonwealth and into fifteen years of isolation. In 1977 he was re-elected leader of what had become the Republic of Rhodesia but a demoralizing guerrilla war forced him into British-sponsored peace talks

11. Sir Roy Welensky, the prime minister of the ill-fated Central African Federation, speaking at the Institute of Directors' annual conference in London in November 1961. African opposition to the federation ended any hopes of unifying Nyasaland and Northern and Southern Rhodesia under multi-racial rule

12. Fighting for Freedom I. The Mau Mau campaign was one of the bloodiest guerrilla conflicts during the last days of colonial rule in Africa. Bound by strict blood oaths hundreds of Kikuyu took up arms against white rule in Kenya – although many of their victims were Africans. 'Somewhere in Meruland', 'Field Marshal' Mwariama inspects the soldiers under his command

13. Fighting for Freedom II. Following rioting in Nyasaland in 1959 the authorities responded with a heavy hand. Hundreds of young men were arrested and detained without trial. A commission of inquiry claimed that the colony was run like a 'police state' but its members were not allowed to take evidence from these detainees at the Kanjedza Prison outside Blantyre

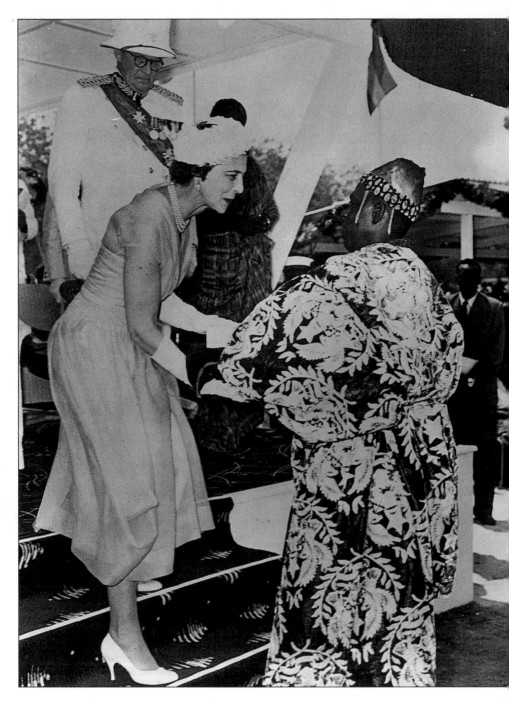

14. First to go. In May 1957 the Gold Coast became independent as Ghana and the first of many carefully stage-managed independence ceremonies was held. The transfer of power took place at midnight with the Union Jack being replaced by the new national flag, usually in front of a member of the British Royal family. The Duchess of Kent represented the Queen in Ghana

5. A familiar sight. The Duke of Kent, dressed in the uniform of the Royal Scots Greys,
represents the Queen at Uganda's independence celebrations in October 1962.
Walking beside him under the ceremonial umbrella is the Kabaka, Edward Mutesa II

16. Fight to the finish. During the last stages of the guerrilla war in Rhodesia the white population was a nation in arms and even in Salisbury, the capital, families carried sub-machine guns while shopping

17. Dirty war. The fighting between Rhodesian security forces and ZANLA and ZIPRA terrorists was a brutal and uncompromising confrontation in which thousands – black and white – lost their lives. Amongst the most successful counter-insurgency units were the Selous Scouts, a mixed-race tracker unit

18. The end of the road. Although Rhodesian security forces had been confident of winning the guerrilla war, by 1977 large areas of the country were under terrorist control. In the Cheredzi area of south-east Rhodesia travel was only possible in convoys protected by men of the Rhodesian African Rifles

Suddenly we woke up in the forties and found we hadn't trained them and it was too late. And so you've got the position that we've got the grandsons of slave-traders to administer the South. It was a terrible situation and it was our fault. We simply misjudged the times.

This was a refrain which was to be heard time and time again as the African colonies headed towards independence: the officers in the Colonial Administrative Service felt that they had too little time or opportunity to train the Africans to take responsibility for political power or that the process of Africanization had been introduced too tardily. In the Sudan this was particularly relevant because the South had remained undeveloped and its small number of politicians were fearful of being dominated by the more sophisticated North.

That their concern was justified became clear in 1953 with the signing of the Anglo-Egyptian Agreement which paved the way for self-government. A year earlier, a Constitutional Amendment Commission had recommended the formation of an all-Sudanese Council of Ministers, and a parliament consisting of a Lower House and a Senate. The South was to be granted full representation although the governor-general retained responsibility for the southern provinces. This should have provided adequate safeguards, but Neguib's intervention in the subsequent talks changed everything. When the Anglo-Egyptian Agreement was signed, it contained important amendments calling for immediate Sudanization and the restriction of the governor-general's powers. Significantly, all the Northern political parties signed the agreement and, as Bell argues, 'the ground was cut from beneath the feet of the administration and the British government'.

Those of us who had the future of the Sudan at heart were dismayed. It seemed to us that the Independence parties, in accepting an Egyptian solution, had put the future of their country at risk. The Southerners who formed a third of the population had not been consulted by any of the political parties. The price the

117

Northern Sudanese were ready to pay in thus ignoring the South seemed to us a recipe for disaster, as indeed it proved to be. We were dismayed that the British government, which had always upheld the principle that the Sudan's status should not be changed except after consultation through constitutional channels, had accepted an agreement in which that provision had been ignored.

Even though Egypt failed in its long-term policy of developing close links with the Sudan – in 1955 the recently elected prime minister, Ismail al-Azhari, declared for full independence instead of union with Egypt – the anticipated problems between North and South did not take long to materialize. Under the process of Sudanization, only six out of eight hundred senior posts in the civil service went to Southerners, and in August 1955 the men of the Equatorial Corps of the SDF mutinied against their Northern officers at Torit. In the subsequent violence, several hundred Northerners were killed and the government had to send 8,000 troops into the area to restore order. Although the new parliament promised to give serious consideration to a federal solution to the South, it was not acted upon and the stage was set for a bloody civil war which would continue long after the granting of independence in 1956. Former SDF officers such as Lieutenant-Colonel W.B.E. Brown, who served in the South, felt that the matter had been bungled and that at the time Britain should have included safeguards for the Southerner who 'not only distrusted and feared the Northerner, as he had feared his slave-trading fifty years before, but his feelings were usually even more intense than that'.

> I consider there was a very strong case for allowing the South to develop as a separate region in its own good time, which would have been several years behind the North, using colloquial Arabic as the lingua franca. It would have thus developed as a Southern Region with some regional autonomy within an independent Sudan. Such a policy for the South was unfortunately not given consideration by the Sudan government.

The solution could have provided the South with safeguards, but it is difficult to see how it could have been implemented without the British appearing meddlesome. At the time Britain was keen to negate Egyptian political ambitions and rapid Sudanization of the main services certainly helped to create the conditions for the evolution of an independent Sudan. Unfortunately, the process exploited the Southerners, who were left to fend for themselves against the more sophisticated and aggressive Northerners. Unfortunately, too, Britain's relations with Egypt were bad – by 1954 the Suez Canal Zone garrison was being slowly evacuated – and as Bell reminds us, this meant that 'the circumstances which were to lead to the final transfer of power in the Sudan less than nine years after the end of the war differed in one marked respect from those obtaining in other dependent countries'.

Matters came to a head in 1956 when Britain and France conspired to attack Egypt after the Suez Canal had been nationalized by the new regime led by Colonel Abdel Nasser. It was a shameful episode which brought Britain great obloquy and discredited its policies in the Middle East. Not only did the world combine to denounce the 'imperialist aggression', but Britain lied to the US and lost its reputation for fair play. The day after the landings at Port Said, the US and Australia supported a UN motion calling for an immediate ceasefire and an end to the hostilities. This was a very different response from earlier adventures in the heyday of empire, when Britain could intervene on the pretext of restoring order to a country's internal affairs: as the historian of empire James [now Jan] Morris remarked, 'Even a Wog had a voice at the United Nations now, and all the splendours of the past, assembled in such a pitiful pastiche in the familiar waters of the Mediterranean, could not save the British from ignominy.'

By then, though, the Sudan had become an independent republic outside the Commonwealth, the flags of Britain and Egypt having been taken down on New Year's Day 1956, and replaced by a new tricolour. Within two years, a military *coup* brought General Abboud to power and his regime began the repression of the South, thereby provoking a bitter secessionist war. Inevitably, the fighting prompted disquiet amongst former officers of the SDF and reopened the concern that the South should have been provided with better safeguards or that more could have been done to unite the country before independence. For Bell, it was a matter of too little too late – he also points out that integration was already underway, thereby making it impossible to sustain the idea of a separate South – but for younger officers such as Elliot Balfour, it was simply a matter of working against the clock and making ends meet.

> I remember being stopped by a very strong-minded Assistant District Commissioner in the Bog who asked me to sign a document to the central government asking them where the hell they thought they were going. I signed the document because I knew the chap. But I knew that we wouldn't get any answer because no British government has ever known where it is going. And that's what happened to us in the Sudan. We went on; native administration proved a stop-gap, and the new elements began to arise and we suddenly realized we were going to get an almighty wallop on the nose and we went. We may not have gone at absolutely the right time – in fact as regards the South we probably didn't – but we hadn't the time to deal with that problem and the Sudan has had to deal with it itself. It's been a very hard and very sorrowful time in some ways. But every nation goes through that. It goes to the making of a nation.

From being one of Britain's best-run dependencies, Sudan quickly degenerated into civil unrest after independence, mainly because the North–South question had never been resolved. In 1963 guerrillas from the South formed the Anya Nya movement and launched a sustained campaign against the regime. Various attempts were made to resolve the crisis – ranging from appeasement to repression and the imposition of a centralized Islamic administration – but the endless fighting and subsequent deprivation turned the country into one of Africa's worst disaster areas and a poor reward for the dedication of the officers of the Sudan Political Service.

> Where we, the administration, misjudged the Sudanese both before the war and particularly after, was in failing to realize the speed and the degree wherewith they were adapting themselves to the modern world and to the influence of developments outside the Sudan and particularly the influence exercised by Egypt. We went wrong in failing to appreciate early enough that in spite of the shortcomings of the Egyptians, Egypt would play a leading part in the political thinking and ambitions of the Sudanese leaders. We underestimated the Egyptians and we underestimated Ismail al-Azhari. We made the mistake of judging the Sudanese, whom we liked and admired, much as we judged ourselves. When we discovered that their thinking differed widely from ours, we were surprised.

Bell's concerns were to be echoed again as other parts of Africa achieved independence from Britain, but he is right to stress the importance of Egyptian influence. Sudan was different from the other colonial holdings, in that it was ruled jointly with Egypt, the country with whom Britain had such an unhappy relationship. As decolonization accelerated, the experience of the Sudan during the transfer of power demonstrated the pitfalls of the process: the slow pace of handing over authority followed by a rapid move towards independence before tribal or racial enmities had been resolved. This was very different from 'the minimum of friction, the maximum of goodwill . . . and the greatest possible degree of efficiency' recommended by Cohen in his shelved 1947 report.

The experience of the Sudan also showed that Britain would allow itself to be influenced not just by one country (Egypt) but also by the rest of the world, particularly by the anti-colonialist attitudes of the United States, the Soviet Union and the United Nations. As Trevor Clark saw it in a different context in Nigeria, 'We knew that the Colonial Office in Whitehall wanted to keep the pressure on. They wanted independence, not unreasonably quickly but as reasonably quickly as possible, so that they could continue to maintain this liberal picture which we all wanted to show the outside world.'

So how had it come about that within the space of ten years Britain had changed its colonial ideas from the policy of slow and orderly development to one of rapid movement towards independence? Although never implemented in its entirety, Cohen's 'new approach to Africa' helped to focus minds on the future of the African colonies. Instead of relying on tried and tested partnerships with the tribal chiefs, greater attention would be paid to the nationalist politicians in the legislative and executive councils. To some extent, too, the doctrine of an indefinite period before independence was dropped – officials such as Johnnie McCall in Nigeria began to see that self-government would now come sooner than expected.

> Throughout the fifties we were being prepared all the time for independence and I for example by that time had reached the posi-tion of Resident in charge of Delta, a province in the western part of Nigeria, the middle part, Benin. And there we were desperately pursuing a policy and practice of independence within a few years. [Sir John] MacPherson was the governor and he was going to have independence just as soon as he could get it.

During this period many officials likened the process to a horse race on which high stakes have been bet – exhilarating as it flashes by, but impossible to judge the outcome. In private, most estimated that it would still take a dozen or so years to train their Africans fully so that they could take over government service, but in practice Africanization had to be concertinaed into a handful of years, or even months. Even so, as Cohen had warned, it was better to advance the process than to run the risk of losing everything through delay and obfuscation.

The passing of the years had also produced a difference, if not in policy, then certainly of attitude. The experience of the bloodshed which had accompanied the transfer of power in India had unnerved many politicians and there had been widespread dismay at the violence which led to the ending of Britain's control of the mandated territory of Palestine in 1948. This was followed by a Communist uprising in Malaya, the so-called 'emergency', and by the outbreak of the UN war in Korea in 1950, both of which made heavy demands on British service personnel. Many were conscripted National Servicemen and although most admitted to enjoying a period of service abroad, the experience of helping to maintain an imperial garrison contributed in the mid-1950s to a growing intellectual dissatisfaction with the need to maintain a world empire. John Osborne's play *Look Back in Anger* (1957) was one example of a new anti-establishment view of the empire and imperialists in general; William Golding's anti-colonial parable *Lord of the Flies* (1954) another. The Suez fiasco also implanted the first doubts about Britain's position as a world power – even though the newspapers and Pathé Pictorial newsreels of the period continued to emphasize Britain's leading role in international affairs.

Of course, this growing cerebral restlessness did not intrude on the Colonial Office or unduly affect its policies, but it did presage the feelings of shame with which younger intellectuals would view the colonies a decade later. From being one of the noblest institutions run by man, the colonies were coming to be regarded differently and, in left-wing circles at least, there was a growing sympathy for the African nationalist point of view. Within ten years of the riots in Accra, the Gold Coast had won independence and Nigeria was close to attaining it: this was a bewildering sea-change from Creech Jones's prophecy that it would take a lifetime before any African colony achieved self-rule. After the Gold Coast, there was to be no going back.

5

First to Go

DURING THE PERIOD before the first colonies became independent, their management was a curious mixture of inertia and innovation. Officers bound for the Colonial Administrative Service still completed degrees at Oxford or Cambridge before proceeding to the combined induction term at the University of London; the various churches still trained missionary workers; and companies such as the United Africa Company and the Bank of British West Africa still recruited adventurous young men to work in Africa. When they arrived in the late 1940s or early 1950s, they often encountered physical conditions which had not changed since the pre-war years. When Ian Fraser joined the Bank of British West Africa in the Gold Coast he lived in a bachelor mess in Accra which had no electric lighting and which had only recently been given a kerosene-operated refrigerator. In the bush, or up-country, it could be worse, as he discovered when he was promptly posted to the remote village of Tepa to open a new branch office. Because his bank was anxious to forestall an initiative by Barclay's Bank in the same area, there was little time to give him any training and he was forced to leave behind his new two-seater sports car because the roads were little more than dirt-tracks. Once in Tepa, he quickly discovered that the dividing line between the comforts and facilities of Accra and small-town Africa was only too obvious.

I couldn't take instructions from anybody because if I wished to make a telephone call I used to have to go along to the post office and book it. And he might say, 'Well, ten o'clock in the morning. Come back about three and we might have reached the top of the queue by then.' Because there was one wire and very basic, if a call was coming out there couldn't be one going back. So there was no question of being able to refer. I had to make decisions.

It was also necessary to develop different procedures to meet the needs of the local population, many of whom were cocoa farmers who could neither read nor write. The contractors who bought their crop usually paid for it in new and unused bank notes which were banked immediately. However, when funds came to be withdrawn, there could be problems if the same notes were not produced – an impossible request in any banking system. Faced by demands that the farmers were 'not going to take any money that was someone else's', Fraser found that he had to develop skills which could never have been taught in Accra. As a National Serviceman, he found that he experienced little difficulty in adapting to the local surroundings – although he admitted that his attitude to banking was tested when he arrived to find the branch office still under construction, with the signpost still unhung. For several days the bank's safe had to be kept on the back of a lorry, but it was all worth it because 'Barclay's were absolutely furious that we'd stolen the thunder from them.'

Others, too, experienced varying degrees of concern when they arrived in a remote outpost to find fairly primitive conditions; but most admit that, as they had been drawn to work in Africa partly out of a sense of adventure, they quickly adapted to the circumstances in which they found themselves. When one Scottish doctor arrived at his first posting in Kongwa in Tanganyika, his house and surgery were simple shacks, but for him that was part of their charm. Other missionaries found that they had to compete with the local witch doctors whose 'ju-ju' was often preferred to modern medicines or counselling.

Because the witch doctor was an integral part of African society, it made little sense to try to dissuade African employees from using them. Indeed, there is ample evidence to suggest that their use of herbal medicines often worked – Ron Hunston, a Church of Scotland printer in the Gold Coast remembered one of his boys being cured of swollen wrists and ankles after visiting his witch doctor in Akripan. To begin with, he was also surprised when his workers 'poured libations on the machines and if anything went wrong it was the god in the machine that was causing it', but on one memorable occasion he was able to turn the power of the witch doctor to his own advantage.

> One glorious morning, I found that we were three numbering machines short. They were small machines, they're very complicated and hugely expensive and there were three short. I announced to the whole staff that I'd got the numbers of these machines, which I had, and if they weren't on my desk on Monday morning I would get the witch doctor in and this time I would prosecute and hand them over to the witch doctor. On Monday morning there were four numbering machines on my desk and I never found where the other came from. Never. They must have pinched it from somebody else.

Of course, there were always a handful who were deterred by what they found. Some missionaries admit that they found it difficult to understand or sympathize with the Africans' attitudes towards sexuality or to the practice of buying wives – which was still a common custom, as the Scottish doctor's family discovered when they were posted to the Gold Coast in 1955. By then, they had served in Nigeria where they had taken on a houseboy who was to remain with them for many years.

> His name was Andrew Cheekbow and although he was seventeen he looked about five, was a very small chap, his English was very poor and I trained him how to polish the floors, to turn out the rooms and to do a certain amount of cooking.
>
> I opened a post office savings account for him and saw that he put so much money into it every week. Now this too turned out

to be a very good thing because his wife had already been chosen for him and when we went to Ghana [Gold Coast] he asked me permission to go back to Nigeria to bring back his wife. The price that was being asked for was £80. Andrew at that time had £40 in his savings bank and off he went and came back again without her. So eventually we upped his wages as time went on and not terribly long afterwards he got the other £40. He then went off again and brought this rather beautiful charming little wife called Fidelia. And £80 was a lot of money because she was a virgin. A divorced woman goes half price!

At least Andrew was more fortunate than the fictional clerk Mr Johnson, who also ran into financial difficulties while buying a wife. In Joyce Cary's novel, the hapless Johnson gets into horrendous financial difficulties created mainly by his own lack of foresight but also by his burning ambition to assimilate himself with the British and their way of thinking.

Some attitudes had changed since Cary served in Nigeria during the First World War. Local democracy was taking over from the paternalism of earlier years and new ADOs arriving in Africa were encouraged to take the Africans in their districts into partnership with them. With elections to the new legislative councils dominating political life in west Africa, there was less need to emphasize the importance of touring. In any case, this peerless activity had itself become easier with the advent of four-wheel drive vehicles such as the American jeep and the British Land Rover. Communications also improved, not just internally with better roads but also with Britain. Instead of travelling by sea it was possible to fly, first in converted military aircraft and later in more modern airliners. In piston-engined aircraft such as the Handley Page Hermes or Bristol Britannia, the journey took many hours and included refuelling stops in north Africa and Rome, but at least it cut out the need for a fortnight's voyage by sea – however pleasant that had been for earlier generations.

The improvements allowed wives to stay with their husbands

and children to spend school holidays with their parents. It also became more common for children to be born and brought up in Africa, thus ending the pre-war problem of the children of colonial servants growing up without knowing one or both of their parents. Single women also became more common, not just as travellers, as had happened in earlier years, but now as missionaries, teachers or doctors. Unlike the colonial officers, most had received only scant training for their work in Africa and found that they had to assimilate most of their knowledge on arrival in the country of their choice. For the missionaries, this also entailed understanding that the old paternalism was disappearing and being replaced by a new equality in which British and African teachers worked together.

The churches also had their own synods or assemblies which were quite separate from those in Britain. There were African bishops and African moderators, but as Jocelyn Murray, a New Zealander, found when she arrived in Kenya in 1954, the recent improvements worked both ways. Although the British missionaries at Fort Hall in Central Province clung on to their 'public school/Oxbridge background', they were still forced to come face to face with the Kenyans' [in this instance, Kikuyu] view of Christianity.

> My real introduction to the Kikuyu Christians came through the 'fellowship meeting'. The Christians who were part of the 'East African Revival Movement' met weekly for hymn-singing, spiritual sharing, Bible study and prayer, held at the church and in the vernacular. When I was first taken by my colleagues, it was suggested that I should 'give my testimony' which, through translation, I did. Afterwards one of the Kikuyu men present, a Christian who was a *fundi* – a stonemason, not a teacher – told me that, like the missionaries, I was not a Christian! This was a considerable shock. I had, without really knowing it, been introduced to the East African Revival Fellowship, and was about to be put through the 'trial by testimony' which has happened to so many young missionaries.

Later, Murray found that the Kikuyu congregation had found her testimony too dull and that they had expected a more red-blooded response with 'guilt, struggle, brokenness', and it was some years before she felt that she was fully accepted by them.

Similar tact, though from a distant standpoint, had to be exercised by the Revd Forrestor-Paton, a missionary in the Gold Coast. Although there was an African moderator, he, as secretary to the assembly, was asked to sit beside him instead of in front and below him – the accepted custom in the Church of Scotland. To Forrestor-Paton, this smacked of paternalism – the white secretary guiding the black moderator – but instead of making it an issue which might have embarrassed his colleague, he simply moved of his own accord and took up his correct position below the moderator in the Assembly Hall.

Unfortunately, the slackening of racial or social segregation also introduced new tensions and misunderstandings. Older Europeans sometimes found it difficult to accept the presence of an African official as an equal, particularly in clubs where membership was decided by a man's rank. In west Africa this was less of a problem because the process of Africanization was more advanced, but in Kenya Jocelyn Murray was certainly struck by the 'accepted social segregation which newcomers found [it] difficult to ignore'. This was not the apartheid of South Africa – which had introduced rigid racial laws between 1948 and 1961 to keep black and white people separate – but it is useless to pretend that boundaries did not exist between the races in the British colonies. When Irene Anderson went out by ship to the Gold Coast to teach at the government school in Achimota in 1948, she found that old settler attitudes died slowly.

> There were five tin-miners going back to Jos and they were terribly rude to us because we were going to educate the 'wogs'. With me, that was just the way to make me more determined that I was going to have nothing to do with that type of European. I was going out

to be a teacher. I wasn't going to have any truck with 'white settlers', as it were.

Once at Achimota, though, Irene Anderson found that the
school's teaching staff was multiracial and that, like most other
closely-knit grips, it had developed its own *esprit de corps*, one
which was built on professionalism and mutual respect.

The staff has been mixed from the word go and one of the
reasons I always think of the Ghanaians rather than the expatriates is that there were several Ghanaians about my own age who
had just come back from the UK. The first batch to be sent to
Britain after the war to get their degrees had come back on the
staff and we were new on the staff together. Two or three of
them had been to Oxford or Cambridge, as I had, and somehow
or other it was perfectly natural for us to have a mixed social life
. . . Sometimes the Ghanaians used to think we expats would
mix with all the white people. I remember one ghastly time
someone asking me if I'd be nice to a couple of chaps who were
visiting. I mean, I had nothing in common with them at all
except we had the same colour of skin. I wouldn't have mixed
with them in this country [Britain].

Achimota demanded high standards – the common entrance
exam was stricter than its British equivalent – and the accent was
on educational and sporting achievement. Fees had to be paid
too and, although companies such as Cadbury and UAC
sponsored scholarships, most families had to make considerable
sacrifices when sending their children, mainly boys, to
Achimota. While the school existed to prepare pupils for higher
education elsewhere, or to train them as pupil-teachers, it was
not completely anglocentric: there were classes in the vernacu-
lar and tribal dancing and pupils were encouraged to take an
interest in their own cultures.

Even so, it was not always easy to avoid racial issues. The main
geography textbook – *Stamp's Geography of the World* – contained
a chapter which claimed that in the southern states of America
corn was grown for natives and pigs. 'They would laugh at it

because Ghanaians have a wonderful sense of humour', claimed Irene Anderson. 'But you can imagine, some of them got really livid and it wasn't very long before we got local textbooks.'

On the whole, though, as Bert Davies had discovered in Sekondi, the Gold Coast suffered few racial problems, partly because there was an educated middle class with whom the white officials and teachers felt a close affinity. In Kenya and Southern Rhodesia it was quite different. Unlike west Africa, where the populations were wholly black and the whites were mostly birds of passage, these were predominantly settler colonies which had seen their white populations increase after the war as farming land was made available to former service-men. And the white communities of both countries believed that many years would have to pass before the black population could play any political role in the countries' political life. Although the Colonial Office held to the view of the 1923 White Paper on Kenya that the 'interests of the African natives must be paramount', they were also sympathetic to the settlers' concerns and it was generally agreed that self-rule in east Africa would lag several decades behind events in west Africa.

In both countries, the whites entertained considerable affec-tion for their black servants and liked to think that they 'knew their Africans'. Indeed, this was the message propagated in a Southern Rhodesian government guide for incoming settlers.

> This little booklet is published as your introduction to the man with whom you are in daily contact in your home and at work – the African – and sets out to tell you a little of the customs and beliefs of his people . . .
>
> The African loves laughter. His needs are few and simple and when he was satisfied them he is inclined to sit back . . .
>
> How then should we deal with this man? We should remember his background and treat him with patience and courtesy. Loss of temper when things go wrong helps no one.

As with many official publications of its kind, the booklet was strong on detail but weak on insight. The relationship between

white and black was presented as being basically paternalistic
– the exhortations often read like an introduction to school life –
and the overall impression was of contented Africans and privileged Europeans living in harmony. This was central to the myth
of white supremacy in Southern Rhodesia and Kenya and the
settlers worked hard to maintain it. The reality was usually
different. Although most white settlers had a deep and abiding
affection for those Africans with whom they had close contact
– their servants and workers – they did not know Africans as a
whole, and for the new and increasingly noisy nationalist politicians they often had nothing but contempt. For Clara Chidarara,
a black Southern Rhodesian political activist, though, this
dichotomy allowed blacks to tell whites what they wanted to
hear and not necessarily the truth.

> When a white man tells you something, you listen. This is where
> the past regime lost out. They never got to understand the African
> because we know how to play polite. No matter what someone
> says, even if we don't agree with it, we pretend to agree. This is
> where the whites lost out. They believed things were working,
> while they were not. As blacks we knew that if we resist we'll be
> detained, so the easiest thing to do was to show you agree, you
> believe – finished. But deep down you're boiling.

The problem of communicating between the races was not
unique to Southern Rhodesia, although its complications were
to last longer: it was common all over the colonial empire in
Africa. All too often, British officials did not understand the burgeoning strength of nationalist feeling and preferred to stick to
the formula that many years would have to pass and more
Africans would have to be trained and educated before the
colonies could be granted full independence. The attitude irri-
tated the growing band of African politicians and not for
nothing did Kenyatta complain that 'while certain British people
are willing to learn from colonials privately – over a cup of tea
– they are unwilling to admit publicly that these people are ready

for self-government'. Conversely, it is true to say that the peasantry and the less-educated Africans were the people who wanted the British to stay, while the educated Africans who were acquiring political power were the people who wanted early independence.

While it is generally true that the British left themselves little time to train and educate the political leaderships before the African colonies became independent, the Gold Coast was in fact reasonably well developed and, indeed, its first leader was a product of the country's educational system. Kwame Nkrumah was born in 1909 in the village of Nkroful in south-west Gold Coast, a member of the Nzima tribe. Little is known about his father, but his mother seems to have had the greatest influence on his early life. It was through her that the young Nkrumah received a good education at the local Catholic mission school, which allowed him to become a pupil teacher in the town of Half Assini. This proved to be a turning-point in his life: in 1926 he was spotted by a schools inspector, Wynne Jones, who thought he had sufficient talent to receive further education at the new teachers' college attached to the government school at Achimota.

> I have never forgotten our meeting since I was suddenly made aware that here was no ordinary teacher. Despite a frenzy of noisy spectators at the open windows, the pupils reacted to his calm, dignified and 'magnetic' manner wholeheartedly. It was an unforgettable inspectorial experience.

Nkrumah spent four years at Achimota, a time which introduced him to the world of ideas – one of his colleagues was the Nigerian nationalist Nnamdi Azikiwe – and encouraged him to continue his education overseas. In 1935 he applied to the University of London, but when he failed the entrance examination – Latin and mathematics proved to be his downfall – he was accepted by Lincoln University in Pennsylvania. It was the beginning of a period of intensive schooling, both at university and in his private life. Because his finances were restricted, he had to work during student vacations and to earn a living he was forced to turn his hand to a variety of menial jobs. He also read voraciously and steeped himself in left-wing political philosophy: in an early pamphlet, 'Towards Colonial Freedom', he claimed that this period of his life laid down the experience for everything that followed.

> The national liberation movement in the African colonies has arisen because of the continuous economic and political exploitation by foreign oppressors. The aim of the movement is to win freedom and independence. This can only be achieved by the political education and organization of the colonial masses. Hence workers and professional classes alike must unite on a common front to further the economic progress and indigenous enterprise of the people which is at present being stifled.

As we have seen, by May 1945 he was in London where he made contact with George Padmore and his fellow members of the Pan-African movement who were the early standard-bearers of organized political nationalism. Two years later, he returned to the Gold Coast to become secretary of the United Gold Coast Convention and to begin the task of 'reconciling the leadership of the intelligentsia with the broad mass of the people'. This proved to be an awkward task. The black 'intelligentsia' to whom Nkrumah referred were mainly lawyers, businessmen and wealthy farmers who shared Britain's belief that independence could only be achieved gradually. At first, Nkrumah thought it would be 'quite useless to associate myself with a movement backed almost entirely by reactionaries, middle-class lawyers and merchants, for my revolutionary background and ideas would make it impossible for me to work with them'. However, as his remit was to built up a broad base of popular support and to create an organized framework for the UGCC, he quickly decided that he should pursue an active political policy, based on socialist principles. This aspect of his work had already caused alarm bells to ring in the Colonial Office: shortly before his departure to the Gold Coast, Creech Jones had been warned by an under-secretary, K.G. Bradley, that Nkrumah's presence in the country would cause nothing but trouble.

> It seems probable that if Kwame Nkrumah, who is about to arrive back in the Gold Coast from the United Kingdom, takes an active part in organizing the Convention, he will seek for it the support of certain Communist organizations in the United Kingdom with which he seems to have been actively associated for some time past. He may be expected also to establish contact with Communist groups in neighbouring French territory.[1]

Although Nkrumah was always liable to overestimate the depth of his left-wing ideology – Padmore thought that his grasp of revolutionary ideas was unsophisticated and C.L.R. James claimed that 'he used to talk a lot of nonsense' – he did understand the importance of creating a broad church of popular support for the UGCC. While its leadership wanted to continue the struggle for independence through constitutional means – the 1946 constitution had provided a legislative council with majority African membership – Nkrumah believed that it was possible to manipulate public support in order to pressurize the British into granting early independence. At first the policy seemed to work. When he toured the country with J.B. Danquah, he met enthusiastic crowds of UGCC supporters who wanted political reform sooner rather than later. There were also numerous complaints about the high price and shortage of consumer goods. If this energy could be harnessed, the UGCC could profit; but as Nkrumah discovered, there was still much work to be done before it could call itself a valid political organization.

> I found, on going through the minute-book, that thirteen branches had been formed throughout the country. In actual fact, just a couple had been established and these were inactive. I saw at once

the urgency of a country-wide tour. The results of this were most successful, for within six months I had established 500 branches in the [original] Colony alone. I issued membership cards, collected dues and started raising funds.

The reform of the party's organization proved to be the first step in Nkrumah's rise to political power; the Accra riots of 1948 provided the second. The unrest was small beer when compared to the riots and terrorism which had accompanied the transfer of power in India and Palestine, but it still came as an unpleasant surprise to the colonial government. It began in January 1948 as little more than a country-wide boycott of European and Lebanese firms, and had a successful outcome – despite the lack of government intervention, the retailers agreed to reduce prices for a trial period beginning on 28 February. All might then have been well but for a demonstration of ex-servicemen, timed to take place on the same day, which was allowed to get out of control, with disastrous results for the local administration.

These were men who had seen service in the armed forces and government departments during the war and who had genuine grievances: their gratuities had been less than generous, unemployment was high and, as was the case in other parts of the world, there was a shortage of supplies and consumer goods. In the eyes of the young Cameron Duodu, a schoolboy witness of the riots, Britain had broken one promise too many.

> When the war ended, even those members of our families who had actually risked life and limb in Burma or East Africa had to resort to rioting in order to force the British to fulfil the promises – mainly about 'democracy' and economic welfare – that these ex-servicemen believed the British had made to them. Poor chaps – they were taught to believe that only a man called Goebbels indulged in propaganda.

However, the police had given them permission to hold the demonstration, which was orderly and good-natured until the men decided to disobey instructions and march to Christiansborg Castle. When they refused to disperse, the police commander, Superintendent Imray, panicked and ordered his men to open fire. Two people were killed and as news of the incident spread there was an outbreak of rioting in Accra. Shops and warehouses were looted and the gates of the jail at Ussher Fort were battered down. As the trouble spread, twenty-nine people were killed, hundreds more were injured, and it took two weeks for the rioting to be brought under control. What had begun as a relatively minor incident had escalated out of control and many people with experience of the Gold Coast believed that the heavy-handed policing had only exacerbated the situation.

Stanley Mowbray had served with the Royal West African Frontier Force since 1938 and he felt that in the first stages of the riot, looting was more important than politics.

> It seemed to me to be a good-natured riot because I had to take the rations down in a jeep to the various posts – and was well known as the quartermaster man – and I saw them carting out crates of whisky, sewing-machines, the lot. They really ransacked the place. I went into one of the department stores, a massive place, and there wasn't a matchbox left. They'd cleared it out completely.

What followed next, though, was a mixture of low farce and over-reaction. A curfew was imposed, press censorship introduced and controls put on movement. Two Royal Navy sloops, HMS *Actaeon* and HMS *Nereide* were despatched from the South African naval base at Simonstown and in Gibraltar the 2nd Cameronians (Scottish Rifles) were put on stand-by for possible deployment in the area. In London, the Colonial Office expressed concern lest the riots spread into Nigeria and the normally unflappable Creech Jones was moved to admit: 'The country is on the edge of revolution. We are in danger of losing it.' His concern had been fired both by the news of the rioting and by the first reports from officials in Accra which suggested that the Gold Coast was on the brink of a Communist uprising.

The general pattern of the developing situation has brought into prominence the activities of the Gold Coast Convention and suggests Communist indoctrination. The Convention and the newspapers supporting it have been at pains to paint the situation as being out of hand and the Convention as being the only people capable of restoring it. As the situation changed, the emphasis was placed on the violence of the Government's methods. Race feelings have been inflamed. The ex-servicemen have been used as tools and as good cover for violent action. The greed and baser feelings generally of the rougher types of the population have been stimulated, but the consequential thieving and destruction has been attributed to the outraged feelings of ex-servicemen.[2]

An examination of the signals which passed between the officials in the Gold Coast secretariat and the Colonial Office makes painful reading, even taking into account contemporary Cold War fears and the fact that Britain was facing a Communist insurgency in Malaya. Not only did the secretary to the executive council, Richard Scott, want to place the blame for the riots on Communist agitators, but he was also keen to implicate the leaders of the UGCC, especially Nkrumah. The chief commissioner, Thorlief Mangin, was also guilty of sending alarmist reports to the Colonial Office. When Creech Jones suggested that Nkrumah might be offered 'positive and constructive work' to sideline him from his political activities, Mangin sent a negative reply, reinforcing the idea that the UGCC secretary was a dangerous political activist.

I fear that it would be impractical to adopt your suggestion of finding employment for Nkrumah. He is obdurately and fanatically withdrawn from communication with Europeans, especially officials. Apart from this, he does pretty well out of his agitation and has recently purchased, for example, an expensive Packard car.[3]

In this respect, both men were inadvertently supported by Creech Jones, who wrote to Creasy on 18 March, requesting that the investigations be kept secret 'until a more precise estimate of the true proportions of Communist activity can be made'. This signal, from Scott, came eight days after he had informed London that the real danger came from Nkrumah.

> It is my considered opinion that it is in his ability to exploit a situation, and not because of any facility for constructive political thinking, that Mr Nkrumah is most dangerous to the peaceful progress of this country. I believe him to be sufficiently intelligent to have assessed correctly the political lessons of the past few months in so far as his own ambition is concerned; and there is no reason to suppose that his ambition does not still reach towards the establishment of a Union of West African Soviet Socialist Republics. I consider that his main objective, since he started his career in this country just over a year ago, has been disruption and that, despite his recent adoption of a frothy nationalism, he has been consistent in the pursuit of that objective.[4]

This was wild talk. During his time in London, Nkrumah had indeed joined the British Communist Party and had also proposed the formation of a masonic group called 'The Circle' to further the cause of independence, but he was not involved in the rioting in Accra. When the riots were taking place, he and the UGCC were in Saltpond, over sixty miles away. True, the UGCC leadership had tried to benefit from the riots by sending a telegram to Creech Jones demanding immediate constitutional change, but it was hardly a subversive move: the message ended with the words 'God Save the King and *Floreat* United Gold Coast'. None the less, six leaders, including Danquah and Nkrumah, were arrested on 12 March, thereby beginning the tradition that all successful African leaders should be 'prison graduates'.

Although the men were quickly released, the damage had been done. Not only did the British distrust Nkrumah but so too did the leadership of the UGCC. When the Watson Commission on the riots proposed fresh constitutional initiatives, including the granting of executive power to the Africans, Nkrumah was sidelined from the working committee and by July 1949 he had severed his links with the UGCC. According to the historian Basil Davidson, one of the reasons given by the UGCC leadership was the discovery in Nkrumah's private papers of the dangerous word 'comrade'. Not that the split weakened his position. Having concentrated on recruiting young people – known as 'youngmen' and 'verandah boys' – into the UGCC, early in 1949 he took them into a party of his own creation, the Convention Peoples' Party (CPP).

By that time, too, there was a new governor, the influential figure of Sir Charles Arden-Clarke, whose first experience of colonial service had been in Nigeria. Like Lugard before him, he was a product of Rossall School and the British Army – as a machine-gunner, he had served in the First World War – but unlike the famous African proconsul he believed that the days of indirect rule had come to an end and that it was time to move west Africa more quickly down the road towards independence. At first he was inclined to accept the received opinion that Nkrumah was an 'extremist leader who is aping Hitler', but in time he was not only to respect the man but also to be instrumental in helping him to take over political power in the country. As he told his wife in a letter of 14 August, he also knew that if traditional racial and social barriers were to be broken down, he had to be a man for all seasons.

> Apparently the announcement I made in my speech that I proposed to get out among the people to see things for myself, followed by the news next day that I am to set out on a short tour on Thursday, has gone down with a bang. What an enormous amount of play-acting there is in all this, the Governor's state, the doctor's bedside manner, the all-in-wrestler's ferocity – and the people see through it and love it.

Equally importantly, Arden-Clarke was a pragmatist whose experience of post-war life in South-east Asia – he had served earlier in Sarawak – told him that the Communist threat in Africa had been over-stressed. This was borne out by the find-

140

ings of the Watson Commission and as a result of its recommendations for the implementation of a greater degree of democracy, a new commission was formed to examine the constitution. Headed by the distinguished judge Sir Henley Coussey, the committee recommended the formation of a nationally elected assembly with seventy-eight members, seventy-two of whom would be elected, and a greater representation of Africans in the Executive Council. To Creech Jones, this represented 'a victory for moderate opinion in the Gold Coast' and, as he told Attlee on October 4, it was now possible to see a peaceful way forward to granting self-rule to the colony.

> If we accept it [Coussey's report] broadly, as I think we should, the Governor hopes to have moderate opinion behind him. If we are not prepared to accept it broadly, moderate opinion will be alienated and the extremists given the opportunity of making trouble. I am satisfied that at this present stage of political development in the Gold Coast, no system would be workable which did not provide, as my proposals do, for a very considerable degree of African participation in the control of policy, while preserving the Governor's ultimate responsibility.[5]

Not unnaturally, perhaps, the moderates welcomed Coussey's proposals because it seemed as if they were to be the recipients of political power. Not so Nkrumah, who immediately called a 'People's Assembly' to debate what he called 'bogus and fraudulent' proposals. To this came the people who would provide him with his power-base – trade unionists, farmers, ex-servicemen and representatives of the youth organizations – and, amongst other demands, they called for immediate self-governing dominion status. Although the call was rejected by Arden-Clarke, Nkrumah had built up a seemingly unquenchable head of political steam. Backed by widespread popular support, he laid plans for 'Positive Action' which would include strikes, boycotts and civil disobedience. An announcement that this would begin on 8 January 1950 was met by a government declaration of a state of emergency and the arrest of Nkrumah. Charged with sedition, he was sentenced on three counts to three years' imprisonment, much to the pleasure of Danquah who declared that 'the wolf had been driven away'.

As it turned out, though, nothing suited Nkrumah's purpose better than to be incarcerated in the prison at James Fort in Accra. Not only did this cement the cachet of his earlier imprisonment, but he had become a symbol of colonial oppression, one which his followers eagerly grasped. Through his political aides, most notably Komlo Gbedemah, he was able to direct the CPP's campaign for the first general election which was due to take place in February 1951 and it could be said that his time in prison afforded him even greater opportunities to get across his message. Through party newspapers, rallies and mass meetings, the young men of the CPP preached a compelling and uncomplicated political slogan: 'Freedom now!'

These youthful supporters were not just rabble-rousers – Scott's and Mangin's portrayal – but literate and intelligent young men and women who had an instinctive grasp of populist politics. As W. C. Benson, an engineer with the United Africa Company at Kumasi, found when he arrived in the Gold Coast in 1952, there was a rapidly growing gap between those who received a bare education and those who wanted to prosper under the new technical training schemes being run by the company.

> We had a lot of chaps could read and write quite well, a lot of them had been to the mission school and they were good, and some of them had been to the state school and these lads were quite good. But the chaps that were a bit backward at reading and writing, they felt it if they sensed that the more educated ones were being picked for these courses.

Inevitably, perhaps, the UAC favoured giving further education and training to the most promising workers and many of these rallied to Nkrumah's cause. When the results of the election were announced, the CPP had swept the board, taking thirty-eight seats to the UGCC's three. From being a political prisoner, Nkrumah found himself the country's first minister, or 'leader of government business'. Five days later, on 12 February, Arden-Clarke bowed to the inevitable and ordered Nkrumah's release from prison. As he admitted, he had no alternative.

> Nkrumah and his party had the mass of the people behind them and there was no other party with appreciable public support to which one could turn. Without Nkrumah, the Constitution would be stillborn, and if nothing came of all the hopes, aspiration and concrete proposals for a greater measure of self-government, there would no longer be any faith in the good intentions of the British Government and the Gold Coast would be plunged into disorder, violence and bloodshed.

For the British, it was a symbolic moment. Both Cohen and Arden-Clarke had wanted to release Nkrumah before the elections took place but they feared that such a move would convince the UGCC that the British supported the CPP. Now that Nkrumah had won the election, though, they had to deal with him and not with the UGCC moderates. In a manner which typified much of the ending of colonial rule in Africa, the Governor found that he had to treat a nationalist rebel as a political equal. True to form, Arden-Clarke measured up to the task when Nkrumah presented himself at Christiansborg Castle to discuss the formation of his first government. As he told Cohen on 5 March, although the initial meeting was awkward, the two men found enough common ground in which to work together.

> I do not yet know what to make of Nkrumah. My first impressions, for what they are worth, are that he is an idealist, ready to live up to his ideals, but I have yet to learn what these ideals really are. Unlike most of his colleagues, he seems quite genuinely to bear no ill-will for his imprisonment and is not venal. He has little sense of humour but has considerable personal charm. He is as slow to laugh as he is quick to grasp the political implications of anything discussed. His approach to questions is more of a psychologist than a

realist. He has proved he can give inspiration and I find him susceptible to receiving it but I fear there is a streak of weakness that may be his undoing. A skilful politician, he has, I think, the makings of a real statesman and this he may become if he has the strength to resist the bad counsels of the scallywags by whom he is surrounded.[6]

This was a very different picture from the portrait of the Marxist revolutionary, and Arden-Clarke was praised for his efforts in helping Nkrumah achieve a smooth transition from imprisonment to political leadership. It was a remarkable display of statesmanship although, privately, Arden-Clarke was still aware that his patronage and support would remain a sensitive issue. Later, he described their behaviour at the first encounter as 'two dogs meeting for the first time, sniffing around each other with hackles half-raised, trying to decide whether to bite or wag our tails'. By the second meeting, though, 'the hackles were down, and before the end the tails were wagging'. Arden-Clarke was fond of canine metaphors when describing his relationship with Nkrumah. Describing his efforts to bolster Nkrumah's leadership and to encourage his political independence from Britain, he told *The Times*'s correspondent Oliver Wood: 'We have only one dog in our kennel and the whole question is whether the tail will wag the dog or the dog the tail. It has a very big tail and not much guts. All we can do is to build it up and feed it vitamins and cod-liver oil, and as soon as the opportunity offers, some of that tail must be docked.'

There was still a long way to go before the Gold Coast achieved independence, but a start had been made when Nkrumah decided to co-operate with the British instead of continuing the confrontation. True, there were limits to his power because Arden-Clarke continued to chair the cabinet and the authority of ministers was limited by civil servants. Some of his political opponents, most notably in the UGCC, argued that it was a sell-out and a compromise which halted the political revolution – Nkrumah also came to believe that a better solution might have been to have gone 'straight forward for independence, even if such a course had demanded armed insurrection' – but at the time it was considered a radical move. And as Basil Davidson recalled, it was also a moment of 'happiness and hope'. Having been offered a peaceful progress towards democratic self-rule, Nkrumah and his ministers showed that they had the maturity to accept it.

> Looking back, there were occasions then that still glow in the mind. They evoke the atmosphere of extraordinary excitement in which a people's destiny unfolds. Frail though it is, the ship of national independence has seized the tide and squared its sails. And the wind blows well.
>
> Only twelve days elapse between the release from James Fort of the leaders of the CPP and their formal meeting in the Legislature. There they take the oath of allegiance and prepare to start their work. Proudly, they are still wearing their white 'prison graduate' caps. One of the few among them who has not come from prison, Archie Casely-Hayford, the gentle and immensely loyal lawyer of Accra who has stood by them while they were in gaol, is wearing a special one of his own. It is labelled 'DVB': 'Defender of the Verandah Boys', another gesture of popular defiance.

After the triumphal coming to power and the pageantry of the opening of the new Assembly, Nkrumah and his colleagues had to begin the slow and at times frustrating business of learning how to govern the country. At their shoulders they had senior civil servants as their permanent secretaries or political advisers. Initially, these were white but a rapid expansion of the civil service was accompanied by the equally hasty process of Africanization. The newcomers were the people who could make or break the process and to observers like the Scottish doctor, it seemed to be a race against time to train the Gold Coasters for positions of authority before independence.

> It was a hard time in many ways for the colonial servants at the top in these transition governments, implementing plans that probably they thought were going too fast and trying to put the brakes on or guide it the right way.

Here both sides were helped by the country's financial stability. The high price of cocoa gave the government a healthy profit – in 1951 the price was £269 a ton; three years later it was £358 a ton – and the funds provided Nkrumah with the opportunity to begin the expansion and modernization of his country' economic infrastructure. Under a complicated system evolved during the war, the Gold Coast's Cocoa Marketing Board kept a reserve fund in London from the profits of the sale of cocoa and in 1953 only 21% of the earnings, or £25 million, were available for expenditure in the Gold Coast. To Nkrumah, the system seemed to be unfair because the cocoa profits gave Britain access to dollars but it did at least provide him with much-needed funds for development. In 1951 he was able to lay plans for the expenditure of £10 million – ten times more than the sum estimated by the Colonial Office.

The boom years provided Nkrumah with a solid basis for learning the art of government: Arden-Clarke's careful tutelage provided him with the means. Not that it was all plain-sailing. It took time and effort for his colleagues to come to terms with the culture and politics of power. All too often, people expected too much too quickly and their appetites were sharpened both by heightened expectations and by the availability of funds. Politicians in the assembly also found that they were expected to favour their immediate and wider families as well as their home communities and that failure to do so was to incur the charge of being worse than the British colonialists. As early as June 1952 Sir Thomas Lloyd, the Colonial Office's Permanent Under-Secretary, warned that the constitutional reform programme might be running out of control.

> It seems fairly clear that the danger in the Gold Coast now is not that of an outburst of anti-European or anti-British feeling but rather that of abuse by a certain section of Africans of the power which we are transferring to them in increasing measures. This danger arises partly out of the tendency of the African to exploit the African if placed in a position to do so, and partly out of the

lessons in the organization of party dictatorship which some of the CPP leaders learnt from their early flirtation with Communism or Communist-penetrated organizations, and which they tend to retain long after they have thrown off such aspects of Communism as may have appealed to them when their desire for power was completely frustrated. If this analysis is correct, then we may at some stage be confronted with a situation in which, on the assumption that the possibility of reinstating a colonial form of government must be ruled out, we are faced with the alternative of clearing out altogether or, by our continued presence, appearing to condone, or even abet, a dictatorial form of government.[7]

With a Conservative administration once again in power in London, there were also doubts about the wisdom of giving so much support to Nkrumah when other political contenders had come to the fore. As was the case in many other parts of colonial Africa, the Gold Coast was a federation of different tribal territories and not all of them were enamoured of Nkrumah. The old aristocratic and regal territory of Asante had not taken kindly to the new administration of mainly southern 'youngmen' and 'verandah boys'; neither had the Northern Territories. Both were to combine in the Northern People's Party which emerged as the main political opposition in the 1954 general election. Affiliated to it was the opposition party in the Volta region which included the British sector of the old German colony of Togoland – it was here that Nkrumah's deputy Gbedemah had his seat.

Despite Nkrumah's ambition to weld the four territories into a single harmonious whole, the federalist cause was also growing. In 1955 a rump of discontented CPP members, Asante chiefs and disaffected intellectuals formed the National Liberation Movement under the leadership of Dr Kofi Busia. Their political aims were clear: a postponement of the moves towards independence and the implementation of a new federalist constitution which would allow a strong region such as Asante to dominate the central government. Soon there were clashes between the NLM activists and Nkrumah's supporters. Compared to the later agitation in Nigeria which quickly disintegrated into bloody civil war, the unrest in the Gold Coast was negligible but it did persuade the British to require a further general election before the transfer of power. This would take place in July 1956 and, as the Colonial Secretary Alan Lennox-Boyd told the House of Commons, this was to be the final test before setting a date for independence.

The ball was now firmly in Nkrumah's court and following a bitter election contest against the NLM, his CPP party won seventy-one seats out of the 104 available, winning 57% of the vote in the process. By any standards it was notable victory and Nkrumah had emerged as a leader worthy of taking his country into independence, but even so there were still doubts about his abilities. In the more conservative sections of the British press, he was demonized as a dangerous radical who would plunge west Africa into political chaos. There were also those who hoped that the federalist NLM would win the election and thereby slow down the independence process. Much of the dislike was prompted by Nkrumah's style. In July 1956 F.E. Cumming Bruce, Arden-Clarke's adviser on external affairs, warned the Colonial Office that ministerial corruption was rife and, worse, alleged – wrongly as it was later found – that Nkrumah 'connived at, and possibly organized, the murder of opponents'.

> The comforting myth that the Gold Coast was likely to be a well-behaved child that would be a credit to its parents has always, as you know, seemed to be to bear little relation to facts. The Government is in the hands of knaves. As African rogues go, they are not very bad ones: they have their saving graces; and it would probably be impossible to muster a dozen honest men in politics to replace them. The practical question now is not whether they are good or bad, but whether we can maintain reasonable working relations with them.[8]

Even western liberals in the Gold Coast felt that the process was too rapid, that independence was being foisted on a people who were not yet ready for it.

As far as education is concerned, I think it was a mistake to Ghanaianize as quickly as they did. There was a mass exodus of British civil servants. Now this meant that any Ghanaian who had scraped through a degree could get a job either as a civil servant or a school-teacher, or something like this. And you were getting very ordinary chaps being made heads. Five years as a graduate and you could qualify to be head of a secondary school. Now this is nothing to do with being Ghanaian. They just weren't up to it.

While it is true that the process of Ghanaianization did not always run smoothly, due mainly to the shortness of the time-scale – the civil service expanded from 200 to 1,000 senior officials during Nkrumah's first term of office – it is difficult to see what other course either side could have taken. Once the decision had been made to hold the 1951 elections, the move towards independence was an unstoppable process. True, some Africans were promoted beyond their capabilities – as Irene Anderson noticed (by this time she was headmistress of Aburi Girls' Secondary School) – but at least the schools were expand-ing. By the time independence came in 1957, there were over 3,000 primary schools, 931 middle schools and thirty-eight sec-ondary schools and even in the field of purely technical courses, W.C. Benson found that the policy of educating the brightest apprentices was beginning to work.

Every year a report had to be written to your manager and these reports would go to the personnel department. The objective ulti-mately was to replace ourselves with Africans. When I started in 1952 there were, roughly speaking, about forty-five expatriates in the [UAC] motor division. When I left in 1976 there were only three. So that was the progress.

The argument about quantity versus quality, especially in the educational field, was to rage beyond independence but even so, the granting of self-rule in 1957 was a watershed in the history of African colonial history. Within three years, on 9 January 1960, a British prime minister, Harold Macmillan, was to refer in Accra to the 'wind of change blowing through Africa'; a phrase which was unnoticed at the time but which caused a sensation when he repeated it a few weeks later in Cape Town. Despite right-wing calls for a return to imperial splendour – increasingly the preserve of outlandish minority groups such as the League of Empire Loyalists – Britain was in no mood to maintain colonial rule in Africa. The humiliation of the Suez War in November had undermined British prestige and influence. The United States and the Soviet Union were anxious to remove British and French colonial rule from Africa, not just for altruistic reasons but also to allow them to carve their spheres of influence. And in British society itself, a younger generation failed to be impressed by the lure of colonial service in far-flung parts of Africa.

For all these reasons, when independence was finally granted on 7 March 1957, there was also a sense that Ghana represented the fulfilment of both a promise and a duty. And that belief was represented in the sonorous celebrations which greeted the granting of independence. Just after midnight the new red, yellow and green flag of Ghana was unfurled on the polo ground in Accra, the bands played, the soldiers stood to attention, fireworks lit the night sky and the people celebrated in the streets. Throughout the 1960s the same scenes were to be repeated in other parts of Africa and were soon to become commonplace, but for Bert Davies in Sekondi, the memory never lost its savour.

> There was singing and shouting and letting off fireworks. And everybody was in a very festive mood and slapping you on the back and the fact that you were white didn't make the slightest difference. Eventually we went to a Ghanaian friend, Betty Vander Puye, and ice-cold beer was produced and west African groundnut stew – marvellous, very hot – and as the afternoon wore on, there we were, sitting, sipping away, just listening to the tumult in the town. It was a great day!

150

Ghana had achieved independence without bloodshed and a standard had been set for other countries to follow. For Nkrumah and his colleagues, though, the moment did not mark the end of the struggle. Britain might have given notice that it was prepared to quit Africa sooner rather than later, but for the Ghanaians the enterprise was only beginning.

6

The Centre Cannot Hold

GHANA WAS A declaration: once the Gold Coast had achieved independence, the remaining west African colonies – Nigeria, Sierra Leone and The Gambia – would all follow suit. In fact, Nigeria had already ventured out on the same road with the granting of a new constitution in 1951 – the year of Arden-Clarke's agreement with Nkrumah – but its progress was to be more measured and troubled because of the internal regional differences in the country. In fact, as early as 1948, referring to British attempts to produce a unitary constitution, Abubakar Tafawa Balewa claimed that 'Nigerian unity is only a British invention', and that the Nigerians were too diverse in culture, traditions and history to allow anything but a federal solution. This echoed the sentiment expressed by the Yoruba leader Obafemi Awolowo who wrote that 'Nigeria is not a nation. It is a mere geographical expression.' As both sides were to discover, it would be a long and difficult process to discover a constitutional solution which suited all the parties and tribal factions which made up Nigeria.

A glance at the ethnic map confirms the extent of the problem. To the north, the Hausa and Fulani regarded themselves as being superior to the people living in the south: theirs was a largely feudal society run by well-bred and frequently autocratic Muslim emirs. It was here that the policy of indirect rule had been happiest, the public-school and Oxbridge-educated British administrative officers and aristocratic northerners having discovered that they had much in common. The south was divided into two regions, each of which had a dominant tribal group. The Western Region was the home of the Yoruba, who had enjoyed the longest and closest links with the British traders and administrators; while the densely populated Eastern Region consisted mainly of Igbo-speaking people, many of them well accustomed to Christian missionaries. Even these tribal distinctions became blurred, however, when the different sub-groupings of little-known pagans, animists and minority clans were taken into account. By the early 1950s, though, distinct political groupings had emerged in the three main regions: the Northern People's Congress (NPC) was led by the Sardauna of Sokoto; Awolowo's Action Group (AG) represented the west; while the east was held by the National Council of Nigeria and the Cameroons (NCNC), led by the same Dr Azikiwe who had influenced Nkrumah's early political development.

There were other differences. The northerners were considered more backward, while the southerners, the Igbo and the Yoruba, were better educated and held superior jobs in the administration and commerce. Many had moved to work as artisans or clerks in the north where their presence was a constant source of irritation, especially if they were the predominantly Christian Igbo. Whereas the emirs of the north still ruled within the ordnances of Islamic tradition, the southerners were generally more liberated and, consequently, more interested in pushing for independence. And, as had happened in the Gold Coast, their ranks contained some vocal ex-servicemen, disgruntled by the low gratuities and lack of work. There were fears, too, that many had been influenced by Communism, although when the Colonial Office reported on the matter in 1950 it was not the problem that had been found in the Gold Coast. Apart from the breakaway Zikist movement started by

Nduka Eze, who owned to Communist sympathies, no evidence of Marxist infiltration was found.

> The chief 'liberation' organizations, the National Council of Nigeria and the Cameroons (NCNC) which stands for the overthrow of British colonial rule and the creation of independent Nigeria, cannot be described as Communist in any sense. Its founder-president Dr Nnamdi Benjamin Azikiwe has stated categorically that he is not a Communist; but he has had talks with Palme Dutt and other British Communists and has visited the Czech embassy in London. According to his own statement, he would be prepared to co-operate on a purely reciprocal basis with any person or group in sympathy with his aims, but would never allow himself to become a tool in other hands. The British Communist Party is critical of Azikiwe and suspicious of his purely nationalistic aspirations. No evidence was found of Communist inspiration behind the rioting at the Government coal mines at Enugu in November 1949.

The Colonial Office's findings were borne out by independent witnesses like Sylvia Leith-Ross, who asked a teacher what Communism might mean to him, only to receive the answer 'money for all'.

> This seemed a grand idea and the teacher was ready to become a Communist at once. When the possibility of having to give up part of his yam crop to the State was put before him, he was no longer so sure.

Although Britain had united northern and southern Nigeria in 1914, both had been treated as separate entities and colonial officers posted to the north still considered themselves to be a cut above their brethren in the south, even though that was the seat of the country's main political power. As we have seen, throughout the colonial empire there was a tendency for administrative officers to support the claims of the people amongst whom they worked. Even as late as the 1950s, Joan Sharwood-Smith, the wife of the North's lieutenant-governor, realized that the divide was as deep as ever.

Lagos had always been isolated from the rest of Nigeria and absorbed in its own sophisticated existence. Of the thousands of white people who were stationed there, a few knew the North but many people never travelled far inland. If they thought about the region at all, it was merely to dismiss it as a land of feudal princes and stuffy British officers. 'Dirt and Dignity' was the slogan used to sum up the North.

Similar arguments had raged throughout British rule in India – which was the better posting, United Provinces or Bengal? – and Nigeria was no different. In the post-war world, though, the trick would be to preserve regional differences while producing a federal constitution which would benefit the country as a whole. In his first speech to the northern regional council in Kaduna on 20 January 1947, the newly elected Abubakar Tafawa Balewa warned the southerners that they should not attempt to impose their ideology on the rest of the country.

> If ever the northern provinces change, as I know they must, I want them to change into a modern Northern Nigeria, but not into some sort of artificial civilization which is neither European or African. The northern provinces are now facing a great danger. Evil ideas are creeping into the north from outside sources . . . I do not know what right those people have to claim to be the voice of the north. We must do something soon in the north to show Britain and the world that these self-styled leaders do not and cannot in any matter or in any way represent us.

Under the terms of the constitution, introduced by the Governor Sir Arthur Richards, each group of provinces was given a regional council which would then elect representatives to an expanded national Legislative Council ('Legco') in Lagos. This allowed the elected members in the regional assemblies to sit with their white resident who would guide them on procedure. Not every member was as confident as Abubakar: Rex Niven, the resident for Borno, realized that Muhammadu Ngileruma, the Wali of Borno, was undergoing an 'ordeal endured by so many thousands of public speakers at the start of their careers'.

155

One of the ablest of the Bornu people and certainly the most eloquent, he was nonetheless terrified by the whole thing and completely tongue-tied. I had to urge him to speak on something he knew about: I felt it vital that the difficulty be broken or we should be forever stuck. He wrote his paragraph, about ten lines, and brought it to me to look at. I smartened it up a bit and made it easier to say. When the time came, he shambled (there is no other word) to his feet. He trembled so much I thought that he would fall flat, and as his hand shook he couldn't read what he had written, but fortunately memory came to his aid. He recited the words in a whisper that could scarcely be heard, and sat down in a collapsed state.

As Niven also admitted, the officials had to adapt themselves to the new system of government whose proceedings were 'far from parliamentary and indeed were almost cosy. The President's rather dingy pith helmet [G.B. Williams was one of the last to wear one] lay on his desk before him, like a strange symbol of office.' The northern meetings took place in the Trades Centre at Kaduna and each delegate sat behind a school-style desk, an unusual setting for a fledgeling democracy, but at least it was a beginning.

The arrangement was expected to last for nine years, but the Gold Coast riots encouraged a change of pace and between 1948 and 1960 Nigeria was to be given four different constitutions, each of which was hotly debated by the political parties. Indeed, the British encouraged widespread discussion of the proposals right down to village level and throughout 1950 the country's public life seemed to have been side-tracked into conferences of varying size and understanding. As the new governor, Sir John Macpherson, told Niven, he wanted political progress to be measured by mutual agreement and not by the kind of violence which had taken place in Accra.

I am never going to be forced into decisions I do not like by screaming mobs round the gates of Government House and in our flower-beds. I will always be one jump ahead of them and in our direction, not theirs. I hope you agree?

Admirable through the sentiment was, Macpherson and his colleagues knew that the consultation process would throw up as many new problems as it solved old ones. As officers in the field soon discovered, bemused Nigerians found themselves being appealed to by politicians to agree policies which seemed, even if they understood them, to have little bearing on their day-to-day lives. Inevitably, many of the disagreements were caused by the regional inability to find common cause. As a recently arrived ADO, Trevor Clark, saw it, the consultation process suffered from the 'chauvinism of the grass roots firmly embedded throughout the whole country'.

> The northern chiefs and commoner representatives agreed their line in the Kaduna police college dining-room, and settled for a central legislature that might vest extra powers in the regional councils. Southern politicians were thus invited to recognize that all tribes, including their own, put their own narrow interests first, and that political parties in the south would ignore this at their peril; but that northern leaders would disclaim the right to speak for any but their home areas. The easterners thought the regions should only have powers that the centre specifically delegated, while the westerners wanted all residual powers to be given to regions which should be based on ethnic divisions.

By autumn, Macpherson's drafting committee had reached a compromise solution. A strong federal legislature would be created, but power would be devolved to the assemblies in the Northern, Eastern and Western regions, which would have their own Executive Council with powers to initiate legislation. The Northern and Western regions would also have an upper House of Chiefs presided over by the lieutenant-governor (previously chief commissioners) and for the first time .there would be African 'ministers'. The assemblies would then choose members to represent them in a central House of Representatives with its own Council of Ministers. In the middle of 1951 a final conference debated the measures in London and new Orders-in-Council were issued to authorize a new constitution. It was the first tentative step towards creating a federation; but far from stilling the political in-fighting, the new constitutional arrangements only seemed to bring into sharper focus the differences between the regions.

> Fortunately, at all times, among all people, humour is never far beneath the Nigerian surface, and even extremists and confirmed nationalists could criticize themselves with engaging frankness.
>
> 'Britain is like a mother carrying a child on her back. The child kicks its mother and shouts: "Go faster! Go faster!" The mother tires and puts down the child. "Now see how fast you can walk!" she says.'
>
> 'Nigeria is like a farmer who wants to make a very big farm. He clears the bush in front of him so quickly that he has not time to look back and see that the bush has grown up again behind him.'
>
> One could not fail to recognize an eminent politician in the swift portrait: 'He is like a dancer who bursts out of the shadows, dances beautifully so that everybody applauds him, then retreats to the shadows till he feels the time has come for him to rush out with a new dance.'

At the age of sixty-three, Sylvia Leith-Ross had returned to Nigeria in 1951 to examine the possibility of establishing an élite finishing-school for the wives and daughters of Nigerian politicians who would soon have to learn western-style political protocol. The scheme failed to find much support when she established it in Onitsha in Eastern Nigeria – one girl told her that it was pointless learning how to set a table as she only had one fork and spoon at home – but, undaunted, she stayed on to observe the first elections for the regional assemblies.

Although she admitted that it was 'a period I would like to forget', and that she could see no end to the jealousies and suspicions between the ethnic groups, she also noticed that a younger group of people, Nigerians and British, were working hard together, confidently and happily, towards the goal of eventual independence. By then, the process of Nigerianization was under way, not just in the colonial administrative service but also

in commercial life – as in the Gold Coast, the United Africa
Company had promoted Africans to responsible positions and
was sending younger men and women on training courses in
Britain. In 1948, three Nigerians were sent to London to be
trained on the Colonial Office's Devonshire administrative
course and two Nigerian officer cadets attended the Royal
Military College, Sandhurst. In the Royal West African Frontier
Force, it was agreed to halt the secondment of British non-
commissioned officers and to accelerate the promotion of
African junior officers. Welcome though these and other
changes undoubtedly were, they did seem to some officials, like
Johnnie McCall, to be too little and too late – of the 3,786
public-sector posts in 1948, only 245 were held by Nigerians.

> We should have done more about training and this was not so much
> for us District Officers in the bush, this was for central government
> in Lagos and in Ibadan and in Enugu. We didn't do enough from a
> training point of view. I had an African ADO who was Nigerian
> and maybe we were a bit slow in the training.

As was the case with many of his senior colleagues, McCall
spent his final days in Nigeria in the central secretariat in Lagos
where, as a permanent secretary, he 'had a minister, an African,
and that was very good preparation for that minister for independence because he had a British permanent secretary telling
him how the office worked and so on and how the government
machine worked, so all that added to his preparation for independence'. Even so, most colonial administrative officers admit
that Africanization was tardily introduced in Nigeria – when Sir
James Robertson became Governor in 1955, following service
in the Sudan, he expressed considerable surprise that the process
was so backward.

One reason for the delay in Africanization was the tight time-
scale. Another was the difference in employment patterns in the
regions, particularly in the north, where there were growing
calls for 'northernization' of jobs held by southern workers who

enjoyed little prestige. It had soon became obvious that, for all its good points, the 1951 constitution was not working because the centre was unable to accommodate the disparate voices in the regions. The crunch came in March 1953, during one of the final sessions of the Lagos House of Representatives, when Anthony Enahoro, an Action Group backbencher, tabled a private member's motion 'that this house accepts as a primary political objective self-government for Nigeria in 1956'. This came as a terrible blow to the northern members who knew that they were not ready for self-government and could not be so by such an early date. They also argued that the motion required prior consultation with their constituents. In vain did the Sardauna of Sokoto put forward a counter-proposal to substitute 'as soon as practicable' for 'in 1956': the motion was introduced, proposed and seconded and, according to one witness, the subsequent debate 'quickly ended in uproar'.

In a carefully orchestrated move, Awolowo and Azikiwe stormed out of the building, followed by their AG and NCNC supporters. Outside, crowds of noisy demonstrators waited to jeer at the northern members who were generally held to have to have halted the move towards independence. Worse was to follow. When the northern members went to Iddo Station to board the special train which was waiting to take them home, they had to face further humiliation from crowds of hooligans – and the same fate awaited them at stations along the route back to Kaduna. With tempers running high, the Sardauna of Sokoto angrily waved his arms and shouted: 'Next time I come, I'll have a sword in my hand!'

Next day, the AG leadership resigned from the Council of Ministers, thereby creating a political crisis and ending any hopes of saving the Macpherson constitution. The unrest in Lagos was followed by violent rioting in Kano, where a *sabon gari*, or reservation, of southerners was attacked by machete-wielding thugs. The police did their best to keep the two sides apart, but it was not until barbed wire was erected to separate the combatants that the fighting stopped. In three days of unrest, thirty-one people died and hundreds more were wounded but, as Rex Niven points out, 'it was not all evil in those three days'.

> There were heroic rescues of Hausas by their Igbo friends and the other way round, and people of one side concealed those of the other side being hunted by furious mobs demanding, and sometimes getting, blood. But no one who was not a Hausa or an Igbo was injured or even put in fear, and no child was hurt – I was told they ran unconcerned among the rioters.
>
> Kano was not a place of bloodshed and terror; usually it was peaceful, quiet and industrious – which, considering the huge population and the tiny police force available to deal with trouble, was just as well. But as in other places the peace was firmly in the hands of the village and ward heads and their elders. We got very few complaints, and there was nothing to stop people coming to us: walking or riding through the villages, we talked to the people in their own language and were sensitive to any 'upset' feeling. The Emir sat outside his gate every fine evening before and during sunset and was available to any person. He did not have alarming numbers of 'courtiers' hedging him about; his people could come to him and say what they wished to say. This was the way it had been for generations.

Not for much longer would those bucolic scenes remain the norm in the north. Unstoppable changes were now on their way for, whatever else had happened in Lagos, the failure of the 1951 constitution had helped to concentrate minds in the NPC. Shortly after their return, the northern members held a special meeting of their assembly which demanded 'complete regional autonomy' and the end of the central legislature. What this meant in effect was a call for full regional control with virtually no central government, apart from the creation of a neutral agency to handle matters such as defence and external affairs. Furthermore, the Sardauna of Sokoto also discussed with officials the possibility of opening a new rail-link to the sea through neighbouring French Dahomey.

The passing of the motion placed the Colonial Office in a quandary because it was still responsible legally for supervising Nigeria's affairs; it could not stand by and allow the country to be Balkanized. Accordingly, the northern resolution was reported in full by Macpherson and, recognizing that the present constitution had prevented the three regions from working closely together, it was agreed to hold a fresh conference in London to begin the process of providing greater regional devolution and to reduce their links with Lagos. As Niven noted, the new proposal was not just welcomed by the north: 'This, of course, pleased the other two regions, which saw possibilities of earlier self-government for themselves by this new turn of events.'

And so it proved. The revised constitution, introduced in 1954 after further consultations in Lagos, gave a greater amount of authority to the three regions, while maintaining a federalist system in the House of Representatives in Lagos. However, under the new system the regions became largely self-governing, with their own executive councils containing a majority of elected ministers, budgets, civil service and courts. With the reforms came other changes. The governor became the governor-general, while in the regions the lieutenant-governors received appointments as governors and further down the line district officers found themselves taking on the new title and responsibility of secretaries to the executive councils. Elections were held first in the East and West and then, later, in the North; and it was agreed that the southern regions would be able to move separately towards self-rule – 1956 was still considered a feasible goal – while the northerners would be permitted more time to bring themselves up to date. During his summer leave, Niven, now the Speaker of the northern assembly, spent time in the House of Commons studying which would be the best parliamentary procedures to introduce to his new role.

The Westminster system is very complicated, having grown up over the centuries, and it became clear that it was quite unnecessary to bring all of it into use at Kaduna. The Northerners were not 'parliamentary' creatures as were the Southerners, and were unlikely to appreciate the more recondite features of the House of Commons. Hence in practice I cut it down a great deal. The two Southern legislatures took parliamentary procedure in their stride, as did the House of Representatives in Lagos: many of their members, it must be remembered, were lawyers and to the manner born (or educated).

Despite misgivings at the time, the 1954 constitution did at least put Nigeria on the path towards eventual independence. Unsurprisingly, given the pace of the changes, not everyone was pleased. The chiefs, in particular, felt that their powers were being eroded and on one occasion the Emir of Bauchi produced a shilling coin and asked Trevor Clark: 'Look, this was made in England. We can't even make our own money yet. If we can't even make our own coinage, how can we expect to progress in other directions?' Other siren voices asked plaintively why the familiar British presence would be withdrawn and warned of impending disaster after it happened. But there was to be no going back. Once Britain had embarked on the crash course in nation-building, complete with Speakers' wigs and Westminster procedures, there was to be no change of heart. As many British colonial servants noticed, once the Nigerians began to gain more political power they became even more impatient for complete independence.

> There was a limit to the amount of development. I think that the intelligent, thinking Nigerian was well aware of this. But so often it's the same – a lot of people think that if Scotland became independent tomorrow we would have much more money to spend. That we could do this, we could do that, we could do the next thing. And I think in the same way there would be limits and people realize – some people realize – there would be limits to what could be done.
>
> It was the same in Nigeria – I think in any of the colonies, people, a lot of people, realized that simply by becoming independent there

was not going to be available a great deal of extra money which there hadn't been before. I think that some thought they would be able to get their hands on it more easily. I think that personal advancement would loom large in the minds of some.

Albert Goodere was serving in the Plateau Province at the time and although he concedes that more could have been done to develop Nigeria before granting independence, the movement towards self-rule had created an unstoppable momentum. During those years of constitutional change Nigeria itself was changing. In place of the largely all-male expatriate society, there were more wives with their families. The introduction of modern prophylactics to combat malaria made it a healthier place, as did the more subtle social changes which accompanied increasing domesticity. Gone, for example, was the heavy drinking at the club which had been the norm for the old coasters before the war. Posted to Ilaro in Western Nigeria in 1939, M.C. Atkinson met older men who had been used to drinking heavily at the club most evenings, with perhaps a brandy and soda at breakfast to restore equilibrium, but the introduction of air transport and the arrival of wives and families closed that particular chapter of colonial history.

These and other factors such as improved housing resulted in an influx of wives and soon after of children. More entertaining began to be done at home and, except for the playing of tennis and golf, the clubs ceased to be the focal point of station life; and drink and home became the rule and for some of us it was father who stayed at home once or twice a week and looked after the bairns while mother played tennis and had the single drink.

Of course, the pace of change was not uniform – social life in the out-stations was different from Lagos or Ibadan – but, as had happened in other parts of the empire, the introduction of greater numbers of women did alter the complexion of service in Nigeria.

When my wife arrived in Ikom about six months after I had been there, we were stopped at villages on the way to Ikom because they had never seen a white child. We had a daughter of about two and they had never seen a white child. As far as my wife was concerned, they wondered if the white went all the way through and they were objects of great curiosity, because they had only seen white men before – if you went into some of the more remote parts of the bush you were greeted as 'father' because the only white men they had seen had been missionaries.

By any standards Ikom, on the Nigerian–Cameroons border, was a primitive place when Ernest Rowand arrived there in 1951 to work as a water engineer and in pre-war days it was unlikely that his wife would have accompanied him. Both make light of the difficulties – no electricity, earth closets and only later were kerosene refrigerators introduced – but there were other changes. Even in the more remote areas, social life was becoming more suburban, the strict protocol of earlier years giving way to the more easy-going social standards of post-war Britain. Not that the new tolerance extended to a complete breakdown in standards: in Ikom, the Forestry Officer would not speak to the District Officer because the latter's servant had stolen aubergines and peppers from his garden. And when the Rowands were posted to Lokoja, the local club was split over the matter of the Forestry Officer's thirteen dogs which were encouraged to join their master for drinks on the verandah, much to the discomfiture of those who had children,

> The great rage at that time was playing Canasta and if you were inviting people to play Canasta you had to be sure they were all doggy-people or they were all children-people.

In some sections of the colonial service, it became more common for men to address one another by their Christian names, a heresy previously unthinkable. Even the more conservative North was not left untouched by the changes. When Joan Sharwood-Smith travelled out to Nigeria in 1939 to join her husband Bryan at Kontagora, by virtue of his position she became the 'senior wife', even though she was still in her twenties. Fifteen years later he was the Governor of the Northern

Region and during that time there had been a sea-change in the local conditions of service.

> By this time, there were a hundred or more white children in Kaduna alone. Many parents could no longer afford the expenses of keeping their children in the UK while they were in Nigeria. Moreover, new ideas in child psychology stressed the harmful effects of separating young children from their parents. Recently developed antibiotics dealt swiftly with such debilitating diseases as typhoid and bacillary dysentery and the new anti-malarial medicines were pleasanter to take than quinine and less devastating to the appearance than mepacrine which made the skin turn yellow. So it was now possible for conscientious parents to keep their offspring reasonably healthy. Nevertheless, although the European children in Kaduna were generally quite fit, they tended to be thin, pale and over-active.

For many people in Nigeria, the seal of modern nationhood came with the Queen's visit in the first two months of 1956. Accompanied by the Duke of Edinburgh, she was the first British Royal visitor for over thirty years – the Prince of Wales had spent some time there in 1925 – and the whole country joined together in celebration, the constitutional difficulties momentarily forgotten. As one of the Northern ministers told Niven, 'If she was here all the time, we could really get on with things without troubles and riots.'

Unusually for such an important Royal visit, little time was allowed for the preparations, which were rapidly – and expensively – executed. The overall total cost to the Nigerian exchequer was £2 million and this included the complete refurbishment of Government House with new baths being flown out from Britain at a cost of £1,500 and the special importation of Scottish salmon for the official dinners. At Kaduna there was a magnificent Durbar complete with a variety of bands which played as the people of the provinces marched past the Queen – the Emir of Kano on a camel, snake-charmers and tumblers, and men from the deepest bush. The climax was a full-scale charge towards the royal dais with the horsemen suddenly stopping, wheeling their horses dramatically in the dust and waving their spears and swords in the air.

Never was there such a sight, and such a spectacle of friendship between people not so long ago bitterly opposed to each other: the slavers and the raided, the rich and the poor, purest of Muslims and pagans, plainsmen and people from the High Plateau, the men from the sandy wastes of Bornu and Northern Kano and the stalwarts from the steamy, fertile valleys of the great rivers. All were there and all went home with improbable, and indeed incredible, tales of the young Queen who wore jewels that glittered and flashed in the sunshine, of the people from other countries yet within the bounds of Nigeria, of the languages and songs they had heard, and the dances they had seen.

It was as Rex Niven described. Nigeria was *en fête* for two splendid weeks; power stations had been opened, research institutes visited, troops inspected and loyal addresses read. And, everywhere, happy cheering crowds gave the Royal party a tumultuous welcome. With the pace of independence gathering speed and the realization that their days were numbered, the British in Nigeria tended to regard the Queen's visit as a fitting climax to all their efforts. Nothing was spared to ensure it was a splendid imperial occasion, rivalling even the coronation in London three years earlier.

For the main Nigerian participants, it was also a time of great pride and happiness and yet even as they walked across the stage in their finery, time was already running out for many of them. Of the three ministers deputed to meet the Queen at Ikeja airport, only Kingsley Mbadiwe, the NCNC Minister for Communications, survived into old age. His fellow minister Abubakar Tafawa Balewa, destined to be Nigeria's first prime minister after independence, was murdered in a military *coup* in January 1966. So too was Chief Samuel Akintola, the AG leader of the opposition and a future prime minister of the Western Region. The man who succeeded them in government fared

167

little better. In those heady January days, Major Johnson Aguiyi-Ironsi, an Igbo officer not long out of the Camberley staff college, was the Queen's extra equerry: ten years later he, too, was murdered, a few months after becoming Nigeria's second head of state. As the Sardauna of Sokoto said of the visit in his autobiography, 'It seemed as though a kind of peace, not of this world, came over the country – and it was just as well as it did. It did not endure long after the Queen's departure.' As prime minister of the Northern region, he too was gunned down during the 1966 *coup*.

One reason for the Sardauna's mischievous comment was that the gradual creation of democratic institutions had encouraged confrontational politics and the leading Nigerian politicians had taken advantage of the fact. Although the three regions had become sovereign legislatures capable of passing their own laws and administering their own funds, and a federal body had replaced central government in Lagos, the political battle over the division of federal and regional responsibilities had been hotly contested – as more than one administrator has admitted in his memoirs, the sympathy between the regional peoples was not strong. The disagreements about self-government remained acute between the North and the two southern regions, especially between the North and the Igbo-speaking East, although 1956 passed without any of the regions achieving any form of independence. For many of the British administrators, it was a frustrating period: experienced Colonial Service officers such as Johnnie McCall could see the drift but they were unable to intervene in any meaningful way: 'I was the last British resident of the Delta Province. I pulled down the Union Jack in 1956 because we weren't going to have any more residents with independence coming off.'

In retrospect, many members of the Service – in 1956 renamed Her Majesty's Overseas Civil Service – regret the fact that constitutional change had to be agreed hurriedly and not always painstakingly, or that additional funds were not made available from the home government to further development in Nigeria. It is a natural enough feeling for a group of men who believed that the move towards self-government would be measured and orderly and it was not always easy to answer the question many heard at the time: 'Why are you British leaving us when we are not ready to look after ourselves?' As Trevor Clark admits, this was not just being asked by the simpler or less-educated people but, in the north at least, also by the emirs. '*Mulkin kai* [self-government]?' asked the Emir of Bauchi. 'That is something new that happens in Kaduna and Lagos, the people cannot see it. If it means the DO and other Europeans are to go, we none of us want it, not one.'

However, those sentiments were not always reciprocated in the Eastern and Western regions where the running for self-government was being made by politicians such as the able AG leader Chief Awolowo, whose resignation in 1953 had speeded up the constitutional reforms. By 1955 his legislature passed a resolution calling for self-government within a year, followed by independence for the federation.

It is our belief [he told the western legislature] that every ground won from British rule, no matter how circumscribed in space that ground is, is an accretion to our strength and courage in continuing the struggle for complete liberation. For instance, self-government will mean, in respect of matters within regional competence, the end of the Governor's so-called veto or reserve powers. It will also mean a severe restriction of the Secretary of State's power of interference in our domestic affairs. Above all, it was the immortal Aggrey who said: 'Ask for what you want; get what you are given; keep what you have got, and ask for more.' The people of the Western Region have done no more than to follow this sensible and practical advice of one of the greatest sons of Africa.

The trouble was that the politicians from the regions were frequently pulling in different directions by demanding changes which would suit them but might not always be the correct solution for the federation. Between 1953 and independence in 1960 there was ample opportunity for their views to be aired: there were constitutional conferences in London and Lagos, British MPs visited Nigeria on fact-finding missions, in addition to the official visits made by Colonial Office ministers and civil servants. So frequent were these conferences, and so demanding their schedules, that inevitably they wore down opposition and led to a common desire to create formulas which would allow the country to push forward to statehood. Trevor Clark remembered one elderly official repeating a time-honoured story which seemed to reflect the tenor of the times. An elderly servant, being cross-questioned by his master about his faults, wearily exclaimed: 'Please, sir, dismiss me, fine me, beat me, do anything you want with me, but, sir, please stop asking me questions!' Others were less sanguine. In Lokoja, Ernest Rowand recalled that the visiting parliamentary parties were known as seagulls: 'Fly in and crap on you and fly out again.'

Visiting the country again in October 1957, Sylvia Leith-Ross noticed something else about the British officials, the pain of impending departure, especially amongst the older generation who had served all their lives in Nigeria.

> Among the British officials, as among those in Onitsha and elsewhere in the Eastern Region, the future of Nigeria was endlessly discussed, with confidence, with foreboding, with anxious sympathy, with practical common sense, hardly ever with indifference. The older men were the most apprehensive, for they were the ones who had known Nigeria as an infant and found it hard to believe that adulthood had been reached so soon. It was the older men again who felt, or so it seemed to me, that they were now out of place, that Nigeria was like a bored hostess waiting for the self-invited guests to go. Why had they held on for so long? A good deal for financial reasons no doubt – what other life would there be for them at their age with only specialized experience? Authority and the carrying of responsibility came naturally to them and would be hard to give up. The bond of a common interest with other men

was precious – they often dreaded the loneliness of England after so long an absence.

One senior official found that he could not face such a future: shortly after independence, Sir Algernon Brown, the Chief Justice of the North, committed suicide when his application to serve another term of office was turned down. Others applied to serve elsewhere, in order to stay in the service they loved – Trevor Clark transferred to Hong Kong – and the older officers retired. Amongst the first to go was the Northern Governor Sir Bryan Sharwood-Smith, who was succeeded by Sir Gawain Bell, formerly of the Sudan Political Service, in September 1957. By then, Nigeria had its first federal prime minister, Alhaji Abubakar Tafawa Balewa, the Northern politician whom many British officials had come to regard as the best hope for Nigerian unity once the country became independent on the recently agreed date of 1 October 1960. In many respects it was not a surprise, therefore, when Robertson invited him to become prime minister in the late summer of 1957. As the leader of the majority NPC party in the House of Representatives, he had been a successful federal Minister for Transport. Also, as his biographer Trevor Clark makes clear, 'he was widely respected, and disliked by none' – the first consideration being more important than the second, given the propensity of politicians to dissemble when talking about their opponents in public life.

More to the point, perhaps, he had no serious rivals and was genuinely admired by most southern politicians. His principal opponents Azikiwe and Awolowo had preferred to build up their political power bases in, respectively, the internal self-governing Eastern and Western regions and in 1957 were not seen in the other regions as serious candidates for the federal leadership. Both men were intense rivals, not only because Azikiwe was an Igbo and Awolowo a Yoruba but also because both were desperate for the ultimate prize of federal power. Their mutual dislike was not just a front: when Awolowo wrote his autobiography in 1959, he

171

devoted several pages to describe the anti-Yoruba bias in Azikiwe's newspaper, the *West African Pilot*.

> Apart from failing to give publicity to the achievements of the Yoruba, and holding their public men to obloquy, the *Pilot* always made sure that all their misdoings received due publicity. As many of the unsavoury aspects of Yoruba life as its news-gatherers could muster received banner headlines in the *Pilot*. In contrast to this, care was taken to ensure that any misdoing of the Igbo was kept out of the newspaper.

At the time of the constitutional crisis in 1953, both men had reached a brief understanding but the alliance between the NCNC and AG was short-lived, largely because Awolowo considered there was too wide a gap between what Azikiwe 'believes and what he preaches and between what he preaches and what he practises'. It was perhaps fitting, therefore, that their inability to find common ground denied both men the opportunity to take federal power when the 1959 elections ended inconclusively. The NPC had 142 seats, the NCNC eighty-nine and AG seventy-three. If Azikiwe and Awolowo had formed a coalition, with the former becoming prime minister and the latter his deputy, Abubakar would have been defeated, but opposition from conservatives within both parties stymied the move. In the immediate post-election bartering, Azikiwe decided to throw in the NCNC's lot with Abubakar on the understanding that he would become governor-general after independence. This left Awolowo as the leader of the federal opposition. It was also agreed that the NCNC would be allowed to nominate their own ministers to the federal government, that the Lagos federal territory would be extended and that consideration should be given to creating a new mid-western region carved out of the non-Yoruba peoples of the west. The north-east coalition was to survive into independence but even at that early stage some voices amongst the expatriate population warned that the compromises were stretching tribal loyalties to their limits.

My opinion about independence is that it came too soon or too quickly. There should have been a period of recognizing that the borders of Nigeria were totally artificial; that there was no Nigerian nation nor would there ever be, and there should be some attempt to rationalize boundaries in ethnic groups . . . they should have broken the country up, they should have Balkanized the country back to the tribal groupings that they had, which they didn't know they had, because they were not able to communicate with each other; they didn't know that there were more than 250 languages.

Rowand's ideas were shared by others who lived through that period, not all of whom were British expatriates. During the constitutional talks in the early 1950s, Awolowo constantly argued that the existence of regions 'could not impair the unity of Nigeria or make for a weak Federal Government' and pointed to the fact that Switzerland existed happily enough with its twenty different cantons. 'As far as I know,' he said, 'all these arrangements have earned for Switzerland the praise of being the most democratic country in the world.'

Comforting though that thought was, the situation in Nigeria was different simply because the plurality of tribes was so large. Balkanization was one option but that would have led to the creation of alliances and the probability of further splits and inter-tribal confrontation. At the time, the creation of the federal constitution was considered to be the best solution: although it had been fiercely debated, at least it appeared to balance the country's conflicting major tribal and political interests within a stable parliamentary democracy. Once Britain had accepted the road agreed by the Nigerians themselves, the course had to be followed. As Sylvia Leith-Ross recalled during one of her last visits to the country before independence, a burgeoning sense of optimism subdued the natural alarm felt by those who believed that self-rule was coming too quickly.

To its over-anxious friends, the future of the Federation looked dark indeed. Then I remembered seeing not long before a broken-down lorry being towed by another lorry. Apparently no tow-rope had been available, so the drivers had cut down a young palm tree and the palm trunk, neatly lashed with creepers to the two lorries, had served as a tow-rope. As I watched the two lorries crazily but successfully rounding corners and preparing to race down a crowded street, I was reassured. The country that can tow a large and heavy lorry by means of a palm trunk and a bit of 'tie-tie' can surmount greater difficulties than adaptation to the modern world. When I put forward this illustration to a friend, he instantly agreed. A black man might find ways of doing things quite different to what a European would do, and equally – perhaps, more – effective.

Unfortunately, the harmony masked a growing morass of jobbery, corruption and bitter political enmities, all of which had to be ignored or put out of mind. For every politician with the skills and integrity of Abubakar, there were others who used politics as a means of acquiring the patronage with which to further their own careers as well as those of their supporters and their immediate families. For every letter-writer to the *Daily Times* in Lagos who hoped that self-government would breed self-confidence, there were others who dreamed that independence would be a passport to wealth and a glamorous life-style. Within half-a-dozen years of independence, many of these failings became all too apparent as the façade of unity was broken by a bitter regional scramble for power; but in 1959 the progress towards independence was regarded by the Colonial Office as a peaceful, if inevitable, evolution.

> If we had not brought in democracy with elections and so on, we would have been blamed by the Africans for keeping them from what we thought was the best thing. We regarded democracy as the best solution for government and if we had denied it to the Africans we would have been blamed for that . . . There was a great call from the Africans for the same sort of government as we had in Britain and in fact we regarded it as the best thing for everybody as it was the best thing for us.

Like others in the colonial service, Sir Alan Burns remained cautious both about the timing of independence in Nigeria and the export of the Westminster model but, like others, too, he realized that by the late 1950s Britain had little option but to press ahead with the provision of both. In fact, it seemed to be working. In August 1959, Chief Akintola won control of the Western Region for the AG and served as Awolowo's deputy in the main party. Although this arrangement, too, was to store up trouble for the future, at the time it seemed to be proof that democracy was working and that the establishment of a coherent opposition could only strengthen Nigeria's position. As Burns put it, 'if we had refused to give it [parliamentary democracy] at the time, the Africans would have regarded us as trying to defraud them.'

On 2 April 1960, Abubakar introduced a motion in the House of Representatives, formally requesting Britain to legislate Nigeria's independence; and the final questions of the federal resolve, including defence and foreign affairs, were concluded. The last constitutional conference took place in London a month later and it was agreed that Princess Alexandra of Kent should represent the Queen at the independence ceremonies. As the weeks ticked away towards the great day, the final arrangements were made for the celebrations, which would cost £1.75 million, to launch Nigeria on the world's stage. Fleets of cars were bought, medals struck, eyesores removed and menus arranged for the official banquets. A new flag was designed and a new anthem composed – but as Rex Niven recalled, it was not played until the actual ceremony, with inevitable confusion.

> The last scene was on the racecourse. Princess Alexandra, in sweeping white, presided. Just before midnight the massed bands of the Army, Police and Royal Marines stood waiting. The Prime Minister and Sir James Robertson stood together at the foot of the special flagstaff. The British anthem was played and sung with enthusiasm by the great crowd. The lights went out, and when they came on again the Union Jack had gone and the new Nigerian flag fluttered in its place. The band played the new anthem, with which

the crowd was unfamiliar. The religious leaders prayed in their several ways. Nigeria was independent.

The early confidence even survived the chaos and bloodshed in the Congo which broke out within three months of Nigeria's independence. Unlike the British and the French, the Belgians had never evolved any pertinent system for decolonizing the Congo and their colonial service believed it would be many years before independence could be granted. An outbreak of violence in Leopoldville in January 1959 persuaded the Belgian government to accelerate moves towards internal self-government with the creation of regional assemblies, but these did little to assuage local feelings. As was the case in so many other countries in Africa, tribal and regional rivalries complicated the position and a number of powerful leaders contested the right to absolute political power. In an attempt to defuse the crisis, the Belgians convened a round-table conference of Congolese leaders in Brussels in January 1960 to discuss a gradual movement towards self-rule in four years' time. For once, they combined in common cause and demanded independence in June: faced with the prospect of having to hold the Congo by force, the Belgian government agreed to the demand.

It was a bad move. Not only was the Congo in no position to govern itself – there were only sixteen senior Congolese civil servants in an establishment of 1,400, and no native doctors, engineers, army officers or teachers – but the country was hopelessly fragmented. In the south-east, the province of Katanga demanded independence from the Congo; the Abako leader Joseph Kasavubu wanted to restore the old Bakongo kingdom; and Patrice Lumumba's Mouvement National Congolais wanted independence at all costs. Tragically for the country, the first elections, held before independence, created a coalition government consisting of twelve different parties, with Kasavubu as president and Lumumba as prime minister. It was a recipe for disaster.

Within a week of independence, the army had mutinied and frightened Europeans had started leaving the country to escape the escalating violence. As the confusion mounted, Katanga declared its independence under the leadership of Moise Tshombe. A few days later, on 14 July, the UN Security Council agreed to provide military and technical assistance. For the next four years, the Congo was to be the scene of bloody internecine fighting which exhausted the country and its resources and left thousands dead. Eventually the UN was able to restore a semblance of order but only after their troops had intervened in what turned out to be the largest peace-enforcement operation until the deployment in Cambodia in 1992.

The events in the Congo were watched with considerable anxiety in Nigeria. Aware that it was an African problem, Abubakar wanted to contribute Nigerian troops to the UN force but this was vetoed by Britain and it was not until after independence that battalions of the Queen's Own Nigeria Regiment were deployed as 'an assistance from brother to brother'. Although there were a handful of demonstrations against the continued presence of Belgian troops in the Congo, there was little support for Lumumba and none for the breakaway Katanga state. In that sense, the fighting in the Congo did not immediately influence Nigeria but the experience did reveal the bloody intensity of inter-tribal warfare following the breakdown of organized government.

Thousands died when Tshombe ordered the extermination of the Baluba opposition in 1961 and there was a hideous catalogue of death three years later, when Christopher Gbenye seized control of Stanleyville. Clerks became politicians and sergeants promoted themselves generals. When the Belgian General Janssens refused to accelerate the Africanization of the Congolese army in 1960, he was dismissed and replaced by Victor Lundula, a sergeant. His chief of staff, a clerk called Joseph Mobutu, was later to impose a disastrous military dictatorship when the Congo became Zaire in 1965. The fighting also

spawned a massive refugee crisis and the mayhem in the Congo
stiffened the resolve of the white settlers in Southern Rhodesia
never to surrender themselves to black rule.

Within half-a-dozen years of independence, Nigeria too was
to face the same agonies as the Congo, a fate which many had
secretly feared in happier and more carefree times. As Sylvia
Leith-Ross noted, ahead lay a tragedy of enormous proportions.

> I was too far away to know what slowly dimmed that future, what
> caused the sudden sagging of that bright edifice that both black and
> white had been so proud of. The assassination of Sir Abubakar
> Tafawa Balewa, the Federal Prime Minister, in 1966 came as a per-
> sonal shock; the terrible Northern massacres of Igbo settlers, traders
> and clerks, skilled workmen and civil servants in 1967 may have had
> some reasons but no excuses; the civil war between 'Biafra' and the
> Federal Government, to those of Nigeria's friends who loved her as
> a whole, seemed the end.

As it turned out, Nigeria survived the civil war which saw the
Eastern Region temporarily become the independent but
generally unrecognized state of Biafra, but only after thousands
of people had lost their lives in a frenzy of inter-tribal killing
which matched anything experienced in the Congo. Once
Biafra had been subdued, the federal government assumed
control again but this time enforced its rule through a series of
military and increasingly dictatorial governments. It was a grim
echo of Abubakar's warning words about the nature of power
after the NPC had won the crucial 1959 general election: 'It will
be taken away from us when we leave the path of God – when
we leave the path of God, truth and justice and become corrupt
and unjust and oppressive.'

7

Fighting for Freedom

WITH ITS POPULATION of thirty-five million and its ample resources, Nigeria became Africa's most significant independent country and a glowing example of peaceful decolonization. Not only did it have a settled administration but the transfer of power had been achieved with remarkable goodwill and it seemed to justify Britain's policy of accelerating the preparations for handing over power to the African colonies. Following the euphoria of the celebrations in Accra and Lagos, independence was granted to Sierra Leone in 1961 and the tiny Gambia followed suit four years later. It was not an easy process. Both suffered from the kind of internal racial problems which bedevilled many nascent African countries and both were small and relatively poor, but both had to be granted independence.

Founded at the end of the eighteenth century as a home for freed slaves, Sierra Leone had experienced tribal differences between the Creoles – descendants of the liberated Africans – and the indigenous tribes of the interior, but these seemed to have been overcome by a government of national unity led by Sir Milton Margai. As happened in other countries, though, the harmony was only skin-deep and within a few years Sierra Leone had succumbed to a military *coup* and eventually became a one-party state. The Gambia's position was even more tenuous. Little more than a 292-mile strip of land alongside the

179

River Gambia and surrounded by French-speaking Senegal, it was considered too small and too poor to prosper but with the rest of west Africa free, its independence could not be denied. In time it proved the sceptics wrong and managed to survive on a mixture of foreign aid and international tourism.

As far as the colonies in central and east Africa were concerned, the Colonial Office had envisaged a longer and more leisurely timetable towards independence; but this, too, had to be accelerated to meet the changing needs of the times. In December 1958 Nkrumah had organized an 'All-African People's Congress' to give a coherent voice to the anti-colonial sentiments which were sweeping through Africa. In the final speech, the conference chairman Tom Mboya, a Kenyan trade unionist, spoke for many when he advised the European powers that their day was over and the time had come for them to 'scram from Africa'. A year later, the Colonial Office seemed to disregard his advice when it laid down guidelines for the granting of independence to Tanganyika, Uganda and Kenya: none would achieve self-rule before 1975. Yet this timetable, too, was broken and within the space of two years Tanganyika had achieved independence, followed by Uganda a year later and Kenya in 1963.

Britain had been slow to recognize the strength of African nationalist feeling in east Africa, mainly because it was assumed that the countries were poorer, less developed and lacked the kind of political leadership which had been created in the Gold Coast and Nigeria. There was also the complication of Kenya's 30,000 white settlers who regarded themselves as permanent, albeit privileged, residents and who demanded the provision of a multiracial constitution to protect their interests. Few whites foresaw this stage lasting less than twenty years, while even fewer African nationalists thought that black and white would be able to work in harmony. In Kenya's Legislative Council, the whites held the balance of power and were able to block any moves towards greater African representation. When the Colonial

Office advocated equal representations for the European, African and Asian communities in 1947, the whites argued successfully that white leadership should be paramount and called for the creation of a British East African Dominion incorporating Tanganyika, Uganda and Kenya. Put bluntly, the white argument was: we cultivated the land and made it work, so why should we surrender it to the Africans? In any case, they will only move their goats onto it and plant mealie-maize when the land is God-given for coffee and other dollar-rich crops.

Although there was no official colour bar, post-war Kenya was very much a segregated society with little or no contact between its European, Asian or African communities. Any attempt to harmonize relations was met with derision and most white farmers were distrustful of any 'tampering' by the administration in Nairobi or the Colonial Office in London. Black Kenyans were forced to use identity cards known as *kipande* which also carried their fingerprints and it was unknown to see them in the smarter hotels in Nairobi. (There was almost a rebellion when the Legislative Council attempted to extend the identity-card system to whites in 1949.) For the most part, the settlers' intransigence was a by-product of their pioneering spirit but there were also echoes of the old Muthaiga Club self-indulgence which had given Kenya its distinctive tone.

> As regards actually mixing between the races, I would certainly say in the early days when I went out to Kenya there was virtually no mixing at all. I mean, everybody kept their place. You would go to the cinema, all right you might get Asians there, you would go to parties, you would meet the odd Asian who was wealthy, perhaps some of them were very wealthy indeed and very, very pleasant. To meet an African in the early days up to independence at a social function was very, very rare indeed.

This was not the Kenya of the 1920s, when 'Happy Valley' spawned its own brand of aristocracy, but the Crown Colony thirty years later. John Whitfield arrived in the country in 1952 as part of the British Army's reinforcement of the military garrison and as a Military Police officer enjoyed some status. However, it was impossible to ignore the unofficial segregation which existed in the country. Some restaurants refused to serve blacks and there was a widely held belief that white rule was the best solution for a modern African country. The *laissez-faire* attitude also lay at the heart of government: as late as June 1952 the outgoing Governor, Sir Philip Mitchell, sent his replacement a memorandum on the difficulties of mixing socially with the colony's many divorcees. This was written at a time of growing nationalist disaffection, when Mitchell might have had rather different advice to give his successor.

In fact, that sense of time standing still was typical of white rule in Kenya. Ever since the 1920s and throughout the Delamere period, the white settlers had been able to block moves towards African advancement; even though the Kenyan tribes had solid grievances, not just about political representation but also, more potently, about the ownership of land. Amongst Kenya's most populous tribe, the Kikuyu, there was a genuine feeling that they had lost land to the white settlers in the White Highlands of the Aberdare mountains. Although the Kikuyu had been allocated land elsewhere, it was of poorer quality, a fact acknowledged by the East African Royal Commission in 1955.

> Throughout our inquiry we were impressed by the recurring evidence that particular areas were carrying so large a population that agricultural production in them was being retarded, that the natural resources were being destroyed and that families were unable to find access to new land.

None the less, the white settlers were certainly not prepared to hand over their land to the Africans just because they were demanding it. This was not a matter of stubbornness: the settlers had leased the land for 999 years from the administration and they had worked long and hard to make it work. What had once been uncultivated scrubland had been turned into mature and profitable green acres which helped to give Kenya its wealth. Besides, they regarded themselves as Kenyans, too, and every penny they made was ploughed back into the country. If the Kikuyu had a mystical link with the land through their culture and history, then the white settlers had an attachment which was born of back-breaking work and an ability to improvise. In 1931, Molly Ryan and her husband had left Tipperary to farm in Kenya and by the 1950s they were amongst the country's foremost sheep-breeders. By then, too, they regarded Kenya as their real home.

> The incredible fullness of our lives stemmed from something almost indefinable. Perhaps it was environmental, or perhaps it came from something within ourselves, the steely courage that enabled us to extricate ourselves from the almost impossible situations that beset us constantly. Or maybe it stemmed from the joyousness that accompanied our occasional triumphs, and the surging excitement of watching the panorama of the building of a nation, of being an integral part of that work ourselves. We certainly loved our adopted country with a full heart and we gave it our best, always. The world should know this – we were 'givers' rather than 'takers' always – and we gave with love. Every achievement had been paid for the hard way, and each success had a touch of glory that we savoured to the full. Our achievements never came, ever, without the frustrations and the suffering that first had to be squarely faced.

However, for all that farmers like Tony and Molly Ryan invested heavily in Kenya – not just financially, but emotionally too – and for all that the white settlers had a genuine affinity with Kenya, the land question was a growing point of conflict. The whites refused to give it up and obstinately rejected compromise; while the blacks became ever more resentful at moves to maintain the *status quo*. After the war, the planting of coffee in the southern Kikuyu lands was banned and, to add to the insult, over a quarter of a million acres in the White Highlands were allocated for settlement by white ex-servicemen. At the same time, the ever-expanding Kikuyu population was finding it increasingly difficult to make ends meet on the land which was available to them.

Added to this land-hunger was a high level of unemployment as the Kikuyu farmers fought a losing battle to cultivate the poorer ground while those who moved into Nairobi created a poverty-stricken and homeless underclass. The conditions endured by the Kikuyu made them ripe for exploitation by a new breed of political activists who looked to the leadership of Jomo Kenyatta of the Kenya African National Union (KANU), formed in 1944, to protect black Kenyans' political rights. Like Nkrumah, a veteran of the fifth Pan-African Congress, he had returned to Kenya after the war and had quickly cemented his authority as the country's foremost nationalist leader, not only amongst the Kikuyu but throughout Kenya. At his home at Githunguri, north of Nairobi, he created what is best described as a nationalist training centre which became a focus for disaffected black Kenyans. And as had happened in west Africa, his movement was given impetus by the activists amongst the returning ex-servicemen who felt that their wartime service abroad entitled them to a better living at home in Kenya.

Those who went overseas in Burma came back with a very fresh notion of the Indians who of course they always thought of as pretty rich in comparison to them. It was a great eye-opener for them to see the poverty of Indians in India. We had considerable apprehension about the return of the *askaris* simply because their eyes had been opened in various ways and we didn't know how this was going to affect them, what the political effect would be and so on. I think on the whole it was extraordinary how rapidly they were reabsorbed into the tribal structure. There were a certain number who used their army experience and no doubt picked up ideas out there. I suppose the independence of India in 1947 really did more to roll things along. And above all the growing failure of will-power to run an empire in this country.

184

Charles Meek was serving in Tanganyika at the time, but his point about the restlessness of the returning *askaris* of the King's African Rifles also holds good for Kenya, where it was intensified by the activities of the Kikuyu Central Association (KCA). Originally a focus for the tribe's land grievances – Kenyatta had been its general secretary – it was banned during the war but had lived on as an underground secret society. Out of it was to come the violent and almost unintelligible Mau Mau insurrection which broke out in 1951 and plunged the country into a state of emergency between 1952 and 1957. Centred mainly on the Kikuyu and on elements of the neighbouring Kamba, Meru and Embu tribes, the covert nature of Mau Mau activities created an impenetrable problem – even the name 'Mau Mau' is meaningless in the Kikuyu language and its members were bound together by blood oaths to maintain secrecy. To the canny and mystical Kikuyu mind, these oaths were meant to be taken seriously and as the future politician Mwangi Kariuki remembered, the ceremony itself was a sonorous, if potentially painful, business.

> I took off my trousers and squatted facing Biniathi [the medicine man]. He told me to take the thorax of the goat which had been skinned, to put my penis through a hole that had been made in it, and to hold the rest of it in my left hand in front of me. Before me on the ground there were two small wooden stakes between which the thorax (*ngata*) of the goat was suspended and fastened. By my right hand on the floor of the hut were seven small sticks each about four inches long. Biniathi told me to take the sticks one at a time, to put them into the ngata, and slowly rub them in it while repeating after him these seven vows, one for each stick. After each promise, I was to bite the meat and throw the stick onto the ground on my left side.

An estimated 90% of the Kikuyu population took the oaths, many against their will. To begin with, the practice was a question of binding together the people in common cause over the land question, but by the beginning of 1952 the police discovered evidence of a new 'killing oath' aimed at driving the white settlers from their land and coercing those Kikuyu who refused to join Mau Mau. Having been dismissed as a pseudo-religious cult, Mau Mau began to be taken seriously with growing evidence of forced oath-taking and widespread violence against non-Mau Mau Kikuyu. White farms were attacked and cattle killed or maimed and a pro-government Kikuyu leader, Chief Waruhiu, was assassinated. With the white population fearing a breakdown in law and order, the new governor, Sir Evelyn Baring, ordered a state of emergency on 21 October. British military reinforcements arrived from the Middle East to back up the police and the three resident battalions of the King's African Rifles, and, most significant of all, Kenyatta was arrested together with around two hundred other black Kenyans suspected of directing Mau Mau activities.

It was the beginning of a long and bruising rebellion which soon had all the attributes of a modern guerrilla war and which was to change the course of Kenyan politics. In the short term, it held back the growth of black nationalism, but by the rebellion's end it had shown the white settlers that they could only hold on to political power by relying on British military support. To begin with, though, Mau Mau was more about terrorism than nationalism and as Margery Perham found when she visited Kenya at the height of the rebellion in 1955, the country had been darkened by 'a murderous hate'.

> I have stood on a mission station on a hilltop looking over this glorious [Kikuyu] country, striped with sun and blue cloud-shadows stretching away northwards between the long ridge of the Aberdares and Mount Kenya. It was hard to believe that, as the sun went down, gangs in the forest, and even apparently innocent neighbours in those huts, were preparing to set out not only to murder Europeans but to burn alive or hack to death their own neighbours, with, perhaps, their wives and children. And whereas European farms are now, as far as possible, armed, barricaded and patrolled, and less than a dozen Europeans murdered, the Africans,

scattered in their huts, which are perfect traps and funeral pyres, can hardly be defended and have fallen in hundreds to assassins.

In so far as the Mau Mau had any political philosophy, they can be compared to the Irish Fenians of the nineteenth century who believed that their acts of terrorism would eventually drive the English settler community from their country. But, as Margery Perham pointed out, the attacks on the whites were few and far between: what made the Mau Mau rebellion so terrible to the white population was its indiscriminate nature, particularly amongst those Kikuyu who remained loyal to the government. It was this fear, together with the impenetrable and unseen nature of the organization, which helped to make the Mau Mau such an effective terrorist organization. They lacked the sophisticated command and control systems which made the Communist terrorists in Malaya such formidable enemies and they did not have access to modern weapons, but they still managed to wage a relatively successful guerrilla war against modern army and police forces. By the time the 'emergency' came to an end on 12 January 1960, it had cost the British £20 million and several hundred lives.

At the start of the rebellion, Kenya was an out-station of Britain's military GHQ Middle East and its only regular and territorial troops were those of the King's African Rifles and the Kenya Regiment. By 1956, when the emergency had been contained but the Mau Mau not completely defeated, Kenya had become a separate military command under General Sir George Erskine and eleven British infantry battalions with supporting engineering and signals units had served in the country. In the early days, the presence of the Lancashire Fusiliers on the streets of Nairobi was a dramatic and welcome sign of British support, but when the emergency showed no sign of ending, the settlers' patience with the British Army began to evaporate. As happened in other parts of the empire, the European community looked down on the ordinary British troops, many of whom were conscripted National Servicemen. As John Whitfield observed, here was a reminder that Kenya was dependent on Britain and on a type of soldier who did not always meet the colony's social standards.

> The British soldier, if he wasn't doing his duty, was probably down in Nairobi getting as many beers down him as possible and of course once he had a few beers down he became obstreperous and there were fights and very often fights in public places. The average European out there who would still dress for dinner, black tie, that sort of thing, looked down on him very much . . . I must also say however that up-country a lot of the farmers were very good to the British soldiers, but there was a tendency to look after officers more than the men because the type of farmer up-country probably had been an officer himself.

Once deployed in Kenya on operational duty, though, the British soldiers found that they had more to concern them than the settlers' disapproval. For most of them, new fieldcraft skills had to be learned to counter the Mau Mau. Most battalions were allocated areas of forest and these were divided into sectors which had to be patrolled by men on the ground. Inevitably, mistakes were made as the soldiers came to grips with the new environment. Fires lit to scare away animals revealed their presence to the terrorists, as did the soldiers' tendency to talk and move around noisily. Inexperience led to blunders and even their equipment was not always suitable for jungle warfare.

> The British soldier wasn't terribly good in the forest. The average soldier who came to Kenya had come either from Aden or from Germany or from Britain and it took him quite a long time to be able to move silently and generally not crash around. I think the farmers thought, what the hell is the use of having these soldiers here? I mean, the Mau Mau have gone miles away before they have got anywhere near. They said of one particular regiment, they could hear them coming thirty miles away through the forest.

Not every British unit suffered from the same problems described by John Whitfield. Some, like the Devonshire Regiment, had served in Malaya and already had experience of fighting in the jungle. In time, the battalions were provided with scouts from the Kenya Regiment – settlers who knew the forest as well as the Mau Mau and who were prepared to fight as viciously as their enemy. By a process of trial and error, the British infantrymen adapted to their new roles and were able to contain the terrorists, and then to take them on in their own environment.

> Fighting the Mau Mau is not a very dangerous job compared to the Korean War, but it is a strenuous business none the less. Despite the brutal attacks on their own people and on lonely European farmers and their families, the Kikuyu gangsters will not stand and fight a patrol of six armed soldiers, even at odds of ten to one. In fact, our chief difficulty is to inflict maximum casualties on first contact, before the gang has dissolved into thick jungle. We attack the enemy in three different ways. Patrols try to gain contact with the gangs in the forest which is termed a 'prohibited area'. Here we can shoot on sight. These patrols are usually of twenty-four hours' duration, but sometimes longer, and they carry 'compo' rations and a wireless set. If they make contact with a gang, they follow up as hard as they can, using native trackers.

That Black Watch officer's description of anti-Mau Mau operations was typical of the methods used by the infantry battalions' patrols in co-ordination with the Kenya police force and specially raised 'Home Guard' units: forest patrols to locate enemy hide-outs, followed by sweeps and drives to flush out the Mau Mau gangs. One drive in particular, Operation Anvil in April 1954, netted 16,000 suspects who were kept in detention camps and gradually rehabilitated, once the power of their oaths had been broken by loyal medicine men or witch doctors. As Lt-Col R.C. Glanville of the 6th King's African Rifles discovered, the evolution of these counter-insurgency tactics took time to develop but once in place they did achieve the desired results by breaking down the Kikuyu's support for the Mau Mau terrorist gangs.

> During the Mau Mau campaign we were on a very different task to what we'd been before. We were routing out Kikuyu terrorists who had taken the law into their own hands and were terrorizing their own tribal people who were loyal and trying to impose their will on the country. They resorted to all sorts of tribal customs and magic to frighten the local Kikuyu into subversion. They descended on them from the forest and butchered them where they were defenceless and insisted on defenceless people sustaining them and hiding them on pain of death. By spreading companies about the Kikuyu reserve on the edge of the Aberdare forest at Nyeri, we were able gradually to gain the confidence of the local Kikuyu to withstand these terrorists. And with the help of the administration and the police, small home-guard posts of Kikuyu, armed to a certain extent and barricaded into defensive positions, were able to cope against the Mau Mau themselves. In the forest we tracked and hunted down the Kikuyu Mau Mau. But they were very difficult to catch. And we won the war more by keeping them on the move and preventing them from getting food and sustenance from their local tribesmen than by killing or maiming.

Further initiatives included the designation of 900 square miles of the Aberdares and Mount Kenya as a war zone or 'no-go area', the infiltration of Mau Mau gangs by Special Branch men and the establishment of 'counter gangs', groups of loyal Kikuyu or former Mau Mau terrorists who had been turned and had betrayed their blood oath of allegiance. This was particularly risky, as anyone discovered acting against the Mau Mau in this way would face certain death, but these covert operations played a major role in winning the war. As had happened in Malaya, people at risk were moved into protected villages and suspected terrorists were detained in camps following the security forces' drives through the designated areas. During these operations African beaters armed with machetes were used to clear paths while security-force patrols pursued suspects – and as the Black

Watch officer makes clear, the security forces operated a shoot-to-kill policy. Some units kept a score of the terrorists they killed and there was an unofficial league table. Eventually the practice was forbidden as being too barbarous, but the security forces continued it anyway. As Margery Perham discovered, so terrible were the Mau Mau practices and so outraged was the community, that their methods could not be used 'without a margin of inhumanity'.

> One of the little police posts newly set up in the reserves, for example, I found in charge of two young settlers, recruits to the police reserve, mere boys, just in from the exciting and dangerous job of hunting men. Not far away, a patrol of King's African Rifles, rough tribesmen from northern Uganda, were scouring the bush. Their officer, a fine-looking young settler seconded from the white Kenya Regiment, frankly told me there had been irregularities with prisoners, now remedied, but that he still found it hard to control his men in action against secret enemies dedicated to those hideous methods which have so depressed the friends of this tribe. Yet strictly impartial justice and discipline, openly demonstrated, could do much to rally the wavering majority, torn between their fears of Mau Mau and of its repressors.

It was a dirty little war. Not much quarter was given by either side and some of the incidents such as the massacre of Kikuyu loyalists at Lari in 1953 were horrifyingly brutal. Armed with *pangas* or *simis* – both types of swords or large knives – the Mau Mau burned down the thatched huts and then literally hacked the villagers to death. A policeman investigating the massacre, during which at least eighty-four women and children were slaughtered, described finding 'the trunk of a child, all its arms and legs gone, and came upon one of the legs and an arm with teeth marks in it'. Disgusting though the massacre was, it did not have the desired effect of terrifying either community into submission. While the white community was sickened by the atrocities and had their prejudices confirmed that the Africans were incapable of looking after themselves, the majority of the

Kikuyu became convinced that they should withdraw their support and side with the government. In purely tactical terms, this was one area where the Mau Mau leadership made a considerable mistake. Before turning their attention to ridding Kenya of the white settlers, they believed that they had to unite all the Kikuyu people by killing off those who would not assist them.

Although Kenya was never gripped by the siege mentality which was a feature of Rhodesian life during the long drawn-out 'bush war' against ZANU and ZAPU – only in the more remote areas were white farmers at risk and their casualties amounted to thirty-two – the Mau Mau rebellion did help to polarize attitudes. One man, more than any other, was demonized by the white community and held to be the creator of all the country's troubles: Jomo Kenyatta. Everything about him combined to raise the hackles of the white community. He was intelligent, educated, politically astute and a focus for the nationalist aspirations of the black Kenyans. His links with Communism and his well-advertised friendships with British left-wing intellectuals counted against him. He had also written a book, *Facing Mount Kenya*, which not only explained the culture and anthropology of the Kikuyu but also made it clear that they had their own aspirations for equality in their native Kenya.

> By driving him off his ancestral lands, the Europeans have robbed him of the material foundations of his culture, and reduced him to a state of serfdom incompatible with human happiness. The African is conditioned, by the cultural and social institutions of centuries, to a freedom of which Europe has little conception, and it is not in his nature to accept serfdom for ever. He realizes that he must fight unceasingly for his own complete emancipation; for without this he is doomed to remain the prey of rival imperialisms, which in every successive year will drive their fangs more deeply into his vitality and strength.

This was not the kind of language the white Kenyans wanted to hear from an African and Kenyatta was quickly castigated as public enemy number one. From the whites' point of view, it is not difficult to understand their antipathy. Kenyatta advocated the return of the White Highlands to the Kikuyu and he was a disciple of independence from colonial rule. He also enjoyed widespread support and was clearly an influential figure amongst the Kikuyu. As concern began to mount over the rise of Mau Mau activity, it was not difficult to link them to Kenyatta's politics. But try as they might, the police could find no connection and the legal authorities doubted if any charges could be made to stick. In August 1952 he even denounced Mau Mau during a rally at Kiambu, but as the Kikuyu language contains so many double negatives and ambiguities the authorities were unsure if he meant what he appeared to say.

As the Mau Mau violence began to worsen, so the calls for Kenyatta's arrest increased. Just after midnight on 20 October, a state of emergency was declared by Baring and the police were free to use their powers to arrest Kenyatta at Githunguri. That same day he was flown to Lokitaung in the remote Turkana region where he was kept under heavy guard to await trial. What followed next was a mixture of muddle and bad judgement. Under normal circumstances, much of the evidence against Kenyatta would never have been presented in a British court but tensions were running so high within Kenya that a fair trial was impossible. The main evidence came from a witness, Rawson Macharia, who claimed that he and Kenyatta had administered Mau Mau oaths – this was later found to be perjury – but even though this was denied by reliable defence witnesses, the court was in no mood to compromise. Having dismissed Kenyatta's claim that the government was only exacerbating the situation by arresting him and other moderate Kikuyu leaders, Mr Justice Thacker sentenced him to seven years' hard labour on 8 April 1953.

Kenyatta was imprisoned at Lokitaung and was told that he would never return to his native Kikuyuland. The Kenyan government hoped that by keeping him out of the public eye they would also remove him from the public mind but in this they miscalculated. Instead of being condemned as a common criminal, Kenyatta became a symbol of resistance for black nationalists and an important focus for their aspirations. Worse, his arrest and sentence did nothing to stem the violence. As Kenyatta himself stated at the end of his trial, he and his KANU associates might have been able to exert a moderating influence on the Kikuyu and he accused the government of exacerbating the situation by using him as a scapegoat. This was somewhat disingenuous for, although the question of Kenyatta's alleged membership of Mau Mau remains unproven, he was a symbol of black Kenyan nationalism and had returned to the country with the aim of ending white rule.

Unlike Robert Mugabe's ZANU freedom fighters, who eventually forced the collapse of the white settler regime in Rhodesia in 1980, Mau Mau's use of force did not lead directly to the ending of white rule but it did hasten constitutional change. Once the rebellion was over, the Colonial Office made it clear that Africans had to be brought into government and that property and agricultural reforms had to be introduced to enable the country to develop along multiracial lines. This touched a sore point with the settlers, who believed that they had an inalienable right to the land, but by October 1959 the sale of land in the White Highlands had been opened to all races.

By then, too, the first steps had been taken to educate the Africans in the farming of coffee. Until then it had been the received opinion that the Kikuyu would not have the patience to wait five back-breaking years for the trees to mature and the harvest to make profits which could then be ploughed back into the farm. At Meru on the north-east side of Mount Kenya, the Agricultural Department started a co-operative in which the Africans grew coffee under the direction of white officials. Coffee was sold at 'giveaway' prices to the local farmers, who then grew and tended the trees during the long years of cultivation. One of the officials was John Trestrail, who had arrived in Kenya in 1953 during the Mau Mau emergency. He found that, under white supervision, the black farmers quickly adapted to the new role.

> During the harvest period, the farmer would pick his coffee and he would bring it on his back, on his bike, on his donkey (it could be a distance of five miles, and he'd be bringing in thirty or forty pounds of coffee that he'd picked) and he brought it in every day. It would then be weighed off by the clerk at the factory, all noted, and he would be given a bit of paper (which in any case didn't mean a thing to him – it had all basically to be done on trust) and that coffee would then be processed and it would all be recorded how much each farmer got. At the end of the year the coffee, having been processed, [was] dried, [and sent] off to Nairobi to the mills, and then the price would be ascertained as to the grade of coffee and all the things that went with it. That having been done, it was then sorted out how much money he was going to get for it. That is when they had to be paid up, the money had to be taken out and collected from the bank and taken out to the farmer.

This was a radical change of attitude. Most white farmers believed that the Africans would never be anything more than smallholders, interested in growing enough maize for their own needs but unsuited temperamentally to the long game of investing in crops, tending them carefully and painstakingly and waiting for the best results. For the Europeans who had invested time and money in their own rolling acres, the Kikuyu's conservative methods seemed wasteful and unprofitable. However, as Trestrail and his colleagues discovered at Meru, given the training and expertise, 'the Africans could grow the highest-grade coffee which was being produced in Kenya'.

> The most incredible thing is what can be achieved if people are prepared to work together, with both individualism and the government side. I think the interesting thing was that I don't think anybody thought that the African farmer was able to do as well as he has done.

195

Naturally, perhaps, the whites 'scoffed at it a bit' but they, too, could be conservative when it came to introducing farming reforms in the later 1950s. Molly Ryan was one of the many farmers who struggled to convince the Agricultural Department that the development of sheep-farming could be an integral and rewarding element in Kenya's economy. At first, this was greeted with scepticism. Lord Delamere had been one of the first settlers to attempt to rear a home-grown woolled breed from Maasai ewes and merino studs, but it was not until 1951 that serious thought was put into eradicating the worst diseases – Laikipia lung disease, scab and foot rot – which had hindered the large-scale development of sheep in Kenya. Eventually, with the help of the government laboratories at Kabete, 'there appeared to be nothing on earth to hold back the tide of agricultural progress and success'; although as Molly Ryan remembered, the new methods were a far cry from some the hit-or-miss methods used in the 1930s. One farmer near Naivasha believed that heat-stroke had decimated his herd of lambs and he decided to go straight to the heart of the problem.

> Off went a letter to Italy: 'Please supply urgently 4,000 small straw hats suitable for sheep.'
> I would have given a lot to have witnessed that quite fantastic scene myself – the lovely, green, sparkling grass ley so carefully pre-pared – the incredible sight of four thousand bewildered, restless sheep milling around and wondering what it was all about! On each sheepy head perched a straw hat to which was attached two lengths of tape that tied under the animal's 'chin' hopefully to keep the hat in place! Alas! No photographic evidence! Just one's quite inade-quate imagination! I often wondered what happened to those dear little hats eventually. They probably made very good sheep fodder, as they fell off one by one!

Not all methods were quite so unscientific, but the fact that the farmer at Naivasha attempted the scheme at all is evidence of the pioneering spirit which helped to keep the white-settler community together. By the early 1960s, Kenya was competing with Australia in the international sheep and wool markets. Coffee, too, was secure as a cash crop, as was tea; and as John Trestrail points out, not without pride, Kenya was soon the third-highest tea-producing nation in the world: 'This had come through the incredible amount of hard work which had gone on before and after independence.'

While farmers and development officers of that calibre were prepared to work hard to develop Kenya's agricultural economy, few believed that it would lead to early independence under black majority rule. As more than one settler ruefully admitted afterwards, they might have won the battle against the Mau Mau in the Aberdares, but they were destined to lose the war around the conference table in London. In 1957 the first African elections had brought eight black Kenyans into the Legislative Council and the following year this was increased to fourteen. They were now on equal terms with the white representatives; but even so, no one in Kenya really considered that independence could possibly be achieved before 1975 and perhaps not even by then. But did London understand that? Molly Ryan spoke for many when she said that 'the arguments often ran hot and high and were aggravated by our knowledge that England understood little of Kenya's problems. If she knew and understood anything of them at all, her actions always came too late and too little to be of any avail.'

The mutual suspicion between the white-settler community and the Colonial Office was to be one of the main stumbling-blocks on the road towards independence. The whites believed that their 'blood, sweat and tears' gave them a right to involvement in Kenya's future; the Colonial Office was gradually moving towards the conclusion that the claims of the whites should not stop the development of Kenya as a black African country. Molly Ryan was given a blunt indication of the new thinking when the Conservative politician Reginald Maudling visited Kenya in 1961, shortly after independence had become inevitable.

One night after dinner, chatting in the drawing-room [of the Ryans' friends Sir Anthony and Lady Swann], I said to him, 'You know, Mr Maudling, one can only believe that you in England think of us as wooden pieces on a chessboard, without soul or feeling, to be moved backwards and forwards at the whim and will of our English masters in London.'

I amazed even myself at putting this question so strongly! He came back at me with a rapier-like thrust – 'And what else, indeed, are you, Mrs Ryan! If we didn't think of you in this way, and if we thought of you as flesh and blood, we would never be able to carry out the work that we have set ourselves in England to do!'

I was so flabbergasted at his honesty that I could only gasp, 'Thank you, Mr Maudling, at least now we know' and retired in as good order as I could.

By then, the first Lancaster House conference had taken place and, as Maudling had made clear, there was to be no going back. By then, too, the Conservatives had won the 1959 election with a large majority and although many settlers believed that they would be given a sympathetic hearing, particularly as the new Colonial Secretary Iain Macleod had a brother living in Kenya, they were to be sadly disappointed. Macleod was a Tory Radical who Lord Shaftesbury complained was 'too clever by half' and he was determined to face up to the realities of decolonization by accelerating the process in central and east Africa. Here he enjoyed the support of his prime minister, who was shortly to make his 'wind of change' speech in Ghana and South Africa and who fully supported the idea that Britain should pull out of Africa without further ado.

The first constitutional conference took place at Lancaster House in January 1960 and it was attended by representatives from all the main white and black political groups. On the table was a proposal for a multiracial constitution which would give black Kenyans thirty-five of the sixty-six seats on the Legislative Council, four government ministries to the whites' three, and make provision for a wider franchise. Although the black

Kenyans were hardly united – there was concern amongst the Maasai and Kalanjin people that the main Kikuyu–Luo coalition would dominate an independent Kenya – they managed to speak with one voice. As Molly Ryan had feared, though, the same could not be said of the whites. Not only were they deeply shocked by a proposal which seemed to abandon them without any compensation but they were also divided over the correct response to the crisis.

On the one hand, the United Party spoke of betrayal and a victory for the Mau Mau while its more fiery supporters spoke of creating a resistance movement. At the other extreme, the New Kenya Group, led by Sir Michael Blundell, a well-known farmer, argued that as change was on the way the settlers should face up to it and make provisions to safeguard their interests. Inevitably, the clash between no surrender and compromise was to create tremendous tensions amongst the white community as they struggled to come to terms with this dramatic change of events.

> There were emotional moments after Lancaster House that are pathetic in the telling – moments when self-preservation and self-analysis vied with reason. There were moments when, for many, the deep abiding love born of a lifetime's service for England stunned men into unbelievable anger and contempt for a 'treacherous idol' which, overnight, England had become for them. I have seen proud old men in tears – generals, colonels long since retired, after many years of distinguished service in the far-flung lands of England's colonial empire – men who fought for it, and whose companions died for it.

Despite the anguish noticed by Molly Ryan and others, and despite the high emotions and recriminations, there was to be no turning back. Macleod had agreed on a course of action and he was determined to see it through. After several rancorous debates and walk-outs, the conference ended with the black Kenyans getting their majority on the Legislative Council with elections promised for the following year. On the matter of compensation for any loss of revenue from land sales in the White Highlands, Macleod made it clear that Britain would be unable to help. Despite his misgivings, Blundell agreed to the deal and for his pains he was vilified by the white community. On his arrival at Nairobi airport, a white settler threw a bag of thirty fifty-cent pieces at his feet and denounced him as a traitor. Whenever he appeared in public, rotten eggs were thrown at him and he and his family were ostracized by the membership of the Muthaiga Club.

As more than one settler admitted later, they were so overcome by shock at the unexpected turn of events that they were unable to think clearly about what the future might bring. Some farmers cut their losses, sold up and headed for Southern Rhodesia or South Africa. Amongst these was the Afrikaner settlement at Eldoret who had arrived before the First World War and who were now prepared to trek back into South Africa. Others decided to 'wait and see how things turn out'. Generally they made arrangements to get money out of the country to safeguard their future interests and, alarmed by what was happening in the Congo, they strengthened their personal security for the mayhem which would surely accompany the transition towards black rule. Throughout the summer of 1960, Belgian refugees trickled through Nairobi on their way back to Europe and their account of the violence and madness which had accompanied independence did little to calm the nerves of the settler community.

It never seemed likely that Kenya would have to face a crisis similar to the Congo, but the experience did encourage Britain to give some thought to the problem of resettling the settlers. With some reluctance, money was made available from the World Bank and the Commonwealth Development Corporation, thereby allowing one million acres of land in the White Highlands to be bought by black Kenyans at an economic price. As Tom Mboya reminded a meeting of white farmers at Eldoret, the new

nation of Kenya only wanted true Kenyans: 'To anyone determined to leave, I would say merely – in that historic House of
Commons phrase – "in the name of God, go". Kenya can do
without anybody who has to be persuaded or cajoled to stay.'

> As a young nation, Kenya cannot afford the luxury of squabbles
> with people who do not intend to stay. We have a tremendous
> economic and vocational struggle ahead. Either you are with us or
> you are not even on the field of play. We cannot let ourselves be
> weighed down by people who might cling to Kenya for a while,
> because they like 'the way of life', or because they're making
> money, or – so people often put it – 'to see how things turn out'.
> We cannot give *carte blanche* to benefits, of these or other kinds,
> gained without national investment of dedication, sacrifice and
> strength.

Mboya, a skilful and committed trade unionist, had emerged
as one of the voices of reason in the struggle to create a workable multiracial constitution. Together with younger men such
as Oginga Odinga, a Luo, and James Gicheru, he dominated
Kenyan politics between 1957 and the Lancaster House conference. His crowning moment had come in 1955 when he settled
a dock strike at the port of Mombasa, first by persuading the
men to return to work and then winning a 33.3% wage increase
for them; and he was a great promoter of the role of organized
labour in the task of nation building. Inevitably his high public
profile suggested that he was opposed to Kenyatta and there were
many whites who preferred him to the man who was still in
detention at Lodwar in northern Kenya. Despite every effort to
have Kenyatta released, the new governor, Sir Patrick Renison,
felt that he was still a risk to security and a danger to the nation.
He said as much officially after KANU won the 1961 elections
and named Kenyatta as their president.

> Jomo Kenyatta was the recognized leader of the non-co-operation
> movement which organized Mau Mau. Mau Mau, with its foul
> oathing and violent aims, had been declared an unlawful society. He

was convicted of managing that unlawful society and being a member of it. He appealed to the Supreme Court and the Privy Council. In these three separate courts his guilt was established and confirmed. Here was an African leader to darkness and death.

This was what the white settlers wanted to hear, but Renison was fighting a losing battle. Denied the services of their leader, KANU refused to form a government and in the Legislative Assembly posts had to be filled by nomination and by members of the minority Kenya African Development Union (KADU). Clearly such an arrangement could only be a stopgap and Renison was forced to yield to public pressure. In April 1961, Kenyatta was moved to the hill station of Maralal, north of Nairobi, where he quickly established a kind of emigré court, giving interviews to visiting statesmen and journalists and stressing the need for reconciliation. Four months later, he was released and allowed to return to his home at Gatundu.

With the country entering its final colonial phase, Kenyatta was elected to parliament and took his place as a minister in the Legislative Assembly. In May 1963 he was elected the country's first prime minister and immediately set about the difficult task of persuading the white settlers to stay. A year earlier, Mboya had told the farmers that membership of the new Kenya depended on their commitment to it: either they had to stand up and be counted or they had to quit. Kenyatta took a more conciliatory stance when he addressed four hundred prominent white settlers at Nakuru. The meeting was introduced by Lord Delamere, son of the man who had created white Kenya in his image, and most of those present were deeply sceptical. None the less, Kenyatta rose to the occasion. 'We are going to forget the past and look to the future,' he told them. 'Let us join hands and work for the benefit of Kenya, not for the benefit of one particular community.' As one, the audience rose to acknowledge his speech and many shouted out '*Harambee!*', the Swahili word meaning 'let's pull together!' which was to become the new country's motto.

It was a defining moment in the move towards independence. Not so long ago, many of those present in the hall at Nakuru would have refused to have anything to do with 'this African leader to darkness and death', but now they were eating out of his hand. By then over seventy, Kenyatta was enjoying an Indian summer in his political career. Before the last governor, Malcolm MacDonald, had arrived in the country in January 1963, he had been reliably informed that Kenyatta was a 'wicked old man who was fortunately far past his prime . . . [who] would linger but briefly, since he was a heavy drinker who was rapidly boozing himself to death.' To begin with, he tended to agree with the assessment. Although Kenyatta had given up the heavy drinking which characterized his last years in detention, he seemed to have some difficulty in adapting to the cut-and-thrust of political life. Compared to Mboya and Gichuru, he appeared tired and diffident. His triumph at the May elections changed all that and MacDonald discovered an able politician who 'showed himself not just the nominal chief, but the effective leader of the government'. He, for one, was not surprised by Kenyatta's performance in front of the white settlers.

> One of the qualities in Kenyatta's make-up which this speech revealed was his magnanimity. For many years he had been imprisoned by the British authorities; they had done all in their power to defeat him and destroy his work – and he knew that the crowd of farmers sitting in front of him at Nakuru were among his bitterest foes who had tried to frustrate everything he stood for. They had failed, and he had just achieved triumphant victory. But he never referred to that fact by even one jubilant sentence which might hurt or humiliate them. On the contrary, he greeted them as Kenyan friends and partners.

Under MacDonald's guidance, the constitutional fine-tuning was speeded up, with meetings taking place three times a week instead of on a single morning. It was also agreed that the independence timetable should be accelerated. Initially the Colonial Office wanted a year's grace between the election and independence, but at MacDonald's suggestion this was reduced to a matter of months: the elections would take place in May, internal self-government would follow in June and independence in December. Despite the continuing official disapproval of Kenyatta and KANU, the new Colonial Secretary Duncan Sandys agreed to the proposal and independence day was set for 12 December 1963.

The celebrations lasted two days but, as had become customary, the crowning moment was the ceremony in the stadium when the Union Flag was hauled down and replaced by the black, red and green flag of Kenya. The bands played, the soldiers marched – including a number of Mau Mau 'generals' – and tribal dancers danced. It rained, too, and the car carrying the Duke of Edinburgh got stuck – 'I believe his language was quite something, because he was held up', remembered John Whitfield, who was in the stadium to witness the historic event.

> A great many Europeans were in tears. You know, it was pretty horrible to see it [the Union Flag] pulled down and the Kenya flag put up. The Africans were all just so happy that they had got independence – what it meant to the average African there, probably not a great deal – but the Europeans realized it was the end of an era . . . Sadness on one side, complete joy on the other and you could almost split that down the middle . . . the Europeans basically all bunched up in one area and the rest of the place was just full of Africans.

In the short term, there was little change in Kenya. Government House became State House and MacDonald became Governor-General. Many whites were given positions of authority in the new legislation and even when Kenya became a republic in 1964, there was little surprise or rancour. Everyone seemed to take the changes in their stride because, as John Whitfield points out, things remained much the same.

> I think most of us didn't notice much change. I mean there wasn't any sudden influx of Africans passing into European areas.

Everybody just seemed to do their own job. Our houseboy didn't suddenly say, right, I want to eat in the dining-room. Nothing seemed to basically change . . . you went to the same restaurants, you went to the theatre, you went to the cinema. The Africans had no more money the day after independence than they had before, it wasn't until gradually they began to take over the jobs and got more money that you found more Africans in the cinemas or restaurants. They were the wealthy ones but you didn't get the sort of houseboy types in there. They couldn't afford it. We didn't suddenly have to put up his wages or anything.

John Whitfield lived on in Kenya until 1974 and in that time the country prospered. Nairobi became a wealthy capital city, well-heeled tourists visited the country's game parks and, under Kenyatta's benevolent rule, Kenya became a model of tolerance and self-control. Much of the tranquillity was oiled by the wealth generated by agriculture which was still predominantly in white hands – especially the production of tea, coffee and sisal. But even so, there were still the seeds of future strife. Although three million acres of land in the White Highlands had passed back to the Kenyans, either through the government resettlement schemes or through private negotiation, there were still calls for nationalization of the land. The most prominent critics were former members of Mau Mau who believed that their blood sacrifice had paid for the independence struggle; and two of them, Bildad Kaggia and J.M. Kariuki, built their careers on embarrassing the new government over the land issue.

While Kenyatta lived, their voices carried little political influence – Kariuki was murdered in 1975 – but the general air of contentment in Kenya only helped to disguise some of the country's weaknesses. In addition to the continuing unhappiness over land, graft and corruption in the administration was not unknown and as MacDonald warned, 'soon after gaining power they [ministers and senior civil servants] began to buy (sometimes with money gained by dubious means) large houses, farms, motor cars and other possessions'. The problem was not unique

205

to Kenya, but it did cast a shadow over Kenyatta's last years. He died on 23 August 1978, a grand old man of African politics, and his passing was an occasion for widespread national mourning, not just amongst his native Kikuyu but across the whole of the country. For the man who had once been an extra in the film *Sanders of the River*, there could have been no finer memorial.

8

Failure of the Federation

AT ONE STAGE during the negotiations over Kenya, some white settler leaders had bruited the idea of a British East African Dominion which would also include Uganda and Tanganyika and which would enjoy close ties with Southern Rhodesia and South Africa. The idea had first been raised in 1953 by the Colonial Secretary Oliver Lyttelton, at a time when Britain had created the Central African Federation consisting of Nyasaland, Southern and Northern Rhodesia and when multiracial solutions were very much the order of the day. However, his suggestion was unappreciated in Uganda, where Britain was in treaty with the four main kingdoms and where there had been little settlement of the land by white farmers. To the predominant group, the Baganda people, a proud and monarchical society with a long history and traditions, the proposal smacked of an attempt to impose white hegemony and they bitterly opposed it.

Under the leadership of their king, the Kabaka Edward Mutesa II (otherwise known to the British as King Freddie), the Bagandan people argued that they were a separate nation who had negotiated their own treaty with Britain in 1893. Using this as a lever, they demanded separate independence, not least because they felt themselves to be superior to the other peoples of Uganda, especially the less developed Nilotic tribes of the north. Britain responded by insisting that no form of East African Federation would be introduced without the consent of all Ugandans but there could be no provision for an independent Baganda. As had happened in Nigeria, so too in Uganda it had to be a case of all or nothing. Stung by the British denial of their rights, the Bagandan representatives withdrew from Uganda's Legislative Council and refused to change their minds during subsequent discussions with the governor, Sir Andrew Cohen, who was determined to take a strong line. As the crisis worsened, both sides became more deeply entrenched and in November 1953 Cohen deposed the Kabaka under the terms of the treaty of 1900 which had created the Uganda protectorate. King Freddie was sent into exile in England and did not return until 1955, but the problem did not go away: as Uganda moved towards independence in 1962, the Baganda people still regarded themselves not as colonial subjects but as the equal of the British by means of international treaty.

> Baganda's relationship with Uganda had never been important before. We had dealings with the British and we had friendly neighbours . . . It was not true that, if we were granted federal status, everyone else must get it also. We never had at any time a wish to expand. Nor did it make sense to suggest that I should become Kabaka of all Uganda, though some of my wilder supporters suggested it, which naturally upset the people outside Baganda. We wished to hold what we had, to continue to govern ourselves, as we were demonstrably capable of doing.

The Kabaka's objections on behalf of his people were to no avail. Uganda was granted a federal constitution, although the demoralized Bagandans were allowed to retain their monarchy as well as a measure of internal self-rule with their own parliament, the Lukiko. Following independence, there was a coalition government with the Kabaka becoming head of state while the first prime minister was Milton Obote, leader of the socialist Uganda People's Congress. As was to happen in Kenya, the transfer of power was accompanied by enormous goodwill on all sides but in common with Nigeria, the carefully crafted constitution masked a number of tribal tensions which, all too soon, surfaced and plunged Uganda into civil unrest and eventual military dictatorship.

In retrospect, the officials were to say that Uganda's independence was pushed through too quickly, almost as if Britain were relieved to be rid of an unwelcome burden. Although this was a familiar refrain during the final days of colonialism in Africa – 'too slow off the starting blocks, too quick near the finishing line' – by any standard, the Ugandan timetable was astonishingly rapid. In the Gold Coast, Nkrumah had benefited from eight years of 'tutelage' from Arden-Clarke; the Nigerian constitutional talks had lasted through most of the 1950s and even in Kenya the countdown to independence took place over three years. In Uganda, the first constitutional conference was held in September 1961 and ended with agreement for the transfer of power a year later; hardly the most generous allocation of time for the constitution to be finalized and the elections to be arranged. Under Macleod's leadership, the Colonial Office managed to push through the necessary arrangements but, even so, it was a close-run thing – the actual Order in Council was only granted a week before independence in 1962.

No less rapid, but certainly smoother, was Tanganyika's progress towards independence. Considered by the British to be the most backward of the east African countries, it emerged as the pacemaker and actually achieved independence in December 1961, within three years of agreement that self-government would be by an African majority. That the hand-over should have been so rapid and so trouble-free owed much to the personalities involved – the leader of the Tanganyika African National Union (TANU) Julius Nyerere and the governor Sir Richard Turnbull, formerly Kenya's Internal Security Minister and Chief Secretary.

National cohesion was also helped by the fact that all 120 tribes spoke a common language, Swahili, and that none of them was powerful enough to attain a predominant position in the country.

Educated at Makerere and the University of Edinburgh, Nyerere was in many respects the right man in the right place at the right time. At the San Francisco Conference of 1945, which produced the Charter of the United Nations, the question of the League of Nations' mandates was addressed and it was agreed that 'the freely expressed wishes of the people concerned' should be promoted in Article 76. Tanganyika had been mandated to Britain by the League of Nations after the First World War and the trusteeship agreement was revised and transferred to the UN. In 1954, the year in which Nyerere founded TANU, the UN Mission to Tanganyika set its face against multiracial development and put forward the case for African rule: 'The Africans of this country would like to be assured, both by the United Nations Organization and by the Administering Authority, that this territory, though multiracial in population, is primarily an African country and must be developed as such.' That, too, was Nyerere's aim and just as Kenyatta was to be a decisive influence in convincing Kenya's white settlers that independence would not harm their future prospects, so too did the TANU leader strive to create an atmosphere of trust with the country's white community. He also had to keep in check his party's wilder elements who wanted independence at all costs. So complete was his policy of moderation that in the 1958 elections TANU swept the board and with Turnbull installed as governor, Nyerere felt that the path towards African majority government was now clear.

> We have always waited for a Governor of this country even to indicate that it was the government's policy that, when self-government is eventually achieved, the Africans will have a predominant say in the affairs of the country. Now the Africans have this assurance, I am confident that it is going to be the endeavour of the Africans, if non-Africans have any fears left, to remove them quickly.

The speed with which Nyerere achieved his aim surprised many in the Colonial Service but so infectious was his enthusiasm and forcefulness that difficulties such as the lack of trained personnel were put to one side. Murray Lunan had arrived in the country as an agricultural officer after wartime service in the King's African Rifles and was based at Shinyanga. As was the case with so many officers of his age, the rapidly changing political scene was both surprising and bewildering, even for someone who knew Africa well.

> We knew that we were sliding towards independence. The only thing that we were not prepared for was the speed at which it happened, so that there wasn't the trauma that there was in some of the other countries; the only thing that we didn't realize was how fast it would happen and how unprepared we would be – we were thinking in terms of another twenty to twenty-five years and there would be sufficient Africans to take over and we would eventually withdraw.

Unlike the Gold Coast or Nigeria, Tanganyika possessed only a tiny number of university graduates or secondary school-leavers and the process of Africanization was slow to develop. Even so, once the clock had started ticking towards independence, there would only be three years for black Tanganyikans to be trained up to the necessary standard. Given the country's flimsy resources, it was a tremendous gamble and one that did not always pay off.

> I don't think even people like Nyerere who were calling for independence realized that Britain would grant independence so quickly. I mean, Nyerere himself has admitted that a lot of the trouble that arose soon afterwards was that power was given to the people without the necessary background of education or experience. I mean, when we got the order that the next Director of Agriculture would be an African, our senior African was a Provincial Agricultural Officer. And he was shot up straight to be Director of Agriculture. Now he was a very decent, worthy sort of chap, but he was just lost.

211

The manpower difficulties were obvious to everyone but once multiracialism had been abandoned as a constitutional possibility, with Nyerere's prodding and Turnbull's support, officials found themselves being pulled along by the tide. Shortly before independence, and on Turnbull's recommendation, Charles Meek became Nyerere's Permanent Secretary and his description of the final flurry of activity is reminiscent of many ICS officers' memories of the rush towards independence in India once Mountbatten had named 15 August 1947 as the date for the transfer of power.

> The most fascinating experience of my working life, because there was no reason on the face of it why we should get on. I mean, I didn't enjoy the process. It was all being pushed out years before we ever thought it was going to happen. But if there was any background of suspicion it didn't last beyond the first handshake. Thereafter for those fifteen months we worked like blazes. We hadn't done nearly enough about training. We thought it was our duty to train people for independence – but that will be after my time was the unspoken thought in all our minds and we had to leap into crash-courses of Africanization and job division and back-seat driving . . . but of course I think we went wrong because of instead of Africanizing from the bottom up, they Africanized from the top down which meant I was the first to go . . .

Meek left Tanganyika in 1962, having served as the head of the country's civil service. A year later, the country became a republic, with Nyerere as president; and in 1964 it merged with Zanzibar – granted independence from Britain in 1963 – to become Tanzania.

The rapid progress towards independence in Tanganyika not only put paid to the concept of multiracial constitutions, it also ended any lingering hopes amongst the white Kenyans that an East African Federation would enable them to hold on to power. Only in Central Africa had that concept taken root and it was to prove the least happy of Britain's colonial experiments in Africa. It had begun life in the 1920s as a white proposal to amalgamate the two Rhodesias with Nyasaland to form a powerful British dominion across the Zambezi which would be large enough and wealthy enough to be economically and politically self-sufficient. For the whites, the attractions were obvious: investment would increase and trading links could be built up with South Africa. For the blacks, though, there were equally obvious dangers – they feared coming under the control of white Southern Rhodesia – and after British commissions of enquiry reported in 1929 and 1938, the idea was dropped.

However, the concept of a federation did not disappear completely and it was resurrected once more after the Second World War. All three countries had enjoyed boom years during the conflict. Increased copper production in Northern Rhodesia ensured profits for the industry and well-paid employment for black workers from Nyasaland. Southern Rhodesia's economy benefited from the enhanced production of coal from its Wankie fields and from the demand for tobacco, cattle and maize. In the post-war years, too, whites emigrated to both countries in large numbers – by 1954 the white population of Southern Rhodesia was over one hundred thousand strong and within five years it had expanded to twice that number. One possibility was for Southern Rhodesia to amalgamate with South Africa to become its fifth province, but this was rejected after the right-wing Afrikaner National Party came to power in 1948. The other was to revive the Federation proposal.

It came into being on 1 August 1953, largely as a result of Cohen's patient advocacy in the Colonial Office. To him, the creation of a Federation offered a number of guarantees, as well as safeguards, which could only be of long-term value to the Africans. First, it would act as a counterbalance to an increasingly nationalistic and anti-British South Africa. Second, it would create a viable economic unit; and, third, it would lead to the creation, at some future date, of a multiracial constitution. Unfortunately, the Africans themselves had no

213

voice in the consultation process – which began in March 1951 – and the running was left very much in the hands of the Southern Rhodesian prime minister Godfrey Huggins and the Northern Rhodesian leader Roy Welensky.

Both men argued that a Federation was the only logical outcome because it would allow the black Africans to develop under white tutelage and in secure economic conditions instead of plunging them rapidly into independence. However, neither man believed that this would be an easy or a particularly speedy process. In 1956 Huggins said that 'political control must remain in the hands of civilized people which for the foreseeable future means the Europeans'; while Welensky, a former trade unionist, argued that a universal franchise might take at least a century to come into being. When discussing constitutional matters, he was also fond of reminding audiences that women still did not have the vote in Switzerland and that some US states operated a restricted franchise for black people. To him, Africa was no different.

> Our present difficulty is to secure the time needed to bring enough of our backward people on to counterbalance the heavy pressure there is from those who do not understand what we are doing or do not wish our policy to succeed. The majority of the latter would prefer to replace it with a more facile but insubstantial demagoguery, under which they would find themselves the popular leaders. Our problem is to convince our own people, as well as those who are interested in us abroad, that we are acting in good faith and that our system does indeed provide a better opportunity for the mass of the people and a better solution to the problems of the continent than is being offered elsewhere.

It is not difficult to see that Welensky's arguments would appeal to those Rhodesian white settlers who had worked the land so that their children could inherit it and who therefore considered Africa their home. Like their counterparts in Kenya, the farmers in Southern Rhodesia had a bond with the land and they were determined to hold on to it. The same was true in Northern

214

Rhodesia, but here the matter was complicated by subtle social cadences which had been imported from Britain. To put it bluntly, during the post-war period many of the white immigrants were considered socially inferior to those of earlier years – and certainly further down the social scale from Kenya's white settlers or the Colonial Service officers in Nigeria. Lord Home, Secretary of State for Commonwealth Relations, said as much in his autobiography when he pointed out that the copper-belt immigrants were mainly 'of the artisan class': 'Fresh from wartime austerity at home, they suddenly found themselves possessed of servants and cars and comfort beyond their dreams . . . the newcomer into the North tended to parade his new-found affluence.'

Home's distaste for the copper-belt's pretentious lifestyle was echoed by others who lived in Northern Rhodesia during the Federation. Having served first in the Indian Police Service and then in the Colonial Service in Nigeria, Anthony St John Wood was given a three-year contract in the colony as a 're-employed pensioner' in 1956. He expected to find a sense of partnership but instead found 'an extraordinary lack of humanity . . . accompanied by priggish self-satisfaction and obstinacy'. These drawbacks were discovered more or less uniquely amongst the Europeans – even, to his horror, amongst the secretaries who worked with him in his district office.

On one occasion, sobbing bitterly, she complained that one of the educated young Africans had been rude to her. She wanted a showdown with him in my presence, but I refused to allow her the pleasure of a first-class row. Later the clerk admitted to me that he had been in the wrong but had lost his temper because of the manner in which she spoke to him. On another occasion, after a tiff with my European colleague, she told me, again sobbing bitterly, that 'he spoke to me as if I were an African'.

There was another lady who really loathed Africans. Nevertheless, in order to come out and work for money she did not need (her husband was a qualified man in a steady job), she had to leave her small son, aged four, in the charge of her gardener, an African youth of about seventeen, all day. She is, alas, typical of the modern British settler of the middle and lower class.

St John Wood's comments were written after his retirement but contemporary evidence of a lack of white comprehension is no less damning. A correspondent to the *Sunday Mail of Rhodesia* in 1960 expressed astonishment at the African habit of using European names: 'Not only is this adoption of European names stupid, but it is also an indication of marked inferiority of the African. He is attempting to transform himself into something he will never be – a civilized Christian.' As St John Wood pointed out, comments of that kind from 'Britons fresh from home' were by no means atypical and they are indicative of the gulf which had sprung up between those of his generation who regarded imperial service as a sacred duty and those for whom it was a dead letter.

> The European has betrayed his trust in Central Africa. He has paid too little attention to the physical needs of those under his government, and almost none to their moral and social needs. He has come here for his own benefit and, most unchristianlike, has failed to regard his neighbour as anything but a means to his wealth. Being human, he has accepted his manner of living as right and just, and then reasoned up to it. The greatest point in his favour is that his aggressive self-justification and addiction to very dull 'gay' parties betray an uneasy conscience. His main argument is the benefit conferred by European occupation, and the entirely European basis of the economy. It contains the assumption that groups are internally responsible for their own welfare and progress, and not for those of other groups, however closely interwoven with their own.

Home put it more succinctly when he explained that 'the Northern Rhodesian white was in the first place looking after himself', but St John Wood was no less adamant that the Europeans would have to adapt themselves to Africa if they wanted to survive. Even so it would be a difficult process, so deeply entrenched was the European 'good life'. In the copper-belt in the late 1950s the average white salary was £2,071 a year; for the black it was £203. Until the mid-1950s Northern Rhodesia operated pass laws for blacks to prevent them moving after 5 p.m. and Southern Rhodesia operated a virtual colour bar through its policy of separate development for the black races. Under the terms of its Land Apportionment Act of 1930, forty-eight million acres of prime agricultural land had been granted to the colony's 220,000 whites, while 2.5 million Africans had to make do with thirty-nine million acres of less fertile land. No African could possess land in a European area or own property in a town and, with stringent franchise rules, only 429 Africans were able to vote in the Federation referendum in 1953. For African nationalist leaders such as the Southern Rhodesia African National Congress president, Joshua Nkomo, this was the real threat posed by the Federation: its subordination to the white-dominated self-governing colony of Southern Rhodesia.

> How have the whites been able to hold on to power? By discriminating against Africans in education, employment, and the franchise laws and by denying Africans freedom of expression and movement. The minds of Africans in Southern Rhodesia are deliberately starved of information, especially from outside the country. While the Government spends huge sums of money sending European students to universities in South Africa and the United Kingdom, no Africans are sent to England for education. Why? Because it is feared they will know what Africans are supposed not to know.

Although Creech Jones and his successor James Griffiths had shown some concern for the African objections and were prepared to listen to them, the return of a Conservative government in October 1951 brushed them aside. During the final negotiations, safeguards were built in to protect the rights of black Africans – Northern Rhodesia and Nyasaland still came under the direction of the Colonial Office and an African Affairs Board was established – but to all intents and purposes the new federal government and its instruments of

217

administration were solidly white. Its headquarters and Assembly were in Salisbury; its first two prime ministers were Huggins and Welensky and between the two of them they promoted the concept of the Federation as a separate and independent country. Their eventual aim was dominion status within the Commonwealth and they might have gained it but for the growing strength of African nationalist opinion, especially in Northern Rhodesia and Nyasaland.

In both colonies, two men came to symbolize the escalating demands for African self-government: Kenneth Kaunda and Hastings Banda. They were very different in background and outlook – Banda had worked as a doctor in Britain and the Gold Coast, while Kaunda, a younger man, had a trade union background – but both were to play leading roles in taking their countries to independence. And like so many other African leaders of their period, both were 'prison graduates', Banda having been arrested in February 1959 and imprisoned at Gwelo in Southern Rhodesia, and Kaunda in 1955. The situation in Southern Rhodesia was less fertile for the growth of nationalist movements, but by 1957 Nkomo had revived an African National Congress which was banned two years later; and other activists included Ndabaningi Sithole and Robert Mugabe, both of whom were involved with the ANC's more militant successor, the National Democratic Party.

Their opposition to the Federation was self-evident and they were prepared to use the weapons at their disposal – strikes, boycotts and civil disobedience – to achieve their aims. Just as pointedly, most whites supported the idea of Federation for the simple reason that it seemed to insure their future against an early transfer of political power to the blacks. Their optimism seemed to be justified in economic terms alone, especially in the two Rhodesias where the construction of the Kariba Dam on the Zambezi provided cheap hydro-electricity for the copper mines in the north and the new industries in the south. With both industry and agriculture booming, white Rhodesians continued

218

to argue that the Federation should move confidently towards independence under white-majority rule.

In Nyasaland, though, with its small population of around 4,000 Europeans, support for the white supremacist approach was less pronounced: indeed, many whites were not only anti-Federation but they believed that the country should be developed separately until it was ready for independence. This was largely due to the fact that it was a British protectorate. First explored by Livingstone in 1859, Nyasaland had come under British control in 1893 and it retained strong links with the Church of Scotland whose missionaries had promoted Christ's teachings of equality, love and charity. Blantyre was named after the Scottish explorer's birthplace in Lanarkshire and according to one leading missionary, the Revd Andrew Doig, the people were not left untouched by the kirk's positive and democratic attitudes towards education, law and politics.

> This is not Scottish pride coming out but we've always got to draw the distinction between Scots and other Britishers. It goes back in history. It was the representations of the Church of Scotland that made Nyasaland a protectorate and the church's influence on Malawi has been predominantly from Scotland and the tradition is that Nyasalanders learn to speak their own language with an Aberdeen accent, that kind of thing . . . And I don't think anything will break that link. They did make a distinction between those of us who were Scots and those who weren't.

There were other benefits. Blessed by an absence of inter-tribal rivalry, its peoples enjoyed a reputation as farmers and soldiers – many served as machine-gunners in the East African divisions – and as their officers noticed, their experiences in Burma and India had helped to cement the idea of Nyasa nationhood.

> They went back with a fresh attitude to people and to circumstances – sad to say, some of their idealistic notions of Europeans

were destroyed during the war but on the other hand that meant they came back with a more questioning mind and more objective standard of judgement of individuals and of what individuals were trying to do . . . they came back from the war better able to deal with ideas about their country and its future, aware of abilities within themselves that they had never known before.

Nyasaland's agricultural economy meant that most soldiers returned to the land but they went back different people, alert to the changing political circumstances. Following a constitutional modification in 1956, younger African politicians on the Legislative Council, such as Henry Chipembere and Kanyama Chiume, started demanding universal suffrage and free elections to a black majority government. This, too, was the intention of many of the missionaries who argued that 'the main responsibility on the broad front was that we must accept and learn that we were not primarily there to do things for them but to enable them to do things'. The imposition of the Federation seemed to put an end to this worthy aim for, although the interests of the Nyasas were supposed to be protected by the connection with the Colonial Office and the African Affairs Board, the Federation brought Rhodesians into Nyasaland and with them came a different set of white supremacist attitudes. Many Nyasas had worked in the Northern Rhodesian copper-belt or at the Wankie mines in Southern Rhodesia where they had come into contact with their bosses' hardline attitudes.

It is very important to understand that between 1949 and 1951 a terrible thing happened. Nyasaland was made to join the Central African Federation against its will and Africans really felt betrayed. For the first time, they started being aggressive about independence because up till then they had really thought there had been a nationalist movement for a long time but in many ways a kind of friendly movement. They had complained and they had marches and so on but they really felt it was nudging the old girl [Britain] along a bit more quickly but it was all going to happen. Because on the whole the relationship had been reasonably good in Nyasaland.

Suddenly they were lumbered in federation with the same Southern Rhodesians that many of them knew only too well.

The Revd Dr Andrew Ross's argument that the Federation was only piling up difficulties for the future by ignoring the Nyasas' aspirations was shared by many others in the Scottish missionary community, including the redoubtable Revd Doig who had arrived in Nyasaland in 1939. Following war service as a senior chaplain with the East Africa forces, he became a member of the Legislative Council and when the Federation came into being he was elected to the Assembly to represent African interests in Nyasaland. And that he did with a will: his espousal of the African cause earned the rebuke from the *Rhodesian Herald* that he carried out his political duties with all the fervour of the seventeenth-century Covenanters − those extreme Presbyterians who took to the hills of Scotland to protect their religious principles following the Restoration.

> In a sense, it [Federation] was carried through from London, because many, many colonial officers, as we did in the mission, had a tremendous conviction that being a protectorate really meant something and that we had a responsibility to carry through that order right until the day that we were no longer needed to give pro-tection − in other words, independence; and therefore Federation seemed to us an interference with that promise and a denial of what we saw as the potential emerging from the African community and then we saw the representation offered that just made a nonsense of it.

Welcome though Doig's support must have been, the African politicians in Nyasaland needed an effective leader and they found one in Hastings Banda. The first approach had been made by Chipembere in 1957, when he wrote to Banda suggesting that he had all the heroic qualities to become a 'political messiah'. Just as Nkrumah had emerged as his country's strong man in Ghana − a role shortly to be assumed by Kenyatta in Kenya − so, too, did Nyasaland need a committed and

221

charismatic leader. Almost sixty at the time and living in Ghana, Banda wondered if he would be able to fulfil that role but in the following year he returned to Britain to discuss Nyasaland's future with the Colonial Office. In Edinburgh he met Doig who was on leave and already thinking about resigning from the Federal Assembly because it was doing so little to foster African politics. (Although there were six African members in the thirty-four-seat Assembly, their opinions were largely disregarded.) To change that state of affairs, he believed that two questions had to be answered: 'At what point and for what reasons should Andrew Doig resign from Federal Assembly? At what point in time should Dr Banda go back to meet the independence forces of Malawi?'

Both were answered that summer. Doig resigned from the Federal Assembly over the passing of a Franchise Bill which he believed would undermine the African Affairs Board and Banda returned home after an absence of forty-two years. When he arrived back in Nyasaland in July 1958, a handful of settlers were inclined to regard the slight doctor in his dark suit, Homburg hat and fly-whisk as the devil incarnate. Even before he returned, they held a meeting in Blantyre to discuss their fears and invited all the Europeans, including the missionaries, to attend it. Amongst them was Herbert Bell, a teacher at the prestigious Blantyre Secondary School.

> I think the deep anxiety was among the people in tea, tobacco, that sort of thing. One of the settlers, obviously with the support of some others, got up and warned us of a situation which might arise. It was rumoured that Dr Banda was coming back. It rather looked as if he intended to. Well, he had a right to but we shall expect him to be a doctor in the community, no political nonsense. And yet he warned us of something else. There were people in the community, he didn't mention any names but there were hints that some of them were connected with the Church of Scotland. Now, his call was to resist this, otherwise there is going to be trouble and it's rather serious because there are some among us who, acting in a

rather treacherous way, look like giving these Africans encouragement in their various ideas and yet we know, don't we, that they are
not ready for it, they won't be ready for another hundred years.
They are only just down from the trees.

Although Bell does not say so, the speaker was probably referring to Doig, who continued to be a supporter of African
independence long after his resignation. Even then, he did not
give up the struggle: he was appointed General Secretary of the
Synod of the Church of Nyasaland, in which post he stepped up
the training of Africans for the ministry, a move which did not
attract universal support.

When I was underlining the importance of free scope for African
initiative and representation, they came down like a ton of bricks
on me and it must have been difficult for them for a period. I was
also a minister of the European congregation at Milange which is a
settler district but I think they were very generous about it. We
never lost friendship over it although we might argue pretty
strongly on it.

Doig's colleague the Revd Ross was less fortunate in Zomba.
Having preached a sermon questioning the wisdom of the white
reaction to African nationalism, 'things were made unpleasant,
like if you were in the queue for the checkout at the supermarket
people spoke through you as if you weren't there'. In fact, to
begin with, the settlers' fears were unjustified. Banda did adopt
a reasonable stance and although he engaged in 'political nonsense' his views were moderate and seemed to be confined to
negotiating independence through a reconstructed Nyasaland
African National Congress party.

To begin with, his political meetings were peaceful enough
but he had underestimated his effect on his fellow countrymen.
As Chipembere had forecast, the Nyasas were looking for 'a kind
of hero to be hero-worshipped' and they had found one in
Banda. Soon activists were claiming that Nyasaland needed
Mau Mau to rid them of the Europeans and even reasonably

moderate Africans started shouting out '*Kwacha!*' (dawn), '*Ufuli!*' (freedom) or '*Mtendere!*' (peace) when they passed Europeans. Banda caught the mood of the moment and by the year's end his tactics had changed from conciliation and compromise to talking about setting 'the whole of Nyasaland on fire'. As the settlers had feared all along, Banda's return had consolidated nationalist opposition to the Federation and seemed to hasten the day when Nyasaland would become independent. This was not to the liking of the new pro-Federation governor Sir Robert Armitage and a show-down between him and Banda became inevitable.

When the storm broke, the response to it was as cack-handed as the crackdown following the Accra riots in the Gold Coast in 1948. Following a meeting of the Congress party to discuss non-co-operation, at which the possibility of using violence was freely discussed – Banda himself was not present – Armitage decided to show the mailed fist. As justification, he claimed that there was evidence of a Mau Mau-type rising which would lead to the massacre of the white population. Under the code-name 'Operation Sunrise', a state of emergency was declared, Banda and around 1,200 supporters were arrested, their party was banned and their legal rights suspended. The authorities hoped that the display of firmness would restore the *status quo*, but it had the opposite effect. Africans took to the streets to demonstrate, buildings were set on fire, shots were fired and as the riots got out of control Armitage had to call on the Federation for help. Rhodesian territorial troops and police were rushed into the protectorate, a move which only helped to reinforce the idea that the Federation was dominated by the Salisbury government.

> Well, we thought this was quite unnecessary, we were very much against the Federation anyway, like most Malawians, although the planter-type was mostly pro-Federation. Anyway, our African students just sort of grinned to us as if to say, a show of force, that sort of thing, and they realized that basically we were on their side. And the contact we had with our African teachers was helpful because

we could speak to them – man to man, colour didn't matter at all – and made it clear that we realized independence was coming and a very good thing too. But, of course, we know that in some countries it's been a pretty bloody business and we don't want that, do we? And we were completely agreed that we must – you Africans must – keep it going at a reasonable pace, without being too impatient, and we whites must be prepared to see change and in fact I used to say to them in the school we want to help that change, we wanted to go through smoothly and constructively and we feel we have a part to play.

Herbert Bell's students kept out of the riots but shots were fired near the school. Those who took part were less fortunate: many of the fifty-one people killed by the security forces were unarmed – 'some with bibles in their hands,' claimed Chiume – and the elderly nationalist Chief Gomani died in hospital while waiting for charges to be brought against him. Writing in *The Scotsman* on 14 March, Doig expressed his alarms and concern in a long and passionate article which appealed for 'the utmost restraint on every hand' as the situation worsened.

On Saturday, my wife and I went to call on four families affected by the detentions. In every case there has been a loss of sons and daughters – teachers and a doctor. We can get little or no information about them. One African mother, whose family has done well in education and professional attainment such as she could never know, wept unrestrainedly at the apparent futility of Africans seeking to better themselves and 'have ideas'. There is no lack of evidence of a strong European feeling against the educated African. A graduate was stopped in his car, manhandled and abused in language by men who had nothing of the training that the African had had. Two European women expressed themselves very forcibly regarding African casualties – the more of them, the better.

The crackdown was generally welcomed in Northern and Southern Rhodesia whose white populations wanted to see a show of force, but it seriously embarrassed both the British government and the authorities in Nyasaland. In an attempt to limit the damage, Lennox-Boyd announced in the House of Commons that the governor had been forced to act because his security forces had uncovered a plot to massacre the European and Asian communities and that there was information to suggest the creation of an underground terrorist movement similar to Mau Mau. However, no evidence was produced. This failure and the fact that press censorship had been introduced prompted Labour calls for an official inquiry and three weeks later the government caved in. An independent commission of inquiry headed by Sir Patrick Devlin, a senior high-court judge, was despatched to Nyasaland to listen to evidence and to report back to Westminster. Its findings were announced in July 1959 and they were dynamite.

While Armitage was exonerated for imposing a state of emergency, the police and army were blamed for their rough handling of arrested suspects and the report instanced a number of acts of casual brutality. No evidence was found of any plot to overthrow government. Worse was to follow: as a result of the behaviour of the security forces, there had come into being a 'police state where it is unsafe to make any but the most restrained criticism of Government policy'. Not unnaturally, critics of imperialism at home and abroad jumped on the terminology used by Devlin's commission, but it was not just the reference to political repression which damned Armitage's actions. The report concluded that the root cause of the disturbances was the Africans' dislike of the Federation and that this was not just confined to Congress activists.

> The government's view is that these nationalist aspirations are the thoughts of only a small minority of political Africans, mainly of self-seekers who think their prospects of office will be worse under Federation; and that the great majority of the people are indifferent to the issue. We have not found this to be so. It was generally acknowledged that the opposition to Federation was there, that it was deeply rooted and almost universally held.

This was not the kind of revelation which Macmillan and his colleagues expected to come out of their bold multiracial experiment in central Africa. In an attempt to limit the damage, the Conservative government closed ranks and rejected the report. Even worse, they attempted a cover-up by tampering with Devlin's findings, which had been accidentally sent in proof form to the Colonial Office. As Macmillan's most recent biographer, Richard Lamb, makes clear, the prime minister was furious both with the wording of the report and its main author. In his diary for July 1959, he claimed that the report was only to be expected because it had come from a judge whose 'Fenian blood makes Irishmen anti-government on principle', and behind the scenes, too, he was no less feline. The Colonial Secretary Lennox-Boyd was instructed to hold up publication until a 'full counterblast' had been prepared by Armitage: both were published on the same day, 23 July, and as Lamb makes clear, Armitage's riposte 'served to undermine Devlin's credibility and justify the Government's handling of the crisis'.

Unfortunately for Macmillan, though, the reports coincided with the publication of another damaging white paper which investigated atrocities committed against Mau Mau internees at the Hola detention camp in Kenya. As a result of its findings, the government was forced to accept that eleven Kikuyu detainees had died, not from dehydration – the reason given by the Kenyan authorities – but as a result of 'multiple beatings'. With a general election in the offing in October, the Labour opposition made political capital out of the government's discomfort over its colonial policies and it looked at one point as though Colonial Secretary Alan Lennox-Boyd would be forced to resign. (He had in fact offered his resignation to the Cabinet but it had not been accepted.)

However, when the Devlin Report was debated in the House of Commons, the government won the motion that only part of it should be accepted: its victory was almost entirely due to the fact that querulous backbenchers had been placated by the hurriedly cobbled-together rival report from Armitage. In the October election the government won comfortably, with a majority of 107. Even so, according to Devlin's commission colleague Sir Edgar Williams, the matter of the Devlin Report had been 'a disgraceful episode' and one which gave notice to Macmillan that sooner or later he would have to change his policy towards the Federation. Just as the more experienced colonial officers had warned, the imposition of the Federation had been 'an unmitigated disaster'.

> When we in Nyasaland protested to the Colonial Office that the proposed Federation was completely contrary to the best interests, economic and political, of our African people and that it was selling them down the river to the South African-type whites in Southern Rhodesia, we were told that it was HMG's settled policy to promote federation and that we should shut up and get on with it.

At the time, Kenneth Simmonds was working as the Financial Secretary in Nyasaland but it was not just there that the Federation was losing friends. Suddenly, imperialism in Africa was becoming an unpopular cause in London, both within and outside government. The dislike was fanned by the bloody fighting in Algeria between French forces and the FLN nationalists and there were not ungrounded fears that Britain could become involved in a similar conflict in her own remaining African colonies. Not only had the riots in Nyasaland demonstrated the difficulties and expense of containing any insurrection but the response to them had displayed the extent of the opposition to the maintenance of the *status quo* in central Africa. As Macmillan was to say in his celebrated speech in Cape Town in February 1960, a 'wind of change' was blowing through Africa and 'the growth of [African] national consciousness is a political fact'. But it was not just up to the politicians to accept the changes. Shortly before he left Northern Rhodesia in October that same year, St John Wood argued that the time had come for the whites themselves to 'accept a more realistic standard of living or move on'.

No country can afford to maintain clerks and artisans at a standard where they live in the manner of company directors. Yet they do have their holidays in Europe, picking up a new Peugeot in Paris, touring the Continent in style and bringing the car back with them. They have their cameras and their cine-cameras almost as a matter of course. Oddly enough, they just 'cannot afford' to increase their servants' wages beyond £5 a month. It made us a little sick, on our last journey home, to meet a couple of this class finishing their leave, after a tour of Europe in the said Peugeot, with a tour of the Union of South Africa, and to find that, even as far away as the glass shops of Venice, to be from Rhodesia is to be thought a person of great wealth and taste.

To bring some sense to the future position of the Federation, Macmillan had already appointed Lord Monckton to chair a further commission which would report on the constitution prior to the full review which was planned for 1960. An experienced constitutional lawyer, with something of a reputation as an appeaser – he played a key role in King Edward VIII's abdication in 1938 – Monckton was faced with the weighty problem of reconciling the continued existence of the Federation with the need to extend a multiracial franchise. It was a difficult assignment, not least because the question of secession was not to be addressed and there was a problem over Labour's representation. Uncharacteristically, Macmillan had refused to accept their candidate James Callaghan, the shadow Colonial Secretary, and appointed, instead, Sir Hartley Shawcross who won from Macmillan the private assurance that secession could not be ruled out.

It was a typical piece of juggling from one of the most canny prime ministers of modern times. Welensky had been assured by Macmillan that the question of secession would not be addressed by Monckton's commission, but one of its key members had been told that it could not be left undiscussed. And when he selected his new Cabinet, Macmillan appointed Iain Macleod to the Colonial Office (responsible for Nyasaland and Northern

Rhodesia) while the more cautious Lord Home went to the Commonwealth Relations Office (responsible for Southern Rhodesia), presumably to balance the new Colonial Secretary's enthusiasm for rapid Africanization in the remaining colonies and the release of political detainees. It was the beginning of a period of hot and acrimonious debate, with Welensky fighting tooth and nail to preserve the Federation while Britain struggled to produce a solution which would benefit the Africans while safeguarding the white settlers' interests. In attempting to find a rapprochement, something was bound to give and it proved to be the Federation. As the Revd Doig and others had already discovered, its failure lay in the fact that while it protected white interests it did not afford any representation to black wishes. That drawback alone condemned it amongst the African people of Nyasaland.

> The Federal Assembly had a Hansard like any other parliament and the politically minded and the chiefs and so on, the well-educated teachers, they got Hansard and they read it and when we went round they weren't slow to say, 'Why did you say this?' 'And why didn't you say that?' So this was the only way one could justify having taken the step of membership of the Federal Assembly, if one was to some measure accountable to the people you were representing.

In retrospect, it is possible to see that the Federation's fate had been settled by the riots in Nyasaland and Britain's clumsy response to them. Although it would take another two years before the protectorate was given the right to secede, and British officials and ministers would fight long and hard to find a solution to the question of combining the central African states in a workable union, Nyasaland's opposition had pointed the way ahead. Britain would not support any administration which governed solely through the possession of superior power. And if that meant scrambling out of Africa, then Macleod was certainly the man to oversee the process. Belgium had withdrawn from the Congo and France had granted independence to its west African colonies (while maintaining a strong degree of hegemony): now it was Britain's turn to complete the process.

Macleod set about his task with a will. Writing in *The Spectator* in 1964, he argued that there had been no option but to speed up 'the movement towards independence' because to have done otherwise 'would have led to a terrible bloodshed in Africa'. In his dealings with the Federation, his first concern was to give greater political responsibilities to the Africans in Nyasaland and Northern Rhodesia. Only by increasing the element of political partnership, he reasoned, could the Federation survive; if not as a political alliance, then at least as an economic or customs union. But if Africans were to be given increased political involvement, then the question of the detainees had to be addressed. On 3 December 1959, shortly after his appointment, Macleod told Macmillan that the time had come to release Banda because 'although this may sound paradoxical Banda is the most likely African Nyasa to keep Nyasaland within the Federation'.

In fact it was an ambiguous argument. Banda was committed to secession and, for that reason alone, his release was opposed not just by many whites within the Federation but also by several of Macleod's Cabinet colleagues. Their protests were to no avail: Banda was given his freedom four months later. When he returned to Nyasaland in April 1960, the anticipated violence did not materialize and Armitage was able to lift the state of emergency. From that point onwards, events moved with bewildering speed. That same summer, Macleod convened a constitutional conference on Nyasaland which paved the way for African majority rule in 1961; a year later, in December 1962, the country was given the right to secede from the Federation under Banda's leadership. As Simmonds had foreseen, this was the beginning of the end.

In Nyasaland the ending of the iniquitous Central African Federation was a clear step towards independence for the

Protectorate (and for Northern Rhodesia) even though no date was set . . . In general, independence of every territory sooner or later became inevitable but the actual date was dictated by the march of local events rather than by HMG policy.

In fact, Nyasaland achieved independence in 1964 as Malawi, with Banda appointed its 'president for life'. Somewhat surprisingly for such an austere man, he encouraged white civil servants to stay on to help the fledgeling state in its first years of freedom and the transfer of power was carried through remarkably smoothly.

The same cannot be said of what happened to the rest of the Federation. Welensky and his supporters had been prepared to cave in over Nyasaland's right to secede – its smallness, its relative poverty and the tiny white population always made it the weakest partner in the Federation – but they were prepared to fight over Northern Rhodesia. Not only did it have a sizeable number of white settlers, but its copper-belt was central to the region's economic wealth. This was to be the battleground in the final phases of the Federation: the whites were determined to hold on to power and, with equal determination, the blacks were desperate to acquire it. Both sides were prepared to fight, if necessary, to get what they wanted. At one stage in the increasingly heated negotiations, the leading African nationalist leader Kenneth Kaunda threatened an armed uprising which would make Mau Mau look like 'a child's picnic', and there was more than bluster to Welensky's threats to deploy the white-officered Rhodesian forces in support of the settlers' interests. Given those circumstances, there could be no more multiracial constitutions: as an unnamed senior civil servant in the Colonial Office put it at the time, because the blacks were in the majority and the whites could only hold on to power by resorting to force, there could only be one outcome.

The ball had already been set rolling in October 1959 by the report of the Monckton commission, which recommended a number of far-reaching constitutional changes including equal representation for blacks in the Federal Assembly and a new constitution with a black majority for Northern Rhodesia. It also suggested that a new term be found for the Federation and that individual territories should be allowed to secede. Monckton's findings enraged Welensky and during the next four years the battle for the Federation was to be littered with allegations of broken promises, bad faith and sell-outs, as the whites struggled to retain power while the British government attempted to produce a political solution which would be acceptable to black and white alike.

One by one, the constitutional conferences came and went. There were changes of personnel: in 1961, Macleod was replaced by Reginald Maudling who considered the Federation to be 'a dead duck'; Home went to the Foreign Office and Duncan Sandys took his place at Commonwealth Relations; in 1962 Rab Butler, as Deputy Prime Minister, was given responsibility for Central African Affairs, an office which required him in reality to oversee the last rites of the Federation. A powerful political lobby led by Lord Salisbury and Lord Lambton fought the settlers' corner, in and out of parliament. Welensky proved to be as tough and resilient a scrapper in politics as he had once been a boxer in the ring and at times he showed the surer touch in the increasingly acrimonious public relations struggle. A battle it certainly was. British intelligence planted listening-devices in Welensky's rooms while he was staying at the Savoy Hotel in London; pro-Federation supporters campaigned noisily in the right-wing *Daily Express*; Welensky threw occasional tantrums and berated the British government for its 'act of treachery'; and Macmillan and his fellow ministers were frequently parsimonious with the truth as they attempted to find constitutional solutions which would suit every party.

It was left to Butler to bring the sorry story of the Federation to an end. In his autobiography, he claimed that he accepted the responsibility out of a sense of duty to the country and that he disagreed with Macmillan's and Home's attempts to keep the Federation in being. Initial meetings with Banda confirmed this opinion, and in October 1962 he produced a telling document which argued that, with the secession of Nyasaland, Northern Rhodesia would also demand constitutional change for an African majority government and that their independence would also lead to the country seceding from the Federation. Although Butler continued talks with Welensky about the possibility of creating an association between the two Rhodesias, Kenneth Kaunda, now leading a black coalition government with Harry Nkumbula, was bitterly opposed to any such idea.

The next year, on 4 July 1963, the Federation was finally laid to rest at a reasonably amicable conference held at Victoria Falls. Northern Rhodesia was left free to accompany Nyasaland on its march towards independence, which it achieved in 1964 under its new name of Zambia. Only one other question remained: what was to become of Southern Rhodesia? In 1962, a new Rhodesian Front government had come to power under the leadership of a white farmer, Winston Field. With the breakup of the Federation they, too, wanted independence, but Butler had made it clear that this was impossible unless the constitution contained safeguards for the African majority. Field attended the Victoria Falls conference but, at his insistence, the question of Southern Rhodesia's future was not discussed. That failure left a piece of unfinished imperial business which would torment successive British governments for another seventeen years.

9

Last to Go

AS, ONE BY one, the former colonies and protectorates became independent under African nationalist governments, the people of Southern Rhodesia pondered their own future. Ideally, they would have liked their own independence, too, with the creation of an all-white government which would move slowly towards a multiracial constitution. For the time being, though, what the whites of Southern Rhodesia demanded from their own government was a strong economy backed up by law and order: anything less than that would allow African nationalism to flourish, thereby ushering in a period of instability, rapid disintegration and a general lowering of standards. The election of the Rhodesian Front in December 1962 had helped to concentrate white Rhodesian minds about their future objectives. Not only did they demand independence but they believed it was a right which had been earned by their years of loyal service to the empire and by the stable economic and social conditions which they themselves had brought into being. As the novelist Doris Lessing wrote when she returned to Zimbabwe in 1988, amongst her earliest memories of Southern Rhodesia was the farmers' pride of possession.

> In the old days, visiting a farm, you were 'taken around the place'. It is the settlers' instinct, showing to fellow civilizers what has been achieved, and on behalf of all of them. 'See what I've carved out of

235

the trees, out of the grasslands, see my house, my animals, my plants, my good, strong roof which may very well have to shelter you sometime . . .' So a dog eases itself into a new sleeping corner, fitting his back into a curve, stretching out his legs. He drops his muzzle gently on his paws . . . 'Yes, that's the size of it, that's what it is like, this place of mine.'

Men of that ilk were fond of saying that in most of Britain's African colonial holdings the whites were birds of passage, colonial servants, who retired and went 'home' at the end of their service, whereas they went 'home' every evening at dusk, having done a good day's work.

With the end of the Federation, Southern Rhodesia's status was that of a colony with internal self-government but its constitution still did not protect Africans' rights. In 1961 an attempt was made to introduce a new constitution which would give Africans fifteen places in the sixty-five-seat parliament and in return Britain would withdraw its right to interfere in the country's affairs. In London, the National Democratic Party (NDP) leader Joshua Nkomo had agreed to the settlement but on his return to Salisbury he was faced by such severe dissent within his party that he was forced to go back on his word. Co-operation was withdrawn and there was rioting in the major African townships. In retaliation, the government banned the NDP. Within a week, though, on 18 December 1961, Nkomo formed the Zimbabwe African Peoples Union (ZAPU) and the violence continued. The introduction of the African name for the country signalled a change of attitude: according to Henrik Ellert, who served with the country's British South African Police force, 'it was as if the very name "Zimbabwe" bespoke what was to come'.

The police were hard-pressed to contain the escalating urban violence which threatened to engulf the whole country. Petrol bombing, stoning and mass violence erupted in most of the major African townships of Harare, Bulawayo, Gweru, Masvingo and Zvishavane. Much of the violence was internecine in character and manifested itself in attacks by ZAPU militants against anyone who stood in their way. ZAPU was extremely active against the rural areas of Rhodesia, holding political rallies by day and carrying out acts of political violence by night.

Although the whites were appalled by the violence, there was also an air of self-satisfaction amongst those who had always feared the worst. Didn't we say that this would happen, haven't we always warned that the blacks are untrustworthy and irresponsible? Give them an inch and they'll take a mile. As the violence escalated, so too did the government respond with greater force. The Rhodesian Special Air Service regiment (C Squadron SAS) was called up to reinforce the police, whose own Special Branch began the long and challenging process of infiltrating nationalist groups to gather intelligence. In September 1962 ZAPU was banned and, with the country becoming increasingly tense, the Rhodesian Front government promised the electorate that they would retain the conditions of the Land Apportionment Act, halt plans for integration and win independence from Britain.

For the next two years, the prime minister Winston Field continued his negotiations with Britain against a background of continuing unrest. A new breakaway nationalist party, the Zimbabwe African National Union (ZANU), was formed on 8 August 1963, with Ndabaningi Sithole as president and Leopold Takawira as his deputy; other prominent members included Herbert Chitepo and Robert Mugabe. This marked the beginning of a bitter split in nationalist opinion which was to last long after the country became independent as Zimbabwe in 1980. What kept them together during the seventeen years of struggle was the common goal of liberation, but as Ellert has pointed out, the rivalry often degenerated into gang warfare and in the early 1960s whites were rarely victims of the violence. To the white population, the unrest was further evidence of black immaturity and they failed to understand why Britain would not agree that white rule was not just for the benefit of their own people; it was also the best long-term option for the black Africans.

According to those who knew him, Field was a mild-mannered man, a gentleman farmer who represented the old Rhodesian élite. However, like Whitehead before him, he was considered to be too fair, and too deferential to the perfidious British politicians who kept shifting their ground. Even Welensky had seemed to be too much of a push-over, over-anxious to placate the treacherous men from Whitehall. What was needed was a man with some backbone and the white Rhodesians found him in Ian Douglas Smith, a farmer from Selukwe. Little was known about him apart from the fact that he had flown as a wartime pilot in the Royal Rhodesian Air Force and that he had served under Field as Finance Minister; but he had other attributes in an engaging public modesty, a steely inner determination and a ruthless persistence when it came to fighting political battles both inside and outside Southern Rhodesia. One other distinction singled him out: whereas Field had been born in Bromsgrove, Worcestershire, and Whitehead came from Oxford, Smith was Rhodesian born and bred.

On taking office in April 1964, the little-known Smith made it his business to reassure the white Rhodesians that he would not give in to British demands for a new constitution which would give greater political power to the Africans. On his appointment, one newspaper called him 'the man of the moment', only to change its mind a few days later by renaming him 'the momentary man'; but Smith knew what his fellow whites expected of him and he rarely failed to deliver. 'We shall never surrender to the forces of evil,' became one of the catch-phrases penned for him by his propagandist, the South African Ivor Benson who worked assiduously to promote the concept of 'Good Old Smittie', a father-figure who would always put his country first. (Earlier, Benson had been associated with the British fascist leader Sir Oswald Mosley.) Equally Churchillian was Smith's boast that there would never be black majority rule within his lifetime, a phrase which created considerable offence outside the party when he made it in 1976, but one which he has always insisted was much misunderstood.

> I was asked by a reporter once, 'When will you accept black majority rule in your country?' I thought for a minute and then I said, 'I'm never prepared to accept a government in my country based on race or colour. We've got a lot of good white people here, intelligent people, professional people, experts. Why can't they be part of the government? I support a government in this country based on merit.' So it was with that at the back of my mind when I said, 'In time it will come through merit, not with the colour connotation. So in principle I am unable to accept a black government – never in my lifetime, never in a thousand years could I accept that. It's contrary to the basis of my thinking.' That immediately turned Smith into a racist.

However, the sticking-point with the British government remained Smith's refusal to extend the franchise so that blacks would be given the opportunity to play a fuller role in their country's affairs. Smith insisted that change would only come gradually but his thinking was out of kilter with the times. He maintained that the chiefs were 'the true rulers of the African people', but by the 1960s their power had waned and he was unable to accept the validity of the new ZANU and ZAPU nationalist leadership. 'I don't wish to be unkind, but sixty years ago Africans were uncivilized savages, walking around in their skins,' he said when the number of black members of parliament was increased to sixteen in 1970. 'They have made tremendous progress, but they still have a long way to go.'

By the time Smith came to power, Britain, too, was about to change its government. Hounded by sexual scandal within his Cabinet and with dwindling support in the country, Macmillan had gone into hospital in October 1963 with prostate trouble and had promptly resigned as prime minister. Butler seemed to be the obvious choice as successor but devious plotting by Macmillan and other Tory grandees brought the Foreign Secretary Home into Downing Street. A year later, as Sir Alec Douglas-Home, he fought his first and last general election and a Labour government came to power with Harold Wilson as prime minister. For most white Rhodesians, the news was disastrous. The British might be underhand but at least they were Conservative; now they would have to contend with socialists, not much better in their opinion than the Communists who were busy taking power in the rest of Africa.

From the very outset of the new relationship, Wilson's administration continued to insist on 'the principle and intention of unimpeded progress to majority rule'. He also warned that any attempt to declare independence unilaterally would be illegal and would therefore be punished by the imposition of economic sanctions. Soon after taking over in Downing Street, Wilson asked his Chiefs of Staff about the possibility of using military force if Smith and Southern Rhodesia decided to go it alone, but was told that such an adventure was out of the question. Not only would it take time and huge expense to build up an operational base in Zambia, but senior British officers warned that it was also extremely doubtful if their men would ever be prepared to fight their white 'kith and kin'. The strength of the Southern Rhodesian forces was also taken into account: their soldiers were trained to Nato standards and the air force was equipped with modern helicopters and strike aircraft. MI6 was then ordered to investigate the possibility of unseating the Smith regime, but again, nothing ever came of the idea.

A show-down became inevitable, but this time the white Rhodesians believed that they had found the man for the hour. Using Benson's propaganda skills and the financial backing of a millionaire farmer, Douglas Collard 'Boss' Lilford, Smith was promoted as a leader of national unity, a patriot who would save his country from black rule and the horrors of the Congo. For the *Guardian* journalist Peter Niesewand, he was the epitome of the conservative white leader, 'straight-talking, honest, god-fearing and ordinary'.

> To whites, he was a simple man; but not simple in the sense that he
> could be manipulated by any British Government. Generations of
> white Rhodesians have grown to regard British Governments of
> whatever persuasion as being made up of untrustworthy bastards . . .
> Any leader who could play the British at their own game would
> command overwhelming white Rhodesian support, and Smith was
> such a man. Every time he said 'no' to the British, and they went
> away angry, the spirits of white Rhodesians rose. They were assert-
> ing themselves: they weren't push-overs.

In addition to fighting his corner with Wilson, Smith strengthened his position at home. On 26 August 1964, a state of
emergency was declared in the Highfields township area of
Salisbury; ZANU was banned, as was the People's Caretaker
Council (PCC) which had taken over from ZAPU; and the
leading nationalist leaders were interned. ZANU's leadership,
including Mugabe and Sithole, were imprisoned at Sikombela
camp near Kwekwe, while the ZAPU leaders were restricted in
the remote 'wilderness' area of Gonakudzwinga in the south-
east. Some managed to make good their escape to Zambia to
carry on the struggle from Lusaka, but the crackdown did
nothing to stop a growing number of attacks on white property.
Initially these were little more than irritants but they served to
reinforce the idea within the white community that Smith was
the only leader capable of restoring law and order.

In May 1965 Smith decided to build on that support by
calling a general election which his Rhodesian Front won
handsomely, taking all fifty white seats and obliterating the
opposition. The overwhelming victory greatly strengthened
Smith's hand. Not only did it offer him the political support of
the majority of Southern Rhodesia's whites, but it allowed him
to plan a referendum on independence secure in the knowledge
that he would also win that. He also had the full support of the

security forces and the country's radio and television services. On coming to power, his Minister of Information, P.K. van der Byl, had procured 51% of the voting shares in the commercial RTV channel and had placed government supporters on the board of the independent RBC. He was also able to count on the support of Benson, who used his propaganda skills to argue that the Rhodesians were facing a life-or-death battle against anything which smacked of Communism.

> It is the spiritual and intellectual foundation of what is commonly known as Leftism or Liberalism. Hence, in exactly the same way that the fight against pneumonia is inseparable from a fight against colds and influenza, so is the fight against Communism inseparable from the fight against Liberalism. The war against Communism is ultimately a religious war in which the very thing which makes life worth living is at stake and without which all the material welfare in the world is so much dead fruit . . .

Not everyone was taken in by the propaganda. Notable supporters of the nationalist cause included the former prime minister Garfield Todd, his wife Grace and daughter Judy, who were kept under house arrest on their farm at Hokuni; but the use of disinformation became such an important element of government policy that people in Salisbury would say with no little exasperation: 'We're all members of the Mushroom Club – we're kept in the dark and fed on horseshit!'

With a successful election under Smith's belt and having secured the backing of the white community, the movement towards a unilateral declaration of independence (UDI) became irresistible. Britain would not shift from its position of support for majority rule, while Rhodesia continued to believe that Whitehall was intent on meddling in the country's domestic affairs. In a last-ditch attempt to heal the breach, Wilson travelled to Salisbury in October 1965 for talks with an increasingly intransigent Rhodesian government. Of all Britain's imperial initiatives, this was perhaps the most futile. UDI had almost become a test of Rhodesian virility and it soon became clear that Smith's government could never agree to all of the so-called five principles which enshrined British policy. It also became apparent that they would never agree to a referendum on the acceptability or otherwise of any independence constitution.

Unfortunately the talks were overtaken by farce. At one point, Wilson lost his temper at the treatment meted out to Sithole and Nkomo when they were brought out of detention to join the discussions in Salisbury. Finding that they had been kept in a hot police van and denied food, the British prime minister 'saw red'.

> I told the Governor that if in half an hour from the time I was speaking Sithole and his colleagues were not sitting down to a three-course meal, the menu of which I had personally approved and which would be supervised by my own staff – then I would take a hand. I would personally lead all my staff into the streets of Salisbury, visit every café and snack bar and with our money – I flourished my wallet – we would ourselves buy enough food and would feed my visitors in Government House. What was more, every one of the thousand pressmen and television reporters from Britain, America and the whole free world would be there to see.

The threat worked and the African leaders were given a good lunch, but that was not the end of Wilson's culinary misfortunes. During an official dinner at Smith's residence, the British party was treated to a succession of smutty after-dinner stories including a ribald performance from the expatriate aristocrat the Duke of Montrose. Known in Rhodesia as Lord Graham, he was on the far-right of the Rhodesian Front party and a committed supporter of UDI who hoped to be appointed the country's 'regent' in succession to the British Governor. Wilson made no attempt to disguise his distaste and later spoke witheringly of Rhodesia as 'that land-locked introvert community'; but despite the tensions which surrounded the negotiations, he did come close to solving the deadlock. At a late-night meeting in Smith's house, agreement was almost reached on the creation of a Royal Commission which would make recommendations on the

constitutional issue but this foundered on the question of acceptability, not just to the whites but also to the Africans. For Smith,
this was the last straw.

> Harold Wilson said to me, he said it to me in my house here, you
> and I, Ian, we can easily come to an agreement, but that's not the
> point. What you have to do is to give me an agreement that I can
> sell to the rest of the world and especially to the OAU. But I said,
> Harold, you're telling me that I've got to give you an agreement
> that you can sell to a bunch of Communists? And you're also telling
> me – and this is contrary to what you told me before – you want
> an agreement that is not necessarily the best one for Rhodesia but
> one that will help you? He said, that's a fact of life, my friend.
>
> Contrary to what a lot of people think, I got on better with
> Harold Wilson than with a lot of conservatives because although
> our philosophies were different he was comparatively honest.

Wilson flew back to London on 30 October – as his car drove
through Salisbury, he was amused to see a banner demanding
'Home Rule for Scotland' – and just under a fortnight later, on
11 November, Rhodesia declared UDI with a stirring proclamation whose words deliberately echoed America's declaration of
independence some two hundred years earlier. Within hours,
the Governor, Sir Humphrey Gibbs, symbolically dismissed
Smith's government; but this information never reached the
Rhodesian public because of the strict press censorship introduced by van der Byl.

> I tried to get as much control of the media as was possible. I believed
> that the media should be brought under control because it's largely
> inhabited by people of the Left, the sort of liberal-leaning or social-
> ist philosophy which is the forerunner of Soviet expansionism. You
> get the liberal, and behind the liberal comes the Communist.
> Therefore I did what I could to try and discipline the thing.

This amounted to imposing additional controls on radio and
television and supervising the choice of political news which
appeared in the country's main newspapers: in time, the

country's news media were used for propaganda purposes and during the 1970s several foreign correspondents, including Niesewand, were deported from Rhodesia for breaking the increasingly draconian censorship laws. Other changes were not as dramatic or far-reaching. As had been widely expected, Britain introduced some modest economic sanctions, but these had little impact on the Rhodesian way of life and to begin with there were few shortages of absolute necessities. Even when they became more stringent, to include an oil embargo, the Rhodesians managed to continue importing fuel through Mozambique. In the first stages the sanctions were imposed by Britain alone, but in 1966 the mandatory provisions of the UN's Chapter VII were invoked to allow the Royal Navy to use force to prevent tankers delivering oil to the port of Beira where the vital pipeline stretched into Rhodesia. Although the 'Beira Patrol' was not particularly effective, there was considerable resentment within Rhodesia that Britain had referred the matter to the United Nations.

> Rhodesians felt bitter when the family quarrel was taken to the UN by Harold Wilson – a disgraceful act. The UN contains enemies of Britain as well as our friends and they, the enemies, came to have a say in our affairs. Wilson both misjudged the people and failed to understand our problems. He told our chiefs that they, like the House of Lords, had become an anachronism. Nothing could be further from the truth, the chiefs had spiritual duties as well as acting as arbitrators and judges, their functions were not solely administrative. In fact, Shona chiefs made few decisions. There had to be a consensus of the views of elders and advisers before a chief made a decision, he was the voice of the council, matters which Whitehall and Wilson neither knew nor wanted to know.

It was a familiar argument: the British did not understand the Rhodesian way of doing things and were unduly swayed by unfriendly organizations such as the United Nations or the Organization for African Unity. An experienced African colonial servant, H.E. Sumner, was Provincial Commissioner of

Victoria Province and he believed that the sting could have been taken out of the crisis if Britain had been prepared to give the chiefs a greater role. Like many others in Rhodesia, he believed that they spoke for their people and were more representative of the African point of view than the new nationalist leaders. Ever since the famous *indaba* of 1897 when Rhodes had parleyed with the Matabele leaders in the Matopos Hills to persuade them to end their rebellion, the chiefs had been central to the country's administration and Smith's government wanted to maintain the partnership. However, most nationalists regarded the chiefs as little more than paid stooges who owed their position, power and authority to the Smith regime.

One chief paid a high price for standing up for his people's rights. At the time of UDI, there was a dispute over land and labour in the Eastern Highlands involving the Tangwena tribe. When Chief Rekayi Tangwena refused to sign a new agreement which would declare specified areas to be 'European', he was deposed and the local District Commissioner removed his official red robe, white pith helmet and neck chain and his people were forcibly evicted from their tribal areas. Many crossed over into Mozambique and when the guerrilla war against the Smith regime began in the 1970s Chief Rekayi became both a symbol of resistance and a source of encouragement to the fighters.

The Smith regime only wanted chiefs of their choice so that they could become his puppets. Smith wanted chiefs who accepted money offers since these people would not stand to oppose the government's policies. Instead they would connive with the government.

The regime wanted chiefs who did not know their political rights, those who during the liberation war would locate the freedom fighters' bases so they could be bombed. Certain chiefs did this because they were sell-outs. They were puppet chiefs. All those chiefs have been used by the regime at the expense of their own people. That is why I had to reject all the government's offers like a girl who rejects a boy's advances at first sight and outright.

At the time of the evictions, Brigadier Sam Putterill, head of the country's armed forces, resigned after warning that the policy would only alienate the Tangwena people and that it would create a security problem along the eastern border. His warning went unheeded and the refusal to take advice was typical of a regime which was becoming increasingly intolerant and authoritarian. To Smith and his closest colleagues, though, single-mindedness was required in a country which was fighting for its survival in a hostile world.

> Morale was incredible. Rhodesia was the most united country this world has ever seen, with people charged emotionally to fight for their country and to protect what they believed in, to work over-time without asking for anything in return. It was an incredible nation. It's difficult to describe – you know, it might sound as if one was blowing one's trumpet – but the people who came here and saw what was happening in Rhodesia likened our army to the Israelis'. They said, there isn't a better army in the world from a handful of people like this who can stand up to such incredible pressure. We didn't have what the Israelis had with the most powerful country in the world as its chief backer and supplier. We didn't have a friend in the world but we held on and got stronger, our economy expanded.

With the passing of time, though, that sense of purpose was to turn into intransigence. Attempts to resolve the problem were held on British warships in the Mediterranean – HMS *Tiger* in 1966 and HMS *Fearless* in 1968 – but these broke down on the conditions required for a return to legal rule. As Peter Niesewand saw it, 'they [the Rhodesian people] were too busy refighting the Battle of Britain; basically good people, honestly unaware that this time they were on the wrong side'. Even so, the battle of Rhodesia's survival, albeit as an illegally independent nation, was to last fifteen years and during that time it was to prosper. In spite of the sanctions, the economy boomed and the white population actually increased: by the mid-1970s, it stood at 275,000 and there was no shortage of would-be immigrants. And despite the increasingly dangerous security situation, young men from Britain still flocked to join the country's police, the British South Africa Police Regiment. With the closing of Rhodesia House in London in 1965, the regiment experienced some problems in recruiting from Britain – its traditional supply of manpower – but adventurous young men like 'R' were still prepared to make the effort.

By that time I was pretty determined I was leaving the UK and that Africa was the place I was coming to. I was actually corresponding with a couple of chaps with whom I'd been at school and they certainly encouraged me to persist. So I then wrote to police general headquarters in Salisbury and they said, fine, if you're interested we're actually forming a squad – giving a date in mid-1967 – get yourself over here. I'd really committed myself mentally, the family were aware that I was on the move. By the time the final offer was made, June-ish, I only had two months to sort myself out, get all the inoculations and so on. I came out by South African Airways, all round the edge of the African coast because no one wanted the South Africans flying over them, landing at all those funny little places and then across country to Rhodesia.

Like most young men, 'R' was little interested in the political situation. To him and many others, service in Rhodesia offered an outdoor life, sport and adventure; but he did notice that there was still a sense of loyalty to the British Crown – the Union Flag was flown and the Queen Mother remained the regiment's colonel-in-chief. That sense of unity and loyalty helped to defuse the idea that Rhodesia had engaged in an illegal rebellion and in the first years of UDI the Rhodesian administration backed Smith and helped to maintain a national sense of purpose. Even when the country became a republic in 1969, the links with Britain remained strong: as 'R' points out, most white Rhodesians had family connections in Britain.

Let's put it like this. There were Rhodesians who fought and fell in the First World War; there were Rhodesians who fought and fell in the Second World War; and if a third had come along they would have flocked to the standard again and that's all there is to it. The fight that ensued, it wasn't a rebellion against the Crown as it was portrayed in some quarters, it never crossed anybody's mind that we were doing anything that was going to sever our ties with the UK.

Originally, the British South African Police was more of a military formation than a police force; by 1965, it had changed to a police rank structure but as the unrest continued it became once more a paramilitary organization which worked in tandem with Rhodesia's armed forces. In that role it was to face its severest test. By 1972 the sporadic violence had escalated into a full-blown guerrilla war, when mainly Shona ZANU fighters of the Zimbabwe African National Liberation Army (ZANLA), operating from bases in Mozambique, attacked white farms in the Centenary farming district north-east of Salisbury. Earlier, the armed struggle had centred on the Zambezi valley where Matabele guerrillas fighting under the aegis of the Zimbabwe Peoples' Revolutionary Army (ZIPRA) had crossed over the border from Zambia. However, according to Ellert, this had been a 'defiant yet futile show of force'.

> The Rhodesians considered 1967 and 1968 as happy hunting days . . . Members of the Security Forces reckoned that it was a jolly good war and patrols regularly netted a good bag of terrs (the Rhodesian abbreviation for terrorists). It was common, during those years, to see groups of soldiers and policemen gathered at the popular Makuti Motel overlooking the Zambezi valley, drinking cold beers and boasting of their exploits as their vehicles with the dead bodies of the guerrillas stood waiting outside.

All that was to change with incursions from Mozambique in the mid-1970s. Although the Rhodesian security forces were able to retaliate with a series of formidable counter-insurgency operations, the guerrillas built up a bedrock of widespread support amongst the local population. Not only did this hamper the work of the security forces in picking up information about the guerrillas' movements, but as one district commissioner admitted, 'the effect of the war was to bring our work in the rural areas to a standstill'. Amongst the measures introduced to meet the threat, the most unpopular was the eviction of villagers into protected villages ('PVs') or 'keeps': between 1973 and 1978, over three-quarters of a million people were moved in this way, mainly from the border area. For them it was a humiliating experience but, as van der Byl explained to parliament, as the war became dirtier so too did the tactics have to change.

> If villagers harbour terrorists and terrorists are found running about in villages, naturally they will be bombed and destroyed in any manner which the commander on the spot considers to be desirable in the suitable prosecution of a successful campaign . . . Where the civilian population involves itself with terrorism, then somebody is bound to get hurt and one can have little sympathy for those who are mixed up with terrorists when finally they received the wrath of the security forces.

One reason for the increased ferocity of the fighting in 1972 was the failure of the last best chance for a peaceful solution to the question of Rhodesian independence. The year before, Smith had negotiated a new agreement with Douglas-Home – now Foreign Secretary in Edward Heath's Conservative government – which accepted the principle of majority rule based on the 1969 republican constitution. Predictably, it was denounced as a sell-out by both the Labour opposition in Britain and by nationalists throughout Africa, but the deal did contain an important blocking mechanism: Britain had to be satisfied that the arrangements for independence were 'acceptable to the Rhodesian people as a whole'. A commission of enquiry was set up under the chairmanship of the distinguished judge Lord Pearce and most people, Smith included, thought that it would find enough evidence to cement the agreement.

In this respect they were to be sorely disappointed. The hitherto unfocused nationalist political support harnessed its energies behind Bishop Abel Muzorewa, the leader of the recently created African National Congress and the result was a decisive rejection of the agreement by Rhodesia's black population. When Pearce reported in May 1972, he concluded that 'the people of Rhodesia as a whole do not regard the proposals as acceptable as a basis for independence'. For the whites who claimed to 'know their blacks' it was a cruel blow and there were many in the administration who believed that the British commissioners had been given biased, even untrustworthy, information. When they visited Victoria Falls, H.E. Sumner was called to the famous hotel to meet the commissioners, who included two former African governors, Sir Maurice Dorman (Sierra Leone) and Sir Glyn Jones (Malawi). The meeting was not a success; Sumner was dismayed to find the table 'a-swill with beer and cigarette ends' and that there was little privacy.

> Oh God, we had a fight. I told them what I thought of them. Said something about the agricultural slump of Africa. Little Glyn Jones said, 'Did you know I was governor there?' I said, 'I do indeed. You have nothing to be proud about.' He said, 'I was proud of my command.' We had a real set-to.
>
> I didn't like Glyn Jones and His Lordship may be a very fine man, no doubt, but I disliked him. I ended up by saying that if you dare invade I shall have the greatest pleasure in putting you in the sights of my rifle and killing you both.

For Sumner, a colonial administrator who believed that his efforts were 'directed towards civilizing rural Africans through schools, improved agriculture, better stock farming, irrigation, better health facilities, local government, women's clubs and so on', Pearce's findings represented the voice of a disgruntled minority. To him, and to many others – not all of whom supported the Rhodesian Front – it seemed clear that the Africans had told Pearce and his colleagues only what they had wanted to hear and the silent majority had been ignored. In Britain, too, many Conservatives were dismayed by the report. Not only did they want a solution but they felt that it was morally repugnant to continue sanctions against Rhodesia. Smith was fully aware of the split in Conservative thinking and he believed that Heath was forced to appease his party's liberal wing as the price for taking Britain into the European Economic Community.

> I came to an agreement with Alec Home and we signed it here in Salisbury which would have been the dead right one. But that was upstaged because Ted Heath was going into the Common Market and he bargained that away with the British Liberals. We had agreements and if those had been accepted they could have worked but it was never a plan which was just going to entrench the white man. That's how the case has been twisted against us. Every agreement we made was towards bringing the blacks along that bit more quickly. The British civil servants and our civil servants had worked out that under [Douglas-Home's] agreement blacks would have been in the majority between ten and fifteen years so it was there. But the world believed that Smith was trying to entrench white supremacism.

In fact, taking Britain into Europe in 1973 was the crowning achievement of Heath's government and he had always been prepared to leave the Rhodesian negotiations to Douglas-Home. It is also true that Heath felt little affection for the Commonwealth and certainly did not see it as a viable alternative to the European Community. Comforting though it might be for Smith to believe that the failure of the Pearce Commission lay in political opportunism, it remains valid that no agreement could have stuck without African support and that the test of acceptability had not been passed. In any case, whatever his failings as a prime minister, Heath rarely interfered in the work undertaken by his political colleagues. When the Pearce Commission delivered its verdict, the British government was bound to accept it, and in so doing won the plaudits of many Africans. As Miles Hudson, head of the Conservative Research Department, put it, 'Britain had a fleeting and unusual moment of glory in African and progressive circles'.

★

The Pearce Commission, though, was a turning-point. The guerrilla war intensified with the attacks in the north-east from Mozambique where ZANLA commanders had linked up with FRELIMO guerrillas who were engaged in their own armed struggle against the Portuguese. By this time, the two armies had their own bases and tactical areas of operation. ZIPRA operated from Zambia against targets in western Matabeland, while ZANLA used Mozambique as its base for operations in the eastern and southern provinces. And as Rhodesian intelligence quickly discovered, they were well armed and supported: ZANLA received arms from Yugoslavia, Romania and China, while the bulk of ZIPRA's support came from the Soviet Union and East Germany. The struggle was known as the 'Chimurenga' war after the armed uprising of 1896 and recruits were given special Chimurenga names such as Teruai Ropa ('Shed Blood') or Ropa Rinopfuka ('Blood demands retribution').

I remember when I first saw the comrades. I had heard about them from so many people that I was bored stiff. They were taking so long to come to our area. One day I was going home in a bus and all of a sudden these armed men boarded the bus. I thought, these can't be the soldiers, they are not in uniform, and they don't look or act like soldiers, anyway. So they checked us all and then they exchanged seats with the driver and started driving the bus into the township and then one of them started making the people sing. Everybody was singing as the bus was driving. It was so exciting. It was like all that I had ever heard about being with the comrades but never thought would finally happen to me.

Irene Mahamba took the Chimurenga name of 'Ropa Rinopfuka' because she believed that the situation in Rhodesia 'really demanded that blood be spilled'. As she suffered from polio, she was never able to fulfil her dream of using a gun and worked instead in ZANU's research unit. Others, like Tendai Mujoma who operated under the name of 'Comrade Zeppelin', were given training both in weapons and in psychological

253

warfare. Both armies soon found that it was not enough just to attack white Rhodesian targets, they had to win the support of the local population. Usually this was done by intimidating the tribal elders or brutally murdering 'sell-outs', but the 'comrades' or 'boys' – as the guerrillas were known to black Africans – also made use of the traditional *pungwe* meeting, a Shona word meaning 'all through the night'.

> We would go into an area, study the problems in that particular area, and then teach those people about their problems, and how we can solve them by fighting the enemy. You see, in the north-east, where I was operating, many people were far away from the good farming areas, so we told them that their land was very poor, since it is usually very hot and the soil is non-productive. So we would tell them, 'It's you, the people of Zimbabwe, of this area, who should have been in the areas where there are those farmers who are getting a lot from the rich land. They've thrown you out of the rich land so that you don't get anything', and of course, then the people would like very much to have that land which they did not have. In fact, overall, the land question was our major political weapon. The people responded to it.

The winning over of the local population was a key process in building support from ZIPRA and ZANLA and the security forces made great efforts to counter it. Initially they were given powers to impose collective fines or to move villagers suspected of harbouring terrorists into protected areas. Later, as the war intensified, they developed largely successful counter-insurgency tactics including the creation of Joint Operations Commands (JOCs) to co-ordinate police and army activities, the creation of Operational Areas and the use of élite units such as the Selous Scouts in pseudo-terrorist activities to 'turn' captured guerrillas.

Named after the nineteenth-century big-game hunter Frederick Selous, the Selous Scouts were officially a multiracial tracker unit commanded by Lieutenant-Colonel Ron Reid-Daly. Ninety per cent of its personnel were blacks drawn from the Rhodesian African Rifles, although white territorial soldiers were used later in the conflict for raids into terrorist camps in Zambia and Mozambique. Whatever the colour of their skin, though, all 'troopies' were hand-picked, following a rigorous selection process, and they shared many of the physical and mental attributes of the SAS. The white population regarded them as supermen and they became an important element in the security forces' counter-insurgency war. African nationalists regarded them somewhat differently: in their eyes, the Scouts were little more than desperadoes who were guilty of committing atrocities or stage-managing massacres and blaming them on ZANLA or ZIPRA.

Somewhere in between the two extremes, the Selous Scouts operated as one of the most effective counter-insurgency formations in modern warfare. That they did employ 'dirty tricks' is indisputable – so did ZIPRA and ZANLA. The war against the African guerrilla forces was a sordid one in which compromise was impossible and both sides employed tactics in which the end justified the means and which were usually excused by military necessity. While operating in the bush, the Scouts went to great lengths to disguise themselves by blacking their faces, growing beards and wearing guerrilla uniforms. In this guise they would approach suspected villages and, having pinpointed the opposition, would then call in other forces to engage them. In the early days of the war their primary task was to capture guerrillas and persuade them to change sides, a process which had to be done within twenty-four hours of capture.

The technique of turning or inducing a captured guerrilla to co-operate with the Scouts was achieved in many ways. Firstly he was made aware of the hopelessness of his own situation – death was the only alternative. Secondly, he was put together with other 'captures', some of whom he would recognize from training-camps in China, North Korea, Tanzania or Mozambique. They would explain the many benefits of working with the Scouts – these included a standard kill-bonus of $1,000. Thirdly, the African members of the Selous Scouts subjected the prospective recruit to a crash course in political re-orientation. The turning process was often achieved within twenty-four hours and many successful kills were recorded when a Selous Scouts gang moved into a village using the recent capture to authenticate them and request a guide to the nearest resident group.

As a police officer in Salisbury, Ellert never served in the field but as a disinterested observer his assessment is near the mark. As the war progressed, this élite unit continued to work in close association with the police Special Branch as well as the army's SAS and the Free Force Commando of the Rhodesian Light Infantry who were flown in on French-built Alouette helicopters. One of their most successful conventional operations came in March 1974, when they discovered a large gathering of guerrillas near Ruwani School in the northern Kandeya Tribal Trust Land. Having made the contact, they called in the Free Force Commando from the Mount Darwin base and during the dawn attack fifteen guerrillas were killed and many others captured and turned. It was a classic 'punch-up' – to use the security forces' argot – and in that role the Scouts performed a useful military function. But the fact that they were an autonomous unit with their own budget and chain of command meant that they were free to evolve their own tactics, some of which were not only unconventional but illegal. (These included raids into Mozambique and Zambia, the use of booby traps in radios supplied to the guerrillas and political assassination.) As Ellert concluded in his study of the bush war, the Scouts 'became thoroughly intoxicated with [their] absolute power over life and death and in many ways ran completely out of control.'

None the less, the subsequent notoriety surrounding the Selous Scouts cannot disguise the fact that the war waged between the security forces and ZANLA and ZIPRA was a bloody, low-intensity conflict in which neither side fought with kid gloves. Contrary to popular belief, though, alleged atrocities were always investigated by the senior police officers from the CID and in the early 1970s the Rhodesian security forces still believed that they could contain the incursions and defeat the guerrillas.

> We really thought that our input was absolutely essential. We were given little blocks of the country to look after and you really put your balls on the block. You got out and about and you were left to your own devices to gather intelligence about what the opposition was up to. But throughout, I and my contemporaries thought that what we were doing was right. It might sound naïve, but up until the eleventh hour we never saw ourselves as losing.
>
> The hierarchy would come round on a regulat basis and say, well done lads, you're doing a great job, going forward, don't worry about a thing, old Smithie's going to do this or that. And don't worry, the Brits don't want these bastards in any more than we do. That's the sort of bullshit we used to get.

Much of that confidence was badly shaken after April 1974, when a *coup d'état* in Lisbon brought an end to Portugese power in Mozambique and Angola. Not only did this turn of events open Rhodesia's eastern border to further incursions of ZANLA, but it also exposed South Africa. Ever since UDI, the South Africans had been prepared to support Rhodesia, not out of any fellow feeling – many Afrikaners still resented the British white-settler presence north of the Limpopo – but because along with Angola and Mozambique it formed a line of defence against the forces of nationalism elsewhere in the continent. The *coup* in Portugal changed all that and in 1975 the South African President John Vorster began a series of diplomatic moves to encourage Smith to bring the guerrilla war to an end. Using President Kaunda as a go-between, the South African policy was to encourage the unification of the guerrilla groups to form a united front in discussions with the Rhodesian government. The nationalist leaders, Mugabe, Sithole and Nkomo were released from detention and the first discussions took place in a railway carriage on the Victoria Falls bridge in August 1975. It ended without agreement but Smith realized it was a turning point, that without South African support he would have to find another means of survival.

In fact it was one of the tragedies that it was South Africa, it was Vorster, who pulled the plug on us. We had concrete information – our chaps were talking to terrorist leaders who said we've had enough, we're tired of the bush, we're hungry, we're cold. It was 1975 but then Vorster went off on this campaign of winning the blacks to his side. And in the end we had to do it or else. But we were absolutely on top of the terrorist war, our kill rate was high and that sort of thing and they wanted to come in.

We should never have had that Victoria Falls agreement, because that set us back, but it was Vorster's brainchild. He wanted to save Africa and he wanted to have Kaunda and Nyerere and in exchange they were going to recognize South Africa. He told me that – what a fool. They played into the hands of Nkomo and Mugabe, who said to the terrorists, look, we're winning, Vorster's on our side and without Vorster Smith hasn't got a hope. So they pulled themselves together.

The odds are that the security forces were on top of the situation in 1974, but the length of the border with Mozambique and the arming of ZANLA by eastern-bloc countries meant that the war could only be contained but never won. By 1976 targets were being hit in Salisbury and the guerrillas were still winning over the African population to their side. To meet the new threat, the government called up older reservists and increased taxation and the security forces stepped up their activities along the country's borders. Special Investigation Sections were also established to identify and turn known terrorists before calling in the air force to hit the active service groups.

We were going forward like a bloody train then, we were having tremendous success and people were starting to sit up and take notice. Guys were coming down from Salisbury and asking, how are you managing this? Well, because we were doing it with a handful of guys. We were using police investigation methods and using all this info that we had already accumulated and we would say, right, we're actually going after commander so-and-so. We know this about him and we know that about him. The captured terrs would sit in as well and everybody would have their say about how we should go about this and we'd pull each others' legs. One of them would say, Agh, we're not going because that man is too strong, he's got RPG7s [anti-tank grenade launcher]. And we'd say, don't worry about that because we're not going to actually confront him, we'll pinpoint him, the aircraft will get him. Ah well, they'd say, then that's all right.

After the war, Jerry Mtethwa, a ZIPRA commander, agreed that the deployment of this type of unit 'seriously disrupted' the guerrillas; but for all their successes in the field, 'R' and his colleagues were fighting a losing battle. It was not just that the actual winning of the guerrilla war was probably beyond their resources, but there were increasing international demands for a political solution. Alarmed by the extent of Soviet and Chinese support for the guerrilla armies and fearing that Communist involvement in the internal war in Rhodesia could create a 'domino' effect in the countries of central and southern Africa, the US secretary of state Henry Kissinger entered the fray. Pressure was put on Vorster to cut back on South African military support and the leaders of Zambia and Tanzania were invited to help unite the various Zimbabwean opposition groups. (On 8 October 1976, ZANU and ZAPU had combined in a Patriotic Front, following talks in Maputo, Mozambique.)

During the course of a series of fleeting visits to Africa, Kissinger told Smith that the game was up and that he would have to come to a political settlement. In reply, the Rhodesian leader argued that the west should bolster his country against the threat of Soviet expansionism, but his pleas fell on deaf ears. Eventually he agreed to a two-year transition to majority rule but this was blocked by the PF leadership because the key posts in the new administration would be confined to whites. Following a conference in Geneva, the talks broke down and for the next two years the Americans and the British attempted in vain to reach a constitutional solution which would suit all sides. Meanwhile, the war intensified. Rhodesian security forces made raids into Zambia and Mozambique to hit guerrilla bases – for which they were condemned by the UN – and ZIPRA caused equal opprobrium by shooting down two Air Rhodesia Viscount passenger aircraft with heat-seeking surface-to-air missiles. In the first incident, ten passengers survived the crash but were murdered on the ground; in the second, all fifty-nine passengers on a flight from Kariba were killed.

During this period of so-called *détente*, there was considerable war-weariness on all sides. The whites wanted a return to normality and many had already decided to leave Rhodesia; the guerrilla forces could see no way to final victory; and the countries which supported them, Zambia and Mozambique, were becoming disillusioned because of the cost to their own economies. In a last-ditch attempt to solve the crisis, Smith embarked on an internal settlement in November 1977 by which he reached agreement on majority rule with the moderate leaders Muzorewa and Sithole. Under what was called a 'victory for moderation', the whites would retain twenty-eight out of a hundred seats in parliament as well as control of the security forces and the national exchequer. Following an interim coalition, elections were held in April 1979 with Muzorewa being brought to power: on 31 May the new state of Rhodesia-Zimbabwe came into being. The move was condemned by the UN and Muzorewa's regime went unrecognized by the world community. But by then another player, Margaret Thatcher, had entered the scene and she was determined to solve the long-lasting Rhodesian crisis once and for all.

Elected prime minister of the incoming Conservative government in May 1979, she and her Foreign Secretary Lord Carrington abandoned the old US–British negotiations and called all parties to London for a constitutional conference.

Deploying a mixture of tenacity and brinkmanship, Carrington chaired the Lancaster House conference to a successful outcome on 21 December. Under the terms of the agreement, Muzorewa stood down and a British governor, Lord Soames, would take charge of the country in preparation for 'free and fair elections'; a ceasefire came into being and a multinational Commonwealth force under British command would be deployed to monitor ZIPRA and ZANLA forces at agreed assembly points. Carrington's triumph owed as much to his own diplomatic virtuosity as it did to a general consensus amongst all the parties that a settlement had to be brokered, whatever the cost.

It took courage for a Conservative government to dismiss a pro-western prime minister (Muzorewa) and risk the election of a pro-Marxist contender (Mugabe), but during that transition period the general feeling in Britain and white Rhodesia was that victory would go either to the bishop or to ZAPU's Nkomo. By then, Smith was Minister without Portfolio and although he was still influential the discussions were being led by Lieutenant-General Peter Walls. To this day, Smith believes the army commander and his police and military colleagues were duped by Whitehall's blend of sophistication and guile.

> Carrington told us at Lancaster House – and so did Margaret Thatcher – that my worries were unfounded because when I told them that Mugabe was going to win under that plan they said, no, no, no. The whole plan is to ensure that he doesn't win. All our evidence is to the effect that the next government in Rhodesia is going to be a government of Nkomo, Muzorewa and Smith and, therefore, a Communist government just doesn't have a hope. We were promised that. They promised Walls that. They manipulated Walls who was a soldier and who didn't know anything about politics; they just twisted him around their little finger.

What this plan might have been has never been revealed but there is ample oral evidence of the existence of a number of schemes to prevent Mugabe winning the election. By then, he had emerged as the public enemy number one, a potential

Marxist dictator who would turn Rhodesia into a one-party Communist state with Soviet support. Having returned to the country early in 1980 – to a tumultuous welcome in the Highfields township – he fought his election under the banner of ZANU (PF), Nkomo having registered the name Patriotic Front for ZAPU. Inevitably, perhaps, with so many ZANLA and ZIPRA fighters gathered together at the assembly points there were undeniable allegations of intimidation. This was contrary to the spirit of the Lancaster House agreement and by the beginning of February Soames had sufficient evidence that intimidation in five out of eight provinces was so bad that the elections were in danger of being invalidated.

This led Smith to believe that Soames would either ban ZANU (PF) or disqualify the results where there was evidence of intimidation. With Mugabe sidelined, the way would be open for his Rhodesian Front party to form a coalition with Muzorewa or Nkomo and right until the last minute Smith believed that the British would provide this solution.

I told Soames in Government House ten days before the election, well, I think you've got over a thousand affidavits confirming intimidation by Mugabe and his people, what are you going to do? Oh, we've got a plan, they'll never come in, we're going to disqualify them in those three provinces where there is the most support for them. If that happens, Muzorewa will get a majority. Don't worry. I said, there's intimidation in every province in the country, why those there? Because we can get away with that, the rest of the world will accept it but they won't accept it if we disqualify them in all. Three days before the election I went back to him and said, are we still on course? No, he said, I've had a message from Peter [Carrington], to say forget it. We will not be able to sell that to the OAU. So, forget it. What do you mean, forget it? You're telling me you're not going to honour the agreement? Well, he said, that's my message. I had a certain amount of sympathy for Soames, he wasn't in the driving-seat, he was taking his orders direct from Carrington in London.

In fact, it would have been impossible for Soames to have acted in this way. Not only would the rest of the world have refused to accept the outcome, but Rhodesia itself would have been plunged into unimaginable violence. This was accepted by the Rhodesian Joint Operations Command who advised against the banning of ZANU (PF) and the die was cast. When the elections were held on 21 February, Mugabe was the outright winner with his party taking fifty-seven out of the available 100 seats. As the results began to emerge, many Rhodesians, including Walls, still wanted the election to be invalidated because they could see what was happening to the ordinary voters. At the election points, security forces personnel reported that Mugabe's supporters were shouting 'AK' to electors – a hint that they should not forget the power of the guerrilla's assault rifle when casting their vote – and members of the Youth Wing were active in coercing tribesmen in ZANLA's old operational areas. However, no action was taken, much to the fury of some of the upper echelons of the security forces who still believed that Mugabe had to be kept out of power – however illegal the means.

> The feeling was still the same bullshit. They would pull it out of the fire at the last minute. The Brits, MI5, MI6, you name it, were going to bamboozle all these bastard Communists. Somebody would put pressure on Samora [Machel, president of Mozambique] or whoever was necessary. We were all getting the story, look, if it's necessary we'll actually rig the ballot. And we were practising. We were buggering around doing this sort of thing. There was a house in Salisbury, top-secret Special Branch where we had copies of the ballot papers properly marked – and some properly spoiled – and we had practices as to how we were going to switch them.

Other schemes included two attempts on Mugabe's life, the destruction of the pro-ZANU (PF) newspaper *Moto* and the planting of poisonous snakes at ZANU (PF) rallies. The Rhodesian SAS also had plans to stage a military *coup* by hitting

the headquarters of ZANU (PF) in Salisbury and massacring the
ZANLA and ZIPRA fighters at the assembly points, but
although eight Russian-built tanks were smuggled into the
country nothing ever came of the plot. Later it was widely
believed that the existence of these plans was stage-managed by
senior Rhodesian officers to convince hardliners that 'something
was being done'.

Despite the tensions produced by the election, Mugabe built
up an unstoppable strength of support during the short campaign and the majority of the population swung behind him
either because they felt he was the real victor in the war or
because they were lured by the pledges made by his party.
(While serving as a Special Policeman, Sumner discovered that
the nationalists had promised every supporter ten acres of land,
twenty head of cattle, a free tractor and 'the white woman of
his choice'.) And there is little doubt, too, that intimidation also
accounted for ZANU (PF)'s triumph. On the other hand,
Mugabe's opponents were hardly devoid of support. Huge
amounts of money, much of it South African, were provided
for Muzorewa's campaign, which was run with professional
media and public relations advisers; but the electorate failed to
be impressed by the 'winners' slogan created for his UANC
party.

When it became clear that Mugabe had won, a sense of shock
and disbelief swept through the country's white community.
After some fifteen years of going it alone, they had to confront the reality that a multiracial society had arrived and that
they were now to be ruled by a black majority government
under a man whom their press had castigated as a 'black
Hitler'. The worst affected were the men and women of the
security forces who wondered if the long bush war had been
worth fighting. On the morning of 4 March when the results
were announced, 'R' was back at police headquarters in
Salisbury.

I hadn't heard the news when the results were coming out. I was in the office early and I looked across at a building which was being used by ZANU (PF) as an office and they unfurled a huge flag with a cockerel and various things on it. And I turned to a bloke next to me and said, what the fuck is this? Jesus Christ, what has happened?

And then we thought, well, Christ, we've still got the guys in position. We could hit the assembly points, there was a plan where we were going to hit these camps and take them out, but that was another of the damp squibs which never really came off the ground.

That day at lunch-time we all adjourned to a pub and got rat-arsed pissed and thought, well, what the fuck? We looked at each other and thought, well, what the fuck was it all about? Remember so and so? Well, he's dead, he's in a wheelchair, he's in a funny farm. Absolutely shattered. Shattered. We were shell-shocked, we just sort of wandered about Salisbury for the next six months in a state of shock, getting pissed as often as we could.

Many whites felt that way and made immediate preparations to leave the country for South Africa or Australia. It was an understandable reaction but as it turned out there was no blood-bath and, considering the intensity of the war, there were remarkably few recriminations. Far from being an avenging Marxist dictator or satanic fiend – both favourite white labels – Mugabe asked for a spirit of reconciliation, just as Kenyatta had done in Kenya fifteen years earlier. Not everyone believed him, but it was a start: before the election, he had been advised by Samora Machel not to make the same mistake he had made by expelling the whites from Mozambique in 1974. A month later, the message was repeated at the independence day celebrations which were held in the Rufaro stadium in Salisbury, shortly to be renamed Harare. In the presence of the Prince of Wales and other world leaders, the red, green and gold flag of Zimbabwe replaced the Union Flag and Robert Mugabe, reviled as a Communist terrorist leader, told his new nation that the 'wrongs of the past must be forgiven and forgotten'.

The following day, President Canaan Banana swore in the

new Cabinet, which contained white faces as well as black. After ninety years of white rule, the country claimed by Rhodes from Lobengula had finally passed back into African hands and Britain's colonial connection with the continent was at an end.

10

Aftermath

FOR A BRIEF interlude, independence seemed to work. The new African countries were hopeful and energetic places where committed people worked hard and where the old colonial infrastructure provided a much-needed base on which future prosperity and orderliness could be built. It was a honeymoon period which suggested that all would be for the best in the best of all possible worlds. Even sceptics were forced to admit that in most places a miracle of sorts had happened and that the transition from colony to independent country had been accomplished without undue rancour. Nigeria's wealth and administrative soundness made it a stable and self-confident democracy. Many white settlers had decided to throw in their lot with the new Kenya and its charismatic leader Jomo Kenyatta. Nkrumah regarded himself as an African role-model and became a highly respected international statesman; in 1963 the Organization for African Unity was created to provide a unified African political voice and he became one of Africa's leading international spokesmen. Even Zimbabwe, the last country to gain independence, prospered in its early years and whites who had feared for their lives decided to throw in their lot with the new regime.

Look, we weren't anti-Af, we weren't fighting Africans. We were fighting this bunch of Communist arseholes who wanted to destroy the civilized way of life we were used to. Two-thirds of the lads who fought alongside me were black guys. I mean, I relied on them, we walked into the bush at night, these guys on either side, we never thought twice about it. We'd come out of it and stop at the nearest store in the morning and have a coke and a bun. I'd buy, they'd drink: we'd have a laugh and a joke.

As a member of the security forces, 'R' might have been placed in an invidious position in Zimbabwe but the new country needed a civil infrastructure and some Rhodesian soldiers and policemen stayed on to join former ZIPRA and ZANLA opponents in the newly created Zimbabwe National Army. The same had been true in other parts of the old colonial empire in Africa. While many members of the Colonial Administrative Service were given appointments elsewhere, or took early retirement, others stayed on to serve the new regime, happy to exchange Whitehall for local African rule. In some areas it worked and civil servants or soldiers were able to make substantial contributions to the newly independent countries – in Kenya, John Trestrail noted that 'the most incredible thing is what can be achieved if people are prepared to work together'. Inevitably, though, their positions could only be temporary: few army officers remained in service in Zimbabwe beyond 1982 and in Kenya Colonel Glanville discovered that the rapid process of Africanization in the officer corps bred suspicion and an impatience to get on with the job themselves.

I think that the attitude between black and white was not so trusting as it had been in the past. They obeyed us – those that they liked – unreservedly. But I think some of the newer officers who had come out and went rather rapidly they didn't get to know and there wasn't the same closeness.

In Malawi, though, Dr Banda had made it a point of principle that white civil servants should be allowed to stay and that they would not be replaced until Africans were ready to take over the reins of power. Businessmen were also encouraged to stay on to take advantage of the new markets and there was no shortage of

British military advisers to help in the creation of the new defence forces. Both were to become growth areas although not always to the benefit of the new countries.

In the aftermath of independence, many of the new countries spent large amounts of money constructing modern armed forces. Not only did this place an unnecessary burden on national budgets but it was encouraged by the world's super-powers. With the world still gripped by the Cold War confrontation between the west and the Soviet Union and China, Africa became a happy hunting-ground for arms dealers. Eastern-bloc countries sold weaponry cheaply to the developing countries and also provided military instructors; in time, the ubiquitous AK-47 assault rifle was as mundane a sight as the transistor radio, and Mig military aircraft became commonplace in African skies. The west, too, took advantage of the perceived bonanza and British Military Advisory and Training Teams helped to create new armies formed from units as different as existing regiments such as the King's African Rifles or guerrilla forces such as ZANLA. Having fought with the former during the Second World War, Lieutenant-Colonel R.N. Boyd stayed on in Zambia to serve with a territorial battalion of the newly-formed Zambian Rifles.

> Two of the objects were to give the African confidence that there was an army presence . . . and the other thing was to encourage contact between black and white. And this, we found, was a mar-vellous way of doing it. Many of the Africans had had little contact with Europeans and the same applied the other way round. It's amazing how many of the Europeans' attitudes changed.

Boyd was fortunate. At independence, Zambia suffered a haem-orrhage of white officials and those who stayed were not always encouraged to remain in positions of authority. As happened in many other newly independent countries, a small and tightly-knit ruling élite emerged and under Kenneth Kaunda's leadership the administration drifted towards a one-party state backed up by efficient security forces. In 1964, neighbouring Kenya, Uganda and Tanganyika were rocked by military mutinies which required the intervention of British armed forces. Although the problems were solved and the leaderships of the countries survived the upheaval, the following year saw military *coups* taking place in the former French colonies of Dahomey, Central African Republic and Upper Volta. Suddenly it seemed that powerful armed forces might not always be a blessing as disgruntled military commanders, many trained at Sandhurst, decided to intervene in their countries' politics.

The first casualty in a former British holding was Ghana's Kwame Nkrumah. In the early years of independence he seemed to represent the future, an African leader capable of harnessing his country's wealth to make it a power for good in the world. But behind that international reputation and his pretensions to unite Africa, his domestic economic policies were disastrous. Vainglorious and hugely expensive schemes, such as the creation of a large modern international airline and the construction of huge conference centres, were bankrupting the country and even the lucrative cocoa industry was being run down. Increasingly cut off from reality and frightened of his own associates, Nkrumah cracked down on political opponents and, with Soviet help, strengthened the palace guard. By the early 1960s, those Europeans who had stayed on, such as the engineer W.C. Benson, could see that Nkrumah was a deeply unpopular man.

> I was standing with a manager of a vehicle assembly plant in the port of Tema one day and a young Ghanaian whom he knew well cycled up on his bicycle and started to pass the time of day with us. There were two Russian ships off-loading cement at this particular time. We were watching the operation and this young Ghanaian told us he was building his own home outside Tema but he was refusing to use this Russian cement because it didn't comply with

the British standards that we were used to having in Ghana. And he also said: 'By the way, we've had six years of this man now. Do you think the Queen will have us back?'

One of the many Scottish missionaries also stayed on in independent Ghana and although he considered that Nkrumah was a 'visionary' and 'a very pleasant man', he could understand the frustration felt by many ordinary people who were unable to share in the country's new wealth and political freedoms.

I think many of them looked back with a great deal of pleasure and nostalgia to British rule. When Nkrumah was deposed there were many occasions in which Africans, usually professional men, were so perturbed by what they saw was going on that they looked back with pleasure on the peaceful golden age.

There were demonstrations in Sekondi by the market women who are a very powerful section of Ghana's society. The Mammas were marching along the streets with placards saying BRING BACK THE BRITISH and WE LOVE THE QUEEN. They were roughly handled by Nkrumah's strong men and that was soon broken up.

With several variations, the question posed to the missionary and Benson was to be heard again and again in all the newly independent states. Life was better under British rule: when would the *bwanas* come back to restore order? In Ghana, though, as in several other places, it was not the Queen or the British government who forced change, but the army. In 1966 Nkrumah was deposed in a military *coup* while he was visiting President Ho Chi Minh in Hanoi and Ghana was destined to spend the next thirty years under military rule of one kind or another. A similar fate befell Uganda's Milton Obote, who was deposed in January 1971 while visiting the Commonwealth leaders conference in Singapore. Although his usurper, General Idi Amin, was welcomed as a saviour, he soon became feared as one of the most rapacious and iron-fisted dictators in Africa. Obote's supporters amongst the Acholi and Langi tribes were hunted down and the army was bolstered by northerners and Nubians who owed

Amin their loyalty. The following year, he expelled Uganda's 30,000-strong Asian community and the country rapidly descended into bankruptcy and anarchy. Amin was deposed in 1979, only to be replaced in a disputed election by an equally bloodthirsty Obote. Sanity did not return until 1986 when President Yoweri Musaveni came to power, having pledged to 'demystify the gun' and to return the deposed tribal leaders to power.

Equally dismaying was the fate which befell Nigeria. Plunged into a disastrous civil war following the secession of Biafra in 1967 it went on to endure several military dictatorships which failed to capitalize on the country's increasingly profitable oil economy. Corruption, lawlessness and nepotism were rife and the military leadership of General Sani Abacha caused grave international offence in November 1995 by executing nine Ogoni political activists, including the writer Ken Saro-Wiwa. Before that incident blackened its history, Nigeria had managed to live up to its promise of being Africa's 'sleeping giant' and on the diplomatic front it was an influential focus for African opinion during the negotiations for Zimbabwean independence and the ending of apartheid in South Africa. In fact, the country's powerful civil service remained in place throughout the disruption and the various military administrations were no more dictatorial than many other one-party states in Africa.

In Zambia, Kaunda remained in office until 1991; while Tanzania's Julius Nyerere did not step down from presidential office until 1985. In Zimbabwe, Robert Mugabe has held power since 1980, first as prime minister and then as president. Despite increasing provocation, though, whites continue to play a role and a disenchanted Ian Smith still lives in Harare with his memories and his regrets.

When the elections went Mugabe's way, I said, well of course, Smith, you were right and they were all wrong. They all said that I was wrong and they were all right but it proved the reverse. But what could I think? I'm a person who doesn't believe in bitterness and recrimination, I think it's a sterile thing and it blinds you to the truth. I had a very wise old father who used to talk to me like this and I've always believed it. He was a canny Scot with great breadth of wisdom. So I've never let it get on top of me. So I said we've got to make it work and make the most of it.

After independence, Smith continued to serve in the government before retiring from politics to farm in 1982. Initially amicable to Mugabe's policies, he grew disenchanted after proposals were introduced to create a one-party state and the once stable Rhodesian economy, with its rich agrarian sector, began to falter. Political opposition to Mugabe is negligible, national finances depend on loans from the World Bank and the International Monetary Fund and in 1994 inflation was running at 40%. As happened in several neighbouring countries, Zimbabwe failed to avoid internal civil strife, much of it based on age-old tribal rivalries: in 1982, around 20,000 ZAPU supporters were massacred by government forces in Matabeleland. All this was regretted by Smith.

Because of Communism, the country's gone down the drain. The blacks are worse off today than before he came in. The costs have escalated. I have people stopping me in the street saying, we can't feed our families. Why don't you tell Mugabe how to run the economy? You made a success of it. Well, I say, there's an easy answer. How can I tell him when he won't talk to me? Last year inflation was 40%: how can people keep up with that kind of escalation? The Rhodesian dollar used to be worth £1; today the Zimbabwe dollar is worth 7p.

Inevitably, perhaps, throughout Africa the breakdown in civil authority, the internecine wars, the executions of political opponents and the squandering of natural resources caused considerable heartache amongst the men and women who had served in Africa and who considered it in no small measure to be their second home. All too often it was felt that the process of independence had been pushed through too quickly and with

273

too little preparation. At Cambridge in the early 1930s, T.D. Thomson considered a career in the Indian Civil Service but having been told that he would 'work himself out of a job', he applied for the Colonial Service and was posted to Dowa in Nyasaland. Even in retirement, sixty years later, he still held to the view that Britain scuttled out of Africa – to the disadvantage of the people.

> I think the biggest mistake that we made was shrugging off the white man's burden. I thought that in another generation the Nyasa people might be capable of running their own affairs and I have had no occasion to change my mind over that. I think that half the trouble in a great deal of the world has been simply caused by the fact that we have run away from our responsibilities.

This is such a common theme amongst members of the Colonial Administrative Service that it does bear repetition. Wearied and impoverished by the Second World War and facing a future in which its global authority was being questioned, Britain was incapable of sustaining its world empire. No amount of subsidies or talk of the Commonwealth family could save it from the fact that it was slowly breaking up. As James Morris wryly expressed the mood in 1978, 'suddenly the imperial idea seemed not merely distasteful, but preposterous. It was like waking from a dream.' Although it is difficult to believe that the British could have acted otherwise and that to have held on to colonial control would only have created further difficulties, the feeling persists that Britain sold the colonies short and then suffered feelings of guilt about the whole practice of empire.

> Let's be quite honest and not shy and modest about this as we so often are nationally. The Scot and the Englishman out there who were doing government work or any kind of overseeing, usually put his heart into it and very often his life into it; and very often died out there and they put in years of jolly good, honest, straightforward, decent work. They made mistakes but they were not made out of wickedness and evil. They were only made out of ignorance

and accident. They did a damned good job and we have nothing at all to be ashamed of. In fact we built better than we knew out there and the African realized and appreciated it, and he appreciated the honesty. Now his own lads, his own politicians and bosses quite honestly used to line, used to feather their own nests.

Ron Hunston stayed on in Ghana until 1960 and his wife Cathy admits that 'until independence I really never thought of myself as an expatriate. Ghana was where you lived as far as I was concerned'. In Kenya, John Whitfield experienced similar emotions: he lived in the country until 1974 and experienced the old adage that while you can take the man out of Africa you cannot take Africa out of the man.

It must be one of the finest climates in the world. The people, especially the very good friends we had made. There was quite a lot of excitement in it too, and it was still very much a wild country, it was a bit like the wild west. You could travel vast distances without seeing another soul. The beaches down in Mombasa were absolutely unbelievable, there was no tourism and we had them to ourselves. It was just a jolly good life and I certainly wouldn't have missed it for the world.

That sense of belonging, fuelled as much by commitment as by nostalgia is central to most colonialists' views of the countries in which so much of their lives were spent. People continued to feel involved in what was happening in Africa and even if they grieved at news of a massacre or a military *coup*, they still believed that what they had achieved had been worthwhile. Even in the 1960s and 1970s, when colonialism and imperialism were taboo subjects, experienced administrators such as Sir Alan Burns argued that they could not be written off as unmitigated evils.

When one considers colonial rule, one's got to remember what was there before it started in west Africa. Cannibalism, slavery and various other abominations, human sacrifice all existed in Nigeria and the Gold Coast. When we went out there we abolished slavery as far as we could, we abolished human sacrifices as far as we could although it still continues and we abolished various other enormities. I'm quite certain that Colonialism was a good thing from the point of view of the African native himself. It taught him honesty and respect for the law and it taught him also that you could have a democratic government instead of the absolute rule of the chiefs.

With his family background of service to empire – both his father and his grandfather served in the Caribbean – Burns could be said to have had a vested interest, but there is more to his encomium than heartfelt pride. Sadly for some, their efforts seemed to have been in vain when they witnessed the wanton destruction of what they had achieved. In Kenya, the 'officers' mess' of the African empire, some of the die-hard settlers decided to stay on even though most of the highland farms were broken up and divided amongst Kikuyu farmers – often with disastrous results. Trees, planted as windbreaks to halt soil erosion, were cut down for firewood; crop rotation was ignored and fields became barren; and short-term solutions were preferred to the long, hard slog of making the land work. Similar changes were noted in Zimbabwe, where Mugabe's supporters expected to be recompensed for their loyalty with the possession of land owned by the white settlers. As in Kenya, the results were not always happy. By the early 1990s only a handful of so-called white commercial farmers remained in the country to keep alive the entrepreneurial spirit which had made Rhodesia southern Africa's bread-basket. This, too, was part of the price of empire.

Rhodesia did not of course have British rule but it had white rule, in many ways much the same thing. The locals were too polite to tell me what they thought of us but there were ways of judging their opinions. On the whole I would say that they resented control over stock holdings, resented being moved from one area to another, even to a better area, resented having to dip their stock (until dipping services were destroyed and diseases spread so that markets were closed to their stock) and they resented our ignorance, for ignorance it often was, interference in their civil affairs, particularly adultery cases. They also disliked having to conserve the soil, believing, incorrectly, that their old form of shifting cultivation could continue to be used despite an exploding population. They appreciated the peace which white rule brought and the intercourse between tribes which it made possible. They liked our bus services, clinics, schools and, though at first very suspicious of local government, came to enjoy it and take a great interest in the debates of their councillors. They loved agricultural shows and were very appreciative of improved water supplies. So perhaps their views were as mixed as those of voters in Britain!

Whatever the future might have held, most British colonial servants ended their tours of duty with feelings of accomplishment, that they had carried out their tasks to the best of their abilities and that despite the haste and the muddle, they were leaving behind something solid and dependable. Many felt that they were also losing friends, not just the family circle of servants but also close colleagues. And then there was the sense of loss allied to a belief that nothing could ever match up to Africa.

There were lesser attractions too, warmth and sunshine, a servant or two and always, for many, an unavowed love for the country [Nigeria], a boyish touching love, something belonging to boyhood, to King Solomon's Mines and all other tales of adventure, to that strange homesickness so many of us have for a place without bricks or mortar, roads or signposts. Perhaps 'the smell of wood-smoke' are the commonplace words which best sum up that longed-for, vanished world. How often have I heard a man say: 'It's the smell of wood-smoke that gets me' or 'Do you remember the dusk coming down and the scent of burning wood?' An official who had left Nigeria fifteen years ago read one of my books. 'It brought it all back to me as if I were there – that smell of wood-smoke.'

In many respects, Sylvia Leith-Ross never left Nigeria. She revisited several times and remained a pungent observer of events in the country which had been a home since 1906. In that time she had seen the rise and fall of British rule and the

277

emergence of Nigeria as an independent country – not an uncommon experience given the shortness of the British colonial period in Africa. For her and for the small number of people who were colonialists, Africa still casts a long shadow and many were to make return visits, often as honoured guests. In 1992, having written his biography of Abubakar Tafewa Balewa, Trevor Clark paid a visit to Nigeria where he was treated as an important visiting dignitary. Others found return uncomfortable or impossible, not because they would be made to feel unwelcome as former imperial rulers but because the older generation who had taken their countries to independence were no longer alive.

Today, the physical remains of the British empire in Africa are barely discernible. The once stately Muthaiga Club in Nairobi still exists but it is a better place for being multiracial. Many of the neatly fenced farms remain as reminders of Delamere's dream of a white east African dominion, but downtown Nairobi with its high-rise buildings is indistinguishable from any other international capital. The same holds true for Harare or Lagos. In Khartoum, the inquisitive student of architecture can discern elements of Kitchener's grand design for a modern city; the railways of southern Africa still echo to the sound of British-built Garratt steam locomotives; the stately neo-Georgian homes of the governors-general remain as palaces for the new leaders. But such is the pace of change in Africa and the continent's ability to reclaim buildings or land left untended that tangible evidence of the colonial past has all too often simply faded away.

So, too, has much of the faith in parliamentary democracy and the rule of common law. In most of Britain's old African holdings, the Westminster model has been abandoned for the one-party state or rule by unelected military councils. At the time, when transfers of power were being discussed, there were doubts about the wisdom of imposing all the strict procedures of the British parliament but as more than one administrator has admitted, when the question was raised, 'the universal answer I got was that they'd consider they were being palmed off with a sort of cheap version as if they were unworthy of the real thing'. To the dismay of those well-meaning colonial civil servants, their carefully nurtured ideologies were soon tossed aside in favour of something more pragmatic and more suited to local rivalries and power struggles. What had evolved for the northern democracies over several centuries was not always suited to Africa's tribal societies after less than fifty years of independence.

And yet, it was not all administrative failure. English lives on as the lingua franca of most African countries; the west African states produced a lively modern literature in the novels and poetry of writers such as Chinua Achebe and Wole Soyinka; and the introduction of improved secondary and tertiary education systems brought both enlightenment and improvement – both prime considerations of the British imperial system. Paradoxically, perhaps, education also created an atmosphere which encouraged political debate and its wider provision quickened the pace of demands for self-rule. As the population became better educated, particularly in the urban areas, they were no longer prepared to accept the easy paternalism of earlier years and the creation of a skilled and ambitious middle class provided a bedrock of support for the growing band of nationalist politicians. In the Sudan, the Graduates Congress became a focus for the 'call for freedom and self-government' as early as 1938.

The movement [for independence] started way back before the Atlantic Charter. It was the role of Gordon College, although it was a single school, and although it could be criticized from the point of view of the type of education it gave and discipline which prevailed in it. I think it served a very useful and very important function for us, the Sudanese educated class, because we were collected from all parts of the country and Gordon College was really a melting-pot. That was where the beginnings of Sudanese nationalism could be traced.

Khatim Al-Khalifa's comments about the benefits of British education have been echoed by other African leaders, including South Africa's Nelson Mandela, who reminded the world that he had been educated in a British school and that he had not 'discarded the influence which Britain and British history and culture exercised on us'. In that sense, more than the development of democratic and legal institutions, education proved to be a powerful engine of social and political change in Africa.

As the twentieth century approached its conclusion, Mandela's country was the last imperial boil which remained to be lanced. In 1961 it had left the Commonwealth and its policy of apartheid was to become a political battleground not just in the Commonwealth, where Britain stood accused of dragging its heels on sanctions, but also in the United Nations where the Soviet Union used its support of the African Group as a counter in the never-ending confrontations of the Cold War. In fact, the Soviet leadership had no strategic interest in southern Africa and as imperialists themselves, they controlled the huge former Russian empire; but the controversy allowed them to support South Africa's opponents and to pour money and military aid into Africa's many national liberation groups. Not that international disapproval did anything to halt South Africa's progress towards the creation of separate white and black societies. In 1964, the leader of the militant *Umkhonto we Sizwe* movement, Nelson Mandela, was sentenced to life imprisonment and the state security service cracked down heavily on any opposition to the National Party government.

Despite the sanctions and the opposition, the white South African hegemony remained in place until the 1980s, when it simply became unsustainable. The black homelands, or *bantustans*, of Transkei, Bophuthatswana, Venda, Lebowa, Gazankulu, Basotho Qwawa, KwaZulu and Ciskei were refused international recognition. South African forces failed to counter guerrilla forces from the former Portuguese colonies of

Mozambique and Angola; and the crushing of the riots in the township of Soweto in the late 1970s alienated the liberal population. A state of emergency in 1985 failed to solve the crisis and five years later, as the ending of the Cold War changed global strategic imperatives, a new white president, F.W. De Klerk was forced to face reality. The African opposition parties were 'unbanned', apartheid began to be dismantled and Mandela was released from prison. Four years later, amidst scenes of high emotion, the ANC won the country's first multiracial elections, a government of national unity was formed and Mandela came to power as president, with De Klerk as his deputy. In the end, international isolation, war-weariness and the growing strength of the black African opposition movements proved to be too strong for those who still dreamed of prolonging a whites-only South Africa.

This was a turning-point of no little significance in African history. The white supremacists had dreamed that the structures of race discrimination would never be dismantled and that it would be possible to defeat the growing army of ANC activists who were intent on changing the old order. In the mid-1970s, following extensive rioting in the Soweto townships of Johannesburg there was some constitutional tinkering to give a greater voice to the coloured population, but to all intents and purposes apartheid remained in place. Despite the adoption of a 'total strategy' to maintain white rule by hitting ANC camps within South Africa and in neighbouring Namibia and Angola, white supremacy in the continent was on its last legs. Veteran ANC activist Sally Motlana spoke for many Africans when she described the exhilaration of being able to cast her vote for the first time in 1994.

> I never dreamt that one day I would be sitting here with other human beings and regarded as a human being. For all those years I've been made to feel that I was not part of the human race. The only people who made me feel as one of them all the time, who

made me feel as I was a child of God, were the missionaries who brought me up. Otherwise, I felt I was like a piece of dirty rag. Without them, education was out. Every time I moved after the age of sixteen, I knew I would be arrested at any time for failure to produce a piece of paper called a pass.

I was arrested three times, 1976, 1977 and 1978, all because we were outspoken people against the government of this country. We were made to feel, not in our lifetime are we going to ever get a vote; it doesn't matter if you were educated, whether you called yourself a civilized human being, you're not allowed to vote. What a joy when I had to throw in my paper!

By then, the white colonial influence in Africa had all but disappeared and the age of the European scramble for Africa was only a distant memory. Even the equally rapid process of decolonization had become a half-remembered part of history. Paradoxically, though, there were more Europeans working in the continent than there had ever been in the heyday of empire – officials of the World Bank and the International Monetary Fund, aid workers from the UN and other agencies, political and military advisers, businessmen hoping for a share in the new market-oriented economies, teachers and missionaries continuing the tradition of enlightenment. For all that they are a heterogeneous bunch, each with different aims and aspirations, all are working towards the goal of making Africa a more peaceful and self-sufficient place by improving health care, introducing new industries and agricultural methods and bringing comfort and assistance to the poor, the weak and the dispossessed. They would surely understand only too well the memories of a man like the Revd Dr Andrew Ross, who discovered in Nyasaland that true co-operation comes not from dominance but from a mutual recognition of each side's needs.

I had to work to gain my acceptance. They would of course accept you because the African tradition is of great politeness. It's only when you are really at home in traditional politeness and when you play your role there, then essentially people begin to forget and towards the end of my time there, there were groups of people who often really had forgotten I was white. I was so used to being around, I fitted in so completely to their patterns of behaviour. I ate with them, I slept in their houses when I was away from home in the parish which I often was. I simply lived with these friends. I was part of the family set-up and eventually I learned an enormous amount by simply sitting quietly after a meal and listening to family chatter. I learned things I could never have learned by formal quest-ioning. Just by listening to chatter, I learned many things about the recent past I could never have found out otherwise.

There one has it. The British empire in Africa was not just the wicked, grasping and rapacious institution derided by the croakers in the immediate aftermath of its demise. Nor was it simply a force for universal good, a great adventure which ben-efited everyone concerned in its execution. It was too various an organization, too parti-coloured in its complexity to be either a paternalistic anachronism or a revolutionary instrument for change. But somewhere in between, at the point where Sally Motlana exulted in gaining her emancipation and where the Revd Ross found true understanding in an equal exchange of ideas, British colonial rule was generally decent and fair and invariably even-handed. At its best, those ideals inspired the many men and women who enriched their own lives, and the lives of the people they served, in the days when the winds of change swept through Africa.

Bibliography

NOTES AND REFERENCES
In addition to private interviews and discussions with the author, the personal reminiscences are taken from the following sources.

National Library of Scotland, Scottish Decolonization Project, Acc. 10809
E.F. Aglen, Sudan; Irene Anderson, Ghana; Herbert Bell, Nyasaland; W.C. Benson, Ghana; Trevor Clark, Nigeria; A.C. Davies, Ghana; Very Revd A.B. Doig, Nyasaland; Revd Colin Forrester-Paton, Ghana; Ian Fraser, Ghana; Albert Goodere, Nigeria; J.E. Hodge, Nigeria; Ron Hunston, Ghana; Murray Lunan, Tanganyika; J.A.G. McColl, Nigeria; Charles Meek, Tanganyika; Dr E.W.T. Morris, Sudan; Revd Dr Andrew Ross, Nyasaland; Robert Gordon Scott, Tanganyika; Kenneth Simmonds, Kenya, Nyasaland, Uganda; H.E. Sumner, Rhodesia; T.D. Thomson, Nyasaland; John Trestrail, Kenya; John Whitfield, Kenya

Imperial War Museum, Department of Sound Records
Lt.-Col. R.N. Boyd, 4418/8; Sir Alan Burns, 4708/3; Lt.-Col. R.C. Glanville, 4405/5; Lt.-Col. Sir Martin Lindsay, 4341/3; S.J.O. Mowbray, 4400/4

Public Record Office papers (Chapter Five)
1. Bradley to Creech Jones, 12 December 1947, CO 537/3559/2
2. Memorandum on the Gold Coast government's view of the causes of the riots and the steps to be taken to restore law and order, 3 March 1948, CO96/795/6
3. Mangan to Creech Jones, 6 June 1949, CO537/4638/19
4. Scott to Creech Jones, 10 March 1948, CO537/4638/1

284

5. Creech Jones to Attlee, 4 October 1949, PREM 8/924

6. Arden-Clarke to Cohen, 5 March 1951, CO537/7181/3

7. Minute by Sir Thomas Lloyd on constitutional reform, 7 July 1952, CO554/371/26

8. Cumming Bruce to the Colonial Office, 21 July 1950, 'The Failure of the Gold Coast', CO35/6178/17A

SECONDARY SOURCES

Philip Allison, *Life in the White Man's Grave: A Pictorial Record of the British in West Africa* (London: Viking, 1988)

A.J.V. Arthur, 'The District Officer in India and the Sudan', in Deborah Lavin (ed.), *The Condominium Remembered: The Making of the Sudanese State*, vol. I (Durham: Centre for Middle Eastern and Islamic Studies, University of Durham, 1991)

M.C. Atkinson, *An African Life: Tales of a Colonial Officer* (London: Radcliffe, 1992)

Obafemi Awolowo, *Awo: Autobiography of Chief Obafemi Awolowo* (Cambridge: Cambridge University Press, 1960)

Sir John Barrow, *An Account of Travels into the Interior of Southern Africa in the Years 1797 and 1798*, vol. I (London: Cadell, 1801)

Sir Gawain Bell, 'The Growth of Sudanese Nationalism', in Lavin, op. cit.

Hugh Boustead, *The Wind of Morning* (London: Chatto & Windus, 1971)

Alan Burns, *Colonial Civil Servant* (London: Allen & Unwin, 1949)

Clara Chidarara, quoted in Julie Frederikse, *None but Ourselves: Masses vs Media in the Making of Zimbabwe* (Heinemann: London, 1982)

Trevor Clark, *A Right Honourable Gentleman: Abubakar from the Black Rock* (London: Edward Arnold, 1991)

Colonel P.G.L. Cousens, 'Gallabat-Asmara-Kassala, May 1939–July 1940', in Lavin, op. cit.

Lord Cranworth, *Kenya Chronicles* (London: Macmillan, 1939)

W.R. Crocker, *On Governing Colonies* (London: Allen & Unwin, 1947)

Cameron Duodo, 'Looking ahead to 1995', Gemini News Service, 16 December 1994

Anne Louise Dundas, *Beneath African Glaciers* (London: H.F. & G. Witherby, 1924)

Henrik Ellert, *The Rhodesian Front War* (Gweru: Mambo Press, 1989)

Harry Franklin, *The Flag-Wagger* (London: Shepheard and Walwyn, 1974)

Sir Ralph Furse, *Acuparius: Recollections of a Recruiting Officer* (Oxford: OUP, 1962)

Mary Gaunt, *Alone in West Africa* (London: Werner Laurie, 1912)

Cullen Gouldsbury, *An African Year* (London: Arnold, 1912)

Rosemary Kenrick, *Sudan Tales* (Cambridge: Oleander, 1987)

Sir Khatim Al-Khalifa, in Lavin, op. cit.

Mary Kingsley, 'Life in West Africa,' lecture in the Sunday Afternoon Course at the South Place Institute, Finsbury, in Patricia W. Romero, *Women's Voices on Africa: A Century of Travel Writings* (Princeton and New York: Markus Wiener Publishing, 1992)

Sylvia Leith-Ross, *Stepping Stones: Memoirs of Colonial Nigeria 1907–1960* (London: Peter Owen, 1983)

Doris Lessing, *African Laughter: Four Visits to Zimbabwe* (London: Harper Collins, 1992)

Malcolm MacDonald, *Titans and Others* (London: Collins, 1972)

May Mott-Smith, *Africa from Port to Port* (New York: Van Nostrand, 1930)

Tendai Mujoma, 'Comrade Zeppelin', in Frederikse, op. cit.

Jocelyn Murray, in Romero, op. cit.

Peter Niesewand, 'The Smith Machine', *The Guardian*, 22 July 1978

Sir Rex Niven, *Nigerian Kaleidoscope* (London: C. Hurst, 1982)

Joshua Nkomo, in James Duffy and Robert A. Manners (eds.), *Africa Speaks* (Princeton, New Jersey: Van Norstrand, 1961)

Colonel J.H.R. Orlebar: 'The Story of the Sudan Defence Force', in Lavin, op. cit.

Margery Perham, *African Apprenticeship: An Autobiographical Journey in Southern Africa in 1929* (London: Faber, 1974); *Colonial Sequence, 1949 to 1969* (London: Methuen, 1970)

Brigadier R.H.S. Popham, 'Kura Oasis and the Formation of the SDF Brigade, 1942–1943', in Lavin, op. cit.

Ropa Rinopfuka, in Frederikse, op. cit.

Molly Ryan, *Over my Shoulder: Kenya Walkabout* (Dublin: Grange Press, 1987)

Joan Sharwood-Smith, *Diary of a Colonial Wife* (London: Radcliffe, 1992)

Anna Steenkamp, in John Bird, *Annals of Natal*, vol. I (Pietermaritzburg: Natal Society, 1888)

P.K. van der Byl, in Frederickse, op. cit.

Sir Roy Welensky, in Duffy and Manners, op. cit.

Anthony St John Wood, *Northern Rhodesia: The Human Background* (London: Pall Mall, 1961)

GENERAL BIBLIOGRAPHY

Hakim Adi and Marika Sherwood (eds.), *The 1945 Manchester Pan-African Congress Revisited* (London: New Beacon Books, 1995)

Charles Allen, *Tales from the Dark Continent* (London: Andre Deutsch, 1979)

Bibliography

Correlli Barnett, *The Lost Victory: British Dreams, British Realities 1945–1950* (London: Macmillan, 1995)

H.M. Bartlett, *The King's African Rifles* (Aldershot: Gale and Polden, 1956)

Ngwabi Bhebe and Terence Ranger, *Soldiers in Zimbabwe's Liberation War* (London: James Currey, 1995)

Lord Birkenhead, *Walter Monckton: The Life of Viscount Monckton of Brenchley* (London: Weidenfeld & Nicolson, 1969)

E.G. Bradley, *A Household Book for Africa* (London: OUP, 1939)

Lord Butler, *The Art of the Possible* (London: Hamish Hamilton, 1971)

David Caute, *Under the Skin: The Death of White Rhodesia* (London: Allen Lane, 1983)

Colin Cross, *The Fall of the British Empire* (London: Hodder & Stoughton, 1968)

Michael Crowder (ed.), *The Cambridge History of Africa*, vol. VIII (Cambridge: Cambridge University Press, 1984)

Basil Davidson, *The African Awakening* (London: Cape, 1955); *Africa in Modern History* (London: Allen Lane, 1978)

Prosser Gifford and W.R. Louis, *The Transfer of Power in Africa* (London: Yale University Press, 1982); *Decolonization and African Independence* (London: Yale University Press, 1988)

Lord Hailey, *An African Survey: A Study of the Problems arising in Africa South of the Sahara* (Oxford: OUP, 1938, revised 1956)

W.K. Hancock, *Smuts*, vol I (Cambridge: Cambridge University Press, 1962)

J.D. Hargraves, *The End of Colonial Rule in West Africa* (London: Macmillan, 1979)

A.H.W. Haywood and F.A.S. Clarke, *History of the West African Frontier Force* (Aldershot: Gale and Polden, 1964)

Peter Hennessy, *Never Again: Britain 1945–1951* (London: Cape, 1992)

Thomas Hodgkin, *Nationalism in Colonial Africa* (London: Muller, 1956)

Lord Home, *The Way the Wind Blows* (London: Collins, 1976)

Alistair Horne, *Macmillan, 1957–1986* (London: Macmillan, 1989)

Elspeth Huxley, *White Man's Country* (London: Macmillan, 1935); *The Flame Trees of Thika* (London: Chatto & Windus, 1959)

Lawrence James, *The Rise and Fall of the British Empire* (London: Little, Brown, 1994)

G.B. Kay, *The Political Economy of Colonialism* (Cambridge: Cambridge University Press, 1972)

Jomo Kenyatta, *Suffering without Bitterness* (Nairobi: East African Publishing, 1968)

Richard Lamb, *The Macmillan Years, 1957–1963* (London: John Murray, 1995)

Roy Lewis and Yvonne Foy, *The British in Africa* (London: Weidenfeld & Nicolson, 1971)

Bibliography

J.M. Lee, *Colonial Development and Good Government* (Oxford: Clarendon Press, 1967)

P.C. Mazikana and I.J. Johnstone, *Zimbabwe Epic* (Harare: National Archives, 1984)

Tom Mboya, *The Challenge of Nationhood* (London: Andre Deutsch, 1970)

Martin Meredith, *The First Dance of Freedom: Black Africa in the Post-war Era* (London: Hamish Hamilton, 1984)

James Morris, *Farewell the Trumpets: An Imperial Retreat* (London: Faber, 1978)

I.F. Nicolson, *The Administration of Nigeria* (Oxford: OUP, 1969)

Kwame Nkrumah, *Autobiography* (Edinburgh: Thomas Nelson, 1957)

Julius Nyerere, *Freedom and Unity* (Oxford: OUP, 1967)

Roland Oliver and Anthony Atmore, *Africa since 1800* (Cambridge: Cambridge University Press, 1974)

Roland Oliver and J.D. Fage, *A Short History of Africa* (London: Penguin Books, 1990)

Roland Oliver and G.N. Sanderson (eds.), *Cambridge History of Africa*, vol. VI (Cambridge: Cambridge University Press, 1985)

J.D. Omer-Cooper, *History of Southern Africa* (London: James Currey, 1994)

Thomas Pakenham, *The Scramble for Africa* (London: Weidenfeld & Nicolson, 1991)

Anthony Parsons, *From Cold War to Hot Peace: UN Interventions 1947–1994* (London: Michael Joseph, 1995)

R.D. Pearce, *The Turning Point in Africa* (London: Cass, 1982)

Marjory Perham, *The Colonial Reckoning* (London: Collins, 1971); *Lugard*, 2 vols (London: Collins, 1956, 1960)

Ben Pimlott, *Harold Wilson* (London: Harper Collins, 1992)

David Reynolds, *Rich Relations: The American Occupation of Britain* (London: Harper Collins, 1995)

A.D. Roberts (ed.), *The Cambridge History of Africa*, vol. VII (Cambridge: Cambridge University Press, 1986)

David Rooney, *Charles Arden-Clarke* (London: Rex Collings, 1982)

Trevor Royle, *Orde Wingate: Irregular Soldier* (London: Weidenfeld & Nicolson, 1995)

Roy Welensky: *Welensky's 4,000 Days: The Life and Death of the Federation of Rhodesia and Nyasaland* (London: Collins, 1964)

Harold Wilson, *A Personal Record: The Labour Government 1964–1970* (London: Weidenfeld & Nicolson, 1971)

Monica Wilson and L.M. Thompson, *The Oxford History of South Africa*, 2 vols (Oxford: OUP, 1969–1971)

Index

289